Index

Introduction

Our intention in writing this Manual is to provide the reader with all the data and information required to maintain and repair the vehicle. However, it must be realised that special equipment and skills are required in some cases to carry out the work detailed in the text, and we do not recommend that such work be attempted unless the reader possesses the necessary skill and equipment. It would be better to have an **AUTHORISED DEALER** to carry out the work using the special tools and equipment available to his trained staff. He will also be in possession of the genuine spare parts which may be needed for replacement.

The information in the Manual has been checked against that provided by the vehicle manufacturer, and any peculiarities have been mentioned if they depart from usual workshop practice.

A fault finding and trouble shooting chart has been inserted at the end of the Manual to enable the reader to pin point faults and so save time. As it is impossible to include every malfunction, only the more usual ones have been included.

A composite conversion table has also been included at the end of the Manual and we would recommend that wherever possible, for greater accuracy, the metric system units are used.

Brevity and simplicity have been our aim in compiling this Manual, relying on the numerous illustrations and clear text to inform and instruct the reader. At the request of the many users of our Manuals, we have slanted the book towards repair and overhaul rather than maintenance which is covered in our "**Wheel**" series of handbooks.

Although every care has been taken to ensure that the information and data are correct, WE CANNOT ACCEPT ANY LIABILITY FOR INACCURACIES OR OMISSIONS, OR FOR DAMAGE OR MALFUNCTIONS ARISING FROM THE USE OF THIS BOOK, NO MATTER HOW CAUSED.

History and Type Identification

Adam Opel A.G. (German) Company is a branch of the American General Motors Corporation - which is the largest motor manufacturer in the world.

Your Rekord C series first appeared in August 1966 as a development of the B series and incorporates some interesting engineering features.

A brief description of the types covered, together with identification plates, appear below. Also included in the manual is the Ranger for South Africa.

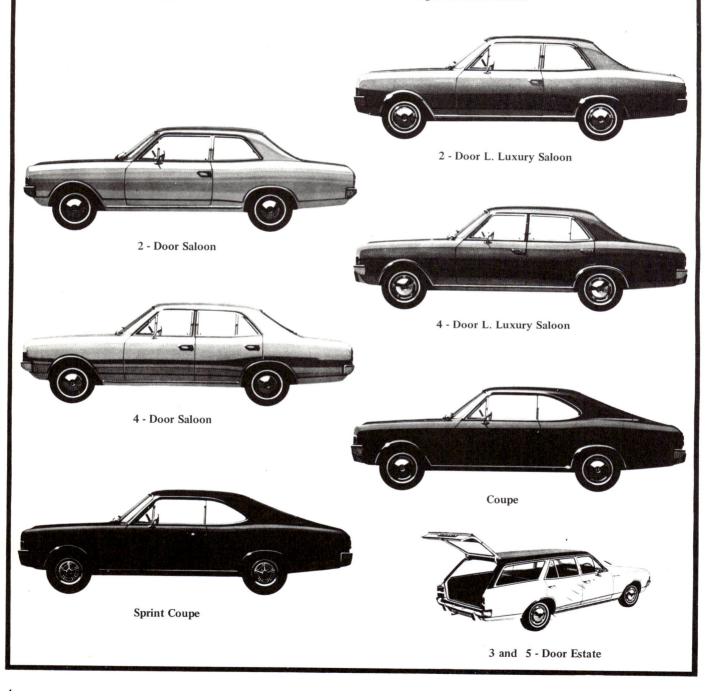

2 - Door Saloon

2 - Door L. Luxury Saloon

4 - Door Saloon

4 - Door L. Luxury Saloon

Coupe

Sprint Coupe

3 and 5 - Door Estate

WORKSHOP MANUAL
for
OPEL REKORD
including
RANGER 2.2/2.5 (S. Africa)

COMPILED AND WRITTEN
BY

PUBLISHED BY
INTEREUROPE LIMITED
AUTODATA DIVISION
NICHOLSON HOUSE
MAIDENHEAD
BERKSHIRE
ENGLAND

SBN 901610 - 29 - 1

Part Names and Alternatives

Certain parts of motor cars are known by other names in different areas and countries. A list of the common alternatives is given below.

ENGINE

Gudgeon pin	Piston pin, small end pin, Wrist pin
Inlet **Valve**	Intake valve
Piston oil control ring	Piston scraper ring
Induction manifold	Inlet manifold, intake manifold
Oil sump	Oil pan, Oil reservoir, Sump tray
Core Plug	Expansion plug, Welch plug, Sealing disc
Dipstick	Oil dipper rod, Oil level gauge rod, Oil level indicator
Silencer	Muffler, expansion box, diffuser
Tappets	Valve lifter, push rods

FUEL

Carburettor choke	Carburettor venturi
Slow running jet	Low speed jet, Idler jet
Volume control screw	Idling mixture screw
Fuel pump	Petrol pump, Fuel lift pump
Air cleaner	Air silencer, Muffler
Fuel tank	Petrol Tank
Accelerator	Throttle

CLUTCH

Clutch release bearing	Throwout bearing, Thrust bearing
Clutch lining	Disc facing, Friction ring
Spigot bearing	Clutch pilot bearing
Clutch housing	Bell housing

GEARBOX

Gearbox	Transmission
Gear lever	Change speed lever, Gearshift lever
Selector fork	Change speed fork, Shift fork
Input shaft	Constant motion shaft, First motion shaft, drive gear, First reduction pinion. Main drive pinion, Clutch shaft, Clutch gear
Countershaft	Layshaft
Synchro cone	Synchronizing ring
Reverse Idler gear	Reverse pinion

REAR AXLE

Rear Axle	Final drive unit
Crown wheel	Ring gear, Final drive gear, Spiral drive gear
Bevel pinion	Small pinion, spiral drive pinion
"U" bolts	Spring clips
Axle shaft	Half shaft, Hub driving shaft, Jack driving shaft
Differential gear	Sun wheel
Differential pinion	Planet wheel

ELECTRICAL

Generator	Dynamo
Control box	Cut out, Voltage regulator, Voltage control, Circuit breaker
Capacitor	Condenser
Interior light	Dome lamp
Lens	Glass
Head lamp ring	Headlamp surround, Headlamp moulding
Direction indicators	Signal lamps, Flashers
Micrometer adjustment	Octane selector
Rear lamps	Tail lamps
Reversing light	Back-up light

STEERING

Drop arm	Pitman arm
Rocker shaft	Pitman shaft, Drop arm shaft
Swivel pin	Pivot pin, King pin, Steering pin
Stub axle	Swivel axle
Track rod	Cross tube, Tie rod
Drag link	Side tube, Steering connecting rod
Steering column	Steering gear shaft
Steering column bearing	Mast jacket bearing
Steering arm	Steering knuckle arm
Stator tube	Control tube
Steering joints	Steering knuckles

BRAKES

Master cylinder	Main cylinder
Brake shoe lining	Brake shoe facing

BODY

Bonnet	Hood
Luggage locker	Boot, Luggage compartment
Luggage locker lid	Boot lid, Rear deck
Mudguards	Quarter panels, Fenders, Mud wings
Roof	Canopy
Nave plate	Wheel disc, Hub cap
Finishing strip	Moulding, Chrome strip
Windscreen	Windshield
Rear window	Rear windscreen, Rear windshield Backlight
Quarter vent	(N.D.V.) No draught ventilator
Bumpers	Fenders
Loom	Harness
Odometer	Trip recorder
Bonnet catch	Hood latch
Kerosene	Paraffin
Boot	Trunk

2

Technical Data

| | SALOON - COUPE - ESTATE | | | | | SPRINT COUPE |
	2 DOOR	2 DOOR L	4 DOOR	4 DOOR L	COUPE	SPRINT COUPE
Overall Length	4550 (179.1)	4574 (180.1)	4550 (179.1)	4574 (180.1)	4574 (180.1)	4574 (180.1)
Overall Width	1754 (69.1)	1754 (69.1)	1758 (69.2)	1758 (69.2)	1754 (69.1)	1754 (69.1)
Overall Height	1456 (57.3)	1456 (57.3)	1453 (57.2)	1453 (57.2)	1426 (56.1)	1420 (55.9)
Turning Circle Diam.		11.74 m	(38.5 ft)			11.8 m (38.7 ft.)
Track - Front and Rear		1410 (55.5)	(55.5)			
Wheelbase		2668 (105.0)	(105.0)			
Ground Clearance (min)		145	(5.7)			
Weight - Kerb	1020 (2249)	1040 (2293)	1045 (2304)	1065 (2348)	1080 (2381)	1135 (2502)
Fully Loaded		1480	(3263)			1510 (3329)
Fuel Consumption (Acc to Din litre/100 km M.P. Imp. Gall.)						
1.5 Litre	9.9 (28.5)	-	9.9 (28.5)	-	-	
1.7 Litre	10.5 (26.9)	10.5 (26.9)	10.5 (26.9)	10.5 (26.9)		
1.7 Litre S	10.8 (26.2)	10.8 (26.2)	10.8 (26.2)	10.8 (26.2)		
1.9 Litre S	10.5 (26.9)	10.5 (26.9)	10.5 (26.9)	10.5 (26.9)	10.6 (26.7)	
1.9 Litre HL					10.4 (27.2)	10.0 (28.3)
2.1 Litre Ranger			NOT AVAILABLE			
2.5 Litre Ranger			NOT AVAILABLE			
Maximum Speed						
1.5 Litre	133 (82.6)	-	133 (82.6)	-	-	
1.7 Litre	138 (85.8)	138 (85.8)	138 (85.8)	138 (85.8)		
1.7 Litre S	148 (92.0)	148 (92.0)	148 (92.0)	148 (92.0)		
1.9 Litre S	160 (99.4)	160 (99.4)	160 (99.4)	160 (99.4)	153 (95.1)	
1.9 Litre HL					165 (102.5)	171 (106.3)
2.1 Litre Ranger			NOT AVAILABLE			
2.5 Litre Ranger			NOT AVAILABLE			

Notes: MM (inches)   KG (lbs.)   KM/H (m.p.h.)

Fig.A.1. Number identifying the cylinder block (17 identifies 1.7 litre)

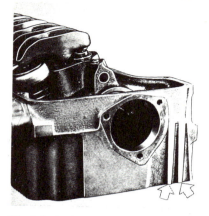

Fig.A.2. Cylinder head identification

Without rib - 1.5 litre
One rib - 1.7 litre S
Two rib - 1.7 litre and 1.9 litre S

Fig.A.3. Engine lifting slings in position

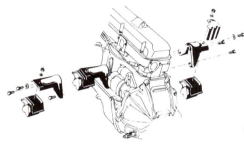

Fig.A.4. Engine supports and heat deflector plate

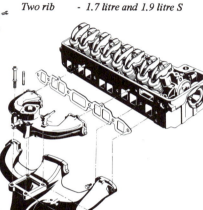

Fig.A.6. Manifold assembly

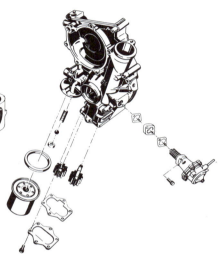

Fig.A.8. Oil filter element, fuel valve and timing case

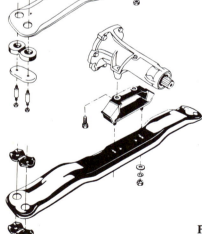

Fig.A.7. Timing case bolt covered by water pump

Fig.A.9. Oil filter and relief valve

Fig.A.5. Transmission cross member, frame and damper block

Engine - Rekord

DESCRIPTION

The following engines are optional equipment on the Opel Rekord - C Series models: -

1.5 litre	-	68 HP
1.7 litre	-	73 HP
1.7 litre-S	-	84 HP
1.9 litre-S	-	102 HP
1.9 litre-HL	-	115 HP

All engines are 4-cylinder in-line camshaft-in-head and all have a stroke of 69.8 mm. The cylinder block is of cast iron and is identified as to type by an embossed number on the left and right-hand side at the front of the block (Fig.A.1.). The cylinder head is of chromium grey cast iron and incorporates wedge shaped combustion chambers and an overhead camshaft supported by three bearings. The head is identified by markings shown in Fig.A.2. The combination of blocks and heads for all five engine types can therefore be easily identified.

The 10 cylinder head bolts form a square to each cylinder bore and the head is centred by two guide pins. The three camshaft bearings are of diminishing size as are the journals and end thrust is controlled at the forward end by the camshaft front bearing seat in one direction and by the front bearing cover in the other direction, the end clearance is adjusted by a nylon bolt in the forward end of the camshaft.

All engines have full skirt "Autothermic" type pistons with horizontal slots in the groove of the oil control ring. This serves to partly separate the head and the skirt and thus maintain contact with the cylinder walls throughout the temperature range.

ENGINE - Removal and Installation

Drain the coolant from the engine and radiator and remove or disconnect the following items: - the windscreen washer hose and then the bonnet, the upper and lower hoses and the radiator (NOTE: on cars fitted with automatic transmission unscrew and plug the oil lines from the angled connectors on the lower radiator tank), disconnect and remove the battery and the carburettor air cleaner. Remove the exhaust pipe from the exhaust manifold and disconnect the cable to the starter motor and the linkages and bowden control wires to the choke, accelerator and heater controls. Ensure that all linkages, pipes, hoses etc, that may impede the removal of the engine are disconnected.

Remove the propeller shaft and its intermediate bearing, then place the cables of the engine lifter sling S - 1220 around the engine as shown in Fig. A.3; the shorter cable (59 inches) should be at the front of the engine and the longer cable (79 inches) at the rear of the engine. Hook the cables on to the lifting sling and raise the hoist to take up the slack on the cables. Ensure that no engine parts are damaged by this operation. Detach the front engine supports from their damper blocks and the heat deflector plate on the right-hand side mounting as shown in Fig. A.4. Remove the bolts securing the transmission cross member to the frame (making a careful note of their positions) and withdraw the cross member and the transmission damper block (an exploded diagram of the cross member and block is shown in Fig. A.5.). Ensure that the engine is now free

to be lifted and raise it far enough to clear the engine supports from the damper blocks. Incline the engine with the forward part higher than the transmission end and then remove the unit from the engine compartment.

Note: Always ensure that the hoist or crane used for removing the engine is of a suitable capacity and that any supports for the hoist are capable of taking the weight.
To install the engine reverse the removal procedure but note the following items:-

Check all attaching parts to ensure that they are fit for re-use. Ensure that the long support is installed on the engine left side. Tighten all engine and exhaust pipe flange bolts and nuts by hand. Ensure that the heat deflector pipe is attached to the engine right damper block. When the engine is correctly positioned, rock it to ensure that it is positioned free of stress and then evenly tighten the securing bolts and nuts, starting with the front.

Check the lock plates of the transmission cross member to frame attaching nuts and replace them as necessary. Refer to Fig. A.55 and tighten the bolts attaching the damper block to the transmission case to 18 lb.ft.

Note, with reference to Fig. A.56 A,B and C, that the arrangement of the engine rear mounting varies due to the three different transmission designs. For 3 speed transmission (Fig. A. 56A) use the first and third threaded hole in the side member. For 4 speed transmission (Fig. A.56B) use the second and fourth threaded hole, and for the automatic transmission use the first and fifth threaded hole (Fig.A.56C). The elongated holes in the cross member are provided for the 3 and 4 speed transmissions and the round holes are for the automatic transmission. An intermediate plate at the side member is an additional requirement for the automatic transmission. Prior to running the engine after installation fill the oil pump with engine oil (Fig.A.57) so that effective lubrication is available upon engine starting.

ENGINE - Dismantling and Assembling

Remove the starter motor and the gearbox from the engine block. Mark the clutch cover and the flywheel clutch assembly with a centre punch or with paint dots to facilitate assembly and then remove the flywheel clutch assembly.

Clamp the engine on to a suitable stand and drain the oil from the engine by removing the threaded drain plug from the sump.

Remove the generator and the V - belt, then the fan and the fan pulley. Remove the bolts securing the water pump and remove the water pump and gasket. Remove the cooling system thermostat. Pull the fuel line connecting hoses from the fuel pump and remove the fuel pump at the flange. Remove the complete carburettor assembly from the inlet manifold then remove the inlet and exhaust manifold from the cylinder head (Fig.A.6.).

Remove the valve rocker gear cover by unscrewing and removing the screws and lifting off the cover and gasket. Remove the distributor assembly and drive as detailed in "Electrical

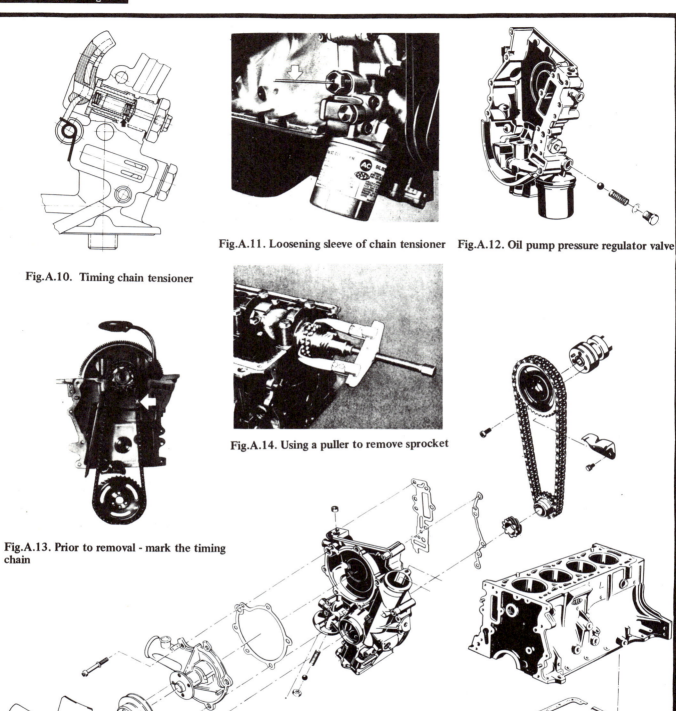

Fig.A.10. Timing chain tensioner

Fig.A.11. Loosening sleeve of chain tensioner

Fig.A.12. Oil pump pressure regulator valve

Fig.A.13. Prior to removal - mark the timing chain

Fig.A.14. Using a puller to remove sprocket

Fig.A.15. Water pump and timing details - exploded diagram

Fig.A.16. Oil sump cover and gasket

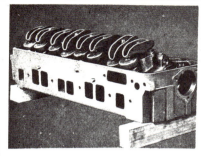

Fig.A.17. Cylinder head supported for bench work

Fig.A.18. Valve rocker and lifter

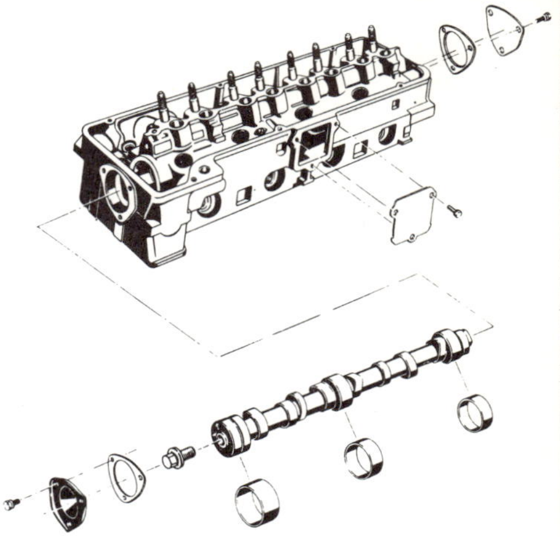

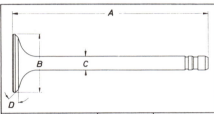

Fig.A.19. Cylinder head and crankshaft - exploded diagram

Fig.A.20. Removing camshaft

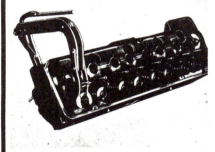

Fig.A.22. Removing valves

			Intake valve	Exhaust valve
A – Diameter		in.	4.84	4.92
		mm	123.0	125.0
B – 1.5 ltrs.,		in.	1.50	1.26
diameter		mm	38.0	32.0
B – 1.7 and 1.9 ltrs.		in.	1.57	1.34
		mm	40.0	34.0
C	Standard	in.	.3538–.3543	.3524–.3530
	(without mark)	mm	8.987–9.000	8.952–8.965
	Oversize 1	in.	.3568–.3573	.3554–.3559
		mm	9.062–9.075	9.027–9.040
	Oversize 2	in.	.3597–.3602	.3583–.3589
		mm	9.137–9.150	9.102–9.115
	Oversize A	in.	.3656–.3661	.3643–.3648
		mm	9.287–9.300	9.252–9.265
D			44°	44°

Fig.A.21. Valve identification and table

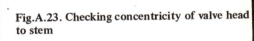

Fig.A.23. Checking concentricity of valve head to stem

Fig.A.24. Checking valve guides for wear

Fig.A.25. Table of valve guides and corresponding valves

Size in. (mm)		Valve guide dia. in. (mm)	Corresponding valve stem dia.		Oversize mark
			Intake valve in. (mm)	Exhaust valve in. (mm)	
Production	Standard	.3553–.3563 (9.025–9.050)	.3538–.3543 (8.987–9.000)	.3524–.3530 (8.952–8.965)	–
Production and Service	Oversize .0030 (0.075)	.3583–.3593 (9.100–9.125)	.3568–.3573 (9.062–9.075)	.3554–.3559 (9.027–9.040)	1
	Oversize .0059 (0.150)	.3612–.3622 (9.175–9.200)	.3597–.3602 (9.137–9.150)	.3583–.3589 (9.102–9.115)	2
Service	Oversize .0118 (0.300)	.3671–.3681 (9.325–9.350)	.3656–.3661 (9.287–9.300)	.3642–.3648 (9.252–9.265)	A

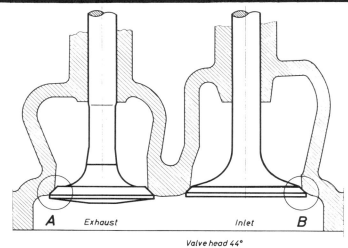

Fig.A.26. Cutters to be used for valve seats

S - 1299 - 1.5 litre intake valve seat cutter 45°
S - 1300 - 1.5 litre intake valve seat correction
cutter 30°
S - 1301 - 1.5 litre exhaust valve seat
correction cutter 30°
S - 692 - 1.5 litre exhaust valve seat cutter
45°
S - 1092 - 1.7, 1.9 litre exhaust valve seat
cutter 45°
S - 1302 - 1.7, 1.9 litre intake valve seat
cutter 45°
S - 1303 - 1.7, 1.9 litre intake valve seat
correction cutter 30°
S - 1304 - 1.7, 1.9 litre exhaust valve seat
correction cutter 30°

A   Exhaust   Inlet   B

Valve head 44°
Valve seat 45°

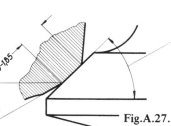

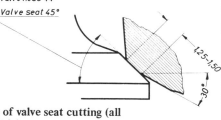

Fig.A.27. Diagram of valve seat cutting (all dimensions are metric)

A   B

Fig.A.28. Cutting a valve seat

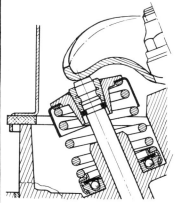

Fig.A.29. Correctly inserted valve and spring

	Fig.A.30. Table of camshaft journal and bearing diameters					
	Grind camshaft journals to in. (mm) diameter			After pressing in, bore bearings to in. (mm) diameter		
	Journal No. 1	Journal No. 2	Journal No. 3	Bearing No. 1	Bearing No. 2	Bearing No. 3
Standard size (Production)	1.926 (48.935) to 1.927 (48.950)	1.916 (48.685) to 1.917 (48.700)	1.906 (48.435) to 1.907 (48.450)	1.929 (49.000) to 1.930 (49.025)	1.919 (48.750) to 1.920 (48.775)	1.909 (48.500) to 1.910 (48.525)
.004 in. (0.1 mm) undersize (Production) *	1.922 (48.835) to 1.923 (48.850)	1.921 (48.585) to 1.913 (48.600)	1.903 (48.335) to 1.904 (48.350)	1.925 (48.900) to 1.926 (48.925)	1.915 (48.650) to 1.916 (48.675)	1.905 (48.400) to 1.906 (48.425)
.02 in. (0.5 mm) undersize (For service only)	1.906 (48.435) to 1.907 (48.450)	1.897 (48.185) to 1.898 (48.200)	1.926 (48.935) to 1.927 (48.950)	1.909 (48.500) to 1.910 (48.525)	1.900 (48.250) to 1.901 (48.275)	1.889 (48.000) to 1.890 (48.025)

The above camshaft journals and bearings are consecutively numbered 1–3 from front (water pump side) to the rear.

* Camshafts with .004 in. (0.1 mm) undersize installed in production are marked with white paint between second and third exhaust cam and the pertaining cylinder head below rocker arm cover.

Equipment" then unscrew the securing screws of the fuel pump and withdraw the pump and associated gaskets from the timing case.

Remove the oil filter element by unscrewing it and then remove the rubber gasket (Fig. A.8.) and element. Use a suitable drift to remove the oil filter pressure relief valve sleeve located below the attaching flange; do not damage the sealing area for the filter element.

Remove the timing chain tensioner (Fig. A.10) by removing the plug and the gasket and then loosen the tensioner body by 2 or 3 turns. Screw out the tensioner body by hand. If it jams at all turn back the tensioner enough to free the plunger sleeve. If it is necessary insert a 3 mm (0.11 in) thin pin (Fig. A.11) and loosen the sleeve. Do not apply force.

Unscrew the oil pump pressure regulator valve and withdraw it from the timing case. Do not damage the seating (Fig. A.12). Remove the bolts securing the oil pump/timing case assembly and remove it from the cylinder block. Do not forget the bolt covered by the water pump.

Remove the sprockets and the timing chain but mark the position (Fig. A.13) for ease of assembly. It may be necessary to use a Kukko puller and thrust piece to remove the sprockets (Fig. A.14).

Remove the bolts securing the cylinder head and lift the cylinder head from the cylinder block. Remove the gasket and clean the sealing area.

Remove the oil sump case by removing the screws securing it and then lowering it from the block. Remove the gasket and clean the sealing area (Fig. A.16).

The assembling of the engine parts is a reversal of the removal procedure but note must be taken of each individual item detailed within this section. A breakdown of individual parts follows.

CYLINDER HEAD - Overhaul

Do not place the cylinder head with installed camshaft and valves with its sealing area on to the work bench as the valves which are held open by the camshaft become distorted. Support the cylinder head with two wooden blocks as shown in Fig.A.17.

Remove the rocker arms and the lateral access hole cover and withdraw the valve lifters (Fig.A.18). Due to the insignificant wear of the valve lifter and guide, no oversizes have as yet been released. Any valve lifter guide showing pitting marks can be smoothed with fine emery cloth at the same time as the valve lifter is replaced.

Carefully remove the camshaft towards the front of the engine supporting the camshaft with one hand through the lateral access hole. Take great care not to damage the bearing surfaces (Figs.A.19 and A.20). If a new camshaft is to be fitted it should be selected according to the chart in this section and must be installed from the front into the cylinder head. Support it in the same way as for removal.

In order not to render the alumetizing of the intake valve seats ineffective, the intake valves must not be refaced or lapped. Therefore, leaky intake valves have to be replaced. The armoured

exhaust valves may be reconditioned twice.

Worn valve guides ensure no concentric valve seat, therefore they must be reamed to the next oversize and new valves installed. The valve head has an angle of 44º and the valve seat has an angle of 45º and the oversize valves are marked near the stem end with the identification 1,2 or A. (see illustration and table at Fig.A.21).

With reference to Figs.A.22 to A.24 remove the valves (illustration Fig.A.22 shows tool MW111). Mark the installation position of individual parts so that re-installation is correct. Check the concentricity of the valve head to the stem: it should not exceed 0,003 in.for the intake valve and 0.002 in.for the exhaust valve. The valve guides should be checked for wear using a dial gauge and an inside calliper.

In case of excessive wear, ream the valve guides to the next oversize. Oversize valves are in rare cases also installed in production, these valves have an oversize mark stamped into the sealing area of the cylinder head opposite the respective valve seat and near to the spark plug aperture. If you are in doubt, measure the guide.

After reaming the guides, obliterate the identification marks with a small chisel and insert the new mark for the oversize used. Always ream the guides from the outside of the cylinder head so that the more accurate bore is attained on the side of the valve head. For a list of valve guides, their corresponding valves and the valve seat cutters refer to Figs. A.25 and A.26.

To produce a good valve seat finish, refer to Figs. A.27 and A.28 and commence cutting with a 45º cutter. Remove as little material as possible and with a 30º correction cutter cut down to the specified seat width (see table in Fig. A.25). Apply red lead to the valve head and insert the valve to check the contact pattern. Recut as required to produce a good seating area. Always apply a uniform downward pressure on the cutter so that a concentric valve seat without "chatter" marks is obtained.

Thoroughly clean the cylinder head and the valve and coat the stems with oil graphite prior to installing the valves into the cylinder head. Refer to Fig. A.29 and note that the narrow windings of the valve springs must show towards the cylinder head. In order to avoid damage to the oil seal ring during installation, place it into the valve stem groove only after compressing the spring with the oil deflector and the valve seat. Ensure that the oil seal ring and the oil deflectors are correctly seated.

Prior to fitting the rocker arms, smooth the surface which contacts the valve stem with a very fine file.

When refitting the camshaft, or fitting a new camshaft, liberally lubricate the journals. Note that cylinder heads with 0.004 in.undersize bearings are marked with a white paint dot below the rocker arm cover near to the front bearing. General Motors Parts Dept. supply camshaft bearings for journals with 0.02.in undersize only: this provides replacement possibilities for all permissible dimensions.

When pressing in the bearings, ensure that the oil bores in the bushings coincide with the oil passages in the cylinder head. The bearings must be bored to standard or to undersize, according to the journal size. After boring, all metal chips should be cleared from oil passages.

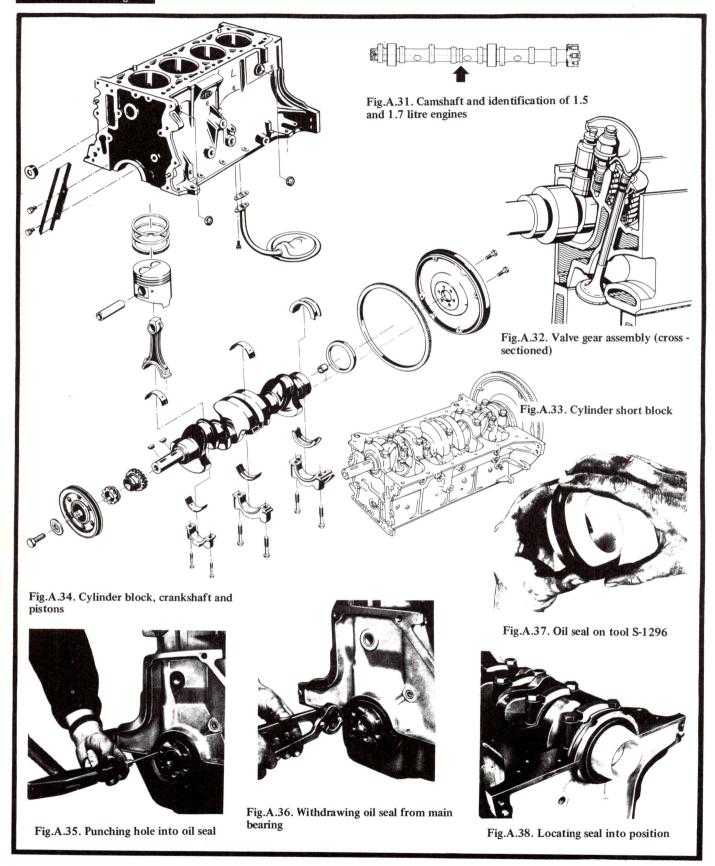

Fig.A.31. Camshaft and identification of 1.5 and 1.7 litre engines

Fig.A.32. Valve gear assembly (cross - sectioned)

Fig.A.33. Cylinder short block

Fig.A.34. Cylinder block, crankshaft and pistons

Fig.A.37. Oil seal on tool S-1296

Fig.A.35. Punching hole into oil seal

Fig.A.36. Withdrawing oil seal from main bearing

Fig.A.38. Locating seal into position

Fig.A.40. Piston and connecting rod assembly

Fig.A.39. Driving oil seal into position

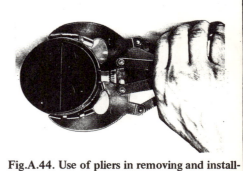

Fig.A.41. Pressing out piston pin

Fig.A.42. Notch in piston and oil hole in connecting rod

Fig.A.43. Correct assembly of connecting rod and piston

Fig.A.44. Use of pliers in removing and installing piston rings

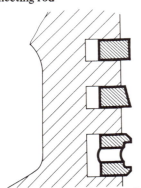

Fig.A.45. Piston ring shapes and positioning

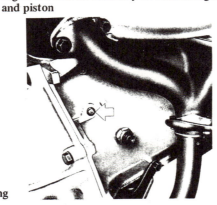

Fig.A.46. Engine coolant drain point

Fig.A.47. Coolant passage gasket (arrowed)

Fig.A.48. Sequence of tightening cylinder head bolts (white numbers)

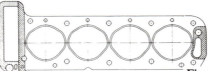

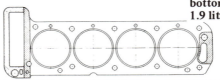

Fig.A.49. Top gasket for 1.5 litre engines; bottom gasket (circular apertures) for 1.7 and 1.9 litre engines

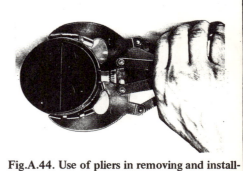

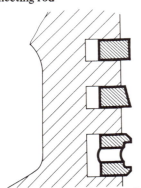

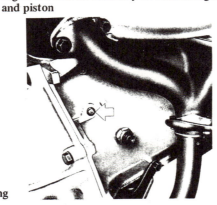

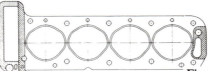

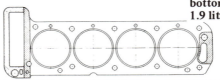

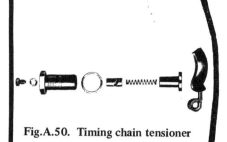

Fig.A.50. Timing chain tensioner

Fig.A.51. Inserting spring with plunger into sleeve

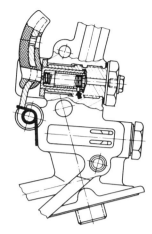

Fig.A.52. Cross section of tensioner assembly

Fig.A.53. Disengaging plunger of chain tensioner

Fig.A.54. Valve clearance adjustment

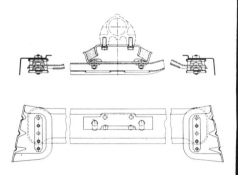

Fig.A.55. Damper block to transmission case attachment

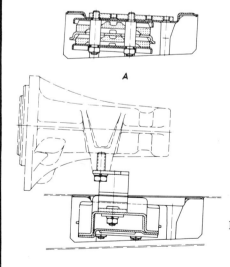

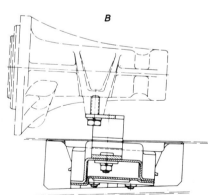

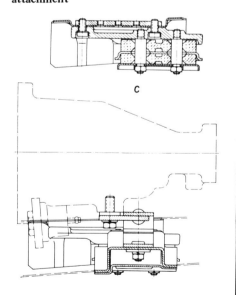

Fig.A.56. A. 3 speed transmission engine mounting
B. 4 speed transmissions engine mounting
C. Automatic transmission engine mounting

The camshaft of the 1.5 and 1.7 litre N engine differs from the camshaft of the other engines. It is distinguished by the bead between the second and third exhaust cam (Fig.A.31). This is visible even when the engine is in-situ by removing the access hole cover.

On reinstallation of the camshaft and the valve gear, amply oil all parts. A sectioned view of the valve gear assembly is shown in Fig. A.32.

REAR MAIN BEARING OIL SEAL - Replacement

Remove the flywheel and then with reference to Figs. A35 to A.37 obtain a suitable punch and punch a hole into the centre of the oil seal (Fig. A.35.) at the engine rear main bearing. Screw a sheet metal screw into the oil seal (Fig. A.36) and then, using a pair of pliers, withdraw the oil seal from its location.

Use tool S-1296 (Fig.A.37) and slide the new oil seal on to the tapered ring of the tool. Ensure that the lip of the oil seal is well coated with lubricant and roate the seal on the tool to ensure that the oil seal lip is not, or does not become, folded back.

Locate the tool and seal, as shown in Fig.A.38, into position on the crankshaft journal. Move the seal so that it goes into position over the journal and then remove the tapered ring. Drive the oil seal into its seating using a tool which gives an even pressure over the complete area of the oil seal.

PISTON AND CONNECTING ROD - Removal and Installation

Remove the cylinder head as previously detailed, drain the engine oil from the sump and remove the oil sump from the cylinder block. Remove the connecting rod bolts and withdraw the lower half of the big end bearing and its shell. Push the connecting rod and the piston up the cylinder bore and remove the assembly from the top of the cylinder block.

For replacing a piston it is recommended that tool S-1297 and electric oven MW 101 be used. General Motors state that all other tools are unsuitable as they cause structural changes and distortions of the connecting rod and piston.

The electric oven has a temperature range of 260 to 700ºF (130 to 370ºc). The red control lamp is lit when the oven is switched on and is extinguished as the set temperature is reached. For installing the connecting rod the temperature setting is 600º F (320ºc). The oven will take about half an hour to reach this temperature.

When replacing either a single connecting rod or a complete set, the weight variation of the individual connecting rods must not exceed 8 grams (0.28 ozs.) For this reason connecting rods are divided, in production, into different weight groups and colour coded. The weight is taken for connecting rods with bearing caps and bolts but without bearing shells. If the colour code paint spot cannot be ascertained, the replacement connecting rods must be accurately weighed. Small variations can be corrected by grinding material off the projection on the connecting rod bearing cap or by adding material to it.

Noting Figure A.40 and with reference to Fig.A.41, place the piston on to a support block which has a hole large enough to take the piston pin.

Use the arbor of tool S - 1297 to press out the piston pin from the piston and connecting rod. The pin is not suitable for re-use.

Place the connecting rod into the oven with the small end pointing toward the rear. Set the oven temperature to 320ºc (600ºF) and switch on and leave until the red light is extinguished.

Select a new piston and piston pin according to the following table:-

Piston Tolerance No.	Paint dot.	Tolerance No.	Piston Pin Paint dot.
1 and 2	Yellow	1	yellow
		2	white
3 and 4	Blue	3	blue
		4	black
5 and 6	Green	5	green
		6	brown

Slide the guide pin and the arbor of tool S - 1297 into the piston pin, which has been well oiled, and place them adjacent to the vice which is to be used for clamping the connecting rod.

When the connecting rod has reached its correct temperature, remove it from the oven with tongs and clamp it into the vice. Note that the piston cannot be fitted on to the connecting rod in a random fashion as the rod is not symmetrical. The piston head is at the front and the oil hole in the connecting rod (Fig.A.42) is on the righthand side when viewed in the direction of driving.

Insert the piston pin into the piston bore and place the piston over the connecting rod small end. Quickly push the piston pin into the connecting rod eye until the shoulder of the installation arbor connects with the piston skirt. The pin is now positioned correctly.

The connecting rod cools down very rapidly, it is therefore essential that the piston pin is located at the soonest possible moment. A correction of the piston pin seat after the connecting rod has cooled is not possible without risking some distortion of the piston.

Check, with reference to Fig. A.43, that the notch in the piston head is towards the front, the connecting rod oil hole is to the right and that when fitted the notch in the connecting rod cap points towards the rear. Fit the piston rings as detailed in the following paragraphs and then insert the assembly through the bore from the cylinder head end. Use new connecting rod bolts and tighten them to a torque of 36 lb.ft. Refit the cylinder head and engine oil sump.

PISTON RINGS - Removal and Installation

Loosen and then remove the connecting rod bolts and remove the piston and connecting rod assembly as previously detailed. Refer to Fig.A.44 and with a pair of piston ring pliers remove the piston rings. Use a piece of broken piston ring to de-carbonize the piston ring grooves: grind the end of the broken piston ring to a wedge shape to aid removal of carbon.

B

Fig.A.57. Pre-oiling the oil pump prior to engine starting

Fig.A.58. Sequence of manifold bolt tightening

Fig.A.59. Tightening the manifold bolts

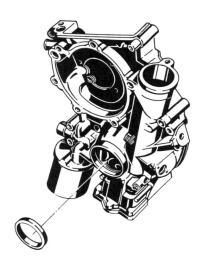

Fig.A.60. Timing case and oil seal

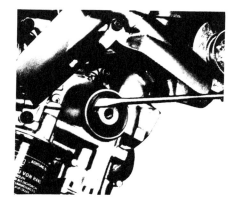

Fig.A.61. Prying out timing case oil seal

Refer to Fig.A.45. and fit the piston rings into their correct grooves. Do not overstrain the rings during installation. The centre ring is identified as to its correct position by having the word TOP stamped on to it.

Check the piston ring gap and its clearance against the following nominal values:-

Engine Type	1.5 litre	1.7 litre	1.9 litre
		Piston ring	
Upper ring	0.0118-0.0177 in.		0.0118-0.0217 in.
Centre ring	0.0118-0.0177 in.		0.0158-0.0217 in.
Lower (oil control) ring		0.0098-0.0157 in.	
		Piston ring clearance	
Upper ring		0.0024-0.0034 in.	
Centre ring		0.0014-0.0024 in.	
Lower (oil control) ring		0.0014-0.0024 in.	

Pistons with the index number "04" and higher which have been installed in production are provided with oversize piston rings.

CYLINDER HEAD GASKET - Replacement

Use a 9 mm articulated socket wrench to drain the cooling system at the engine block (Fig.A.46) and a 13 mm articulated socket wrench to remove the exhaust manifold flange attaching bolts. Note than on the 1.5 litre engine no gasket is fitted at the flange.

Remove the cover from the cylinder head and the sprocket from the camshaft as previously detailed. Remove the cylinder head bolts and rotate the camshaft so that the recesses are in the vertical position: this allows the left-hand row of bolts to be removed.

Prior to installing the cylinder head, rotate the crankshaft so that all pistons are below T.D.C., this aids correct attachment of the camshaft sprocket.

Clean the tops of the pistons and the combustion chambers and all sealing areas. Lightly oil the cylinder walls and install a coolant passage gasket in the timing case (Fig.A.47). Place the new cylinder head gasket (see following paragraphs) without any sealing compound, compensating gasket downwards, on to the cylinder block. Fit the cylinder head and tighten the bolts in the sequence shown in Fig.A.48 to a torque of 72 lb.ft.

Refit the camshaft sprocket, loosening the adjusting nuts of the open valves so that the valves do not touch the piston heads. Adjust all valve clearances.

Fig.A.49. shows the difference between the cylinder head gasket fitted to the 1.5 litre engine and the gasket fitted to the 1.7 and 1.9 litre engine. The latter has circular holes and the former elliptical holes for the cylinder bores.

Retighten the cylinder head bolts after 600 miles, ensuring that the engine is at its normal operating temperature. Tightening torque is 72 lb.ft. Re-adjust all valve clearances.

TIMING CHAIN TENSIONER - Removal and Installation

Remove the plug and gasket and loosen the chain tensioner body by 2 or 3 turns. Screw out the tensioner body by hand. If the body jams turn it back a little and free the plunger sleeve (Fig.A.11), if necessary use a 3 mm pin to loosen the sleeve-do not use force. Check the parts (Fig.A.50) for wear and replace as necessary. If excessive wear is apparent, replace the complete chain tensioner.

Refer to Fig.A.51 and insert the spring with its plunger into the sleeve so that the ratchet peg engages with the helical slot. Insert a 1/8 in Allen Key (Fig.A.53) into the plunger and turn it clockwise until the peg is out of the slot. The plunger is now engaged and the compressed assembly can be inserted into the body.

Screw the body, with its gasket, into the timing case and insert the oiled plunger sleeve with plunger so that the flattened part can slide on the provided area on the timing case. The guide pin must point downwards. Finally tighten the tensioner body with an Allen Key and by turning the plunger clockwise with the Allen Key disengage the plunger. Close the threaded hole with gasket and plug (Fig.A.53).

VALVE CLEARANCE - Adjustment

Run the engine until it is at its normal operating temperature (160°F coolant and 140°F oil). Remove the rocker arm cover and carry out the adjustment of both the inlet and exhaust valve adjustments while the engine is running. Refer to Fig. A.54 and adjust to 0.012 in. by turning the rocker arm nut. Use a feeler gauge to check the gap which when correct will cause the feeler gauge to slide with a feeling of friction.

With the engine running, in the condition shown in Fig.A. 54, oil will be thrown from the timing chain. It is necessary, therefore, to make up a metal deflector plate which can be secured into the two front bolt holes of the rocker arm cover attachment.

When replacing the rocker arm cover attach a new cork gasket to the cover, do not use cement. Adjust the engine idle revolutions to 600 - 650 r.p.m. for 1.5 and 1.7 litre engines and 700 - 750 r.p.m. for 1.7 - S and 1.9 - S litre engines: cars fitted with automatic transmission should idle at 550 - 600 r.p.m. with the selector in the "D" position.

EXHAUST MANIFOLD GASKET - Replacement

Use a 13 mm articulated wrench to disconnect the exhaust pipe from the exhaust manifold. Refer to Fig.A.6 and remove the manifold from the cylinder head; note that no gasket is provided for the two - hole flange on the 1.5 litre engine. Ensure that the scoop is properly positioned and bolt the exhaust manifold complete with the new gasket onto the cylinder head. Tighten the manifold bolts in the sequence shown in Fig. A.58.

Start the engine and run it until the correct operating temperature is attained. Re-tighten all the manifold bolts. Install the bolt with the dished washer in the rear on engines not provided with a scoop.

MANIFOLD INTERMEDIATE GASKET - Replacement

Refer to Fig.A.6 and remove the manifold assembly. Disassemble the manifold assembly and assemble together with the new intermediate gasket. Install the bolts only finger tight and then "tune - up" both manifold surfaces. To do this evenly tighten the assembly with its cleaned contacting areas WITHOUT the gasket, to the cylinder head. Tighten the assembly bolts and then remove the manifold assembly and re-install with the new gasket (Fig.A.59).

TIMING CASE OIL SEAL - Replacement

Refer to Fig.A.60 and remove the fan belt and the crankshaft pulley. Pry out the oil seal (Fig.A.61) by inserting a screwdriver behind the seal and using the crankshaft journal as a levering point.

Lubricate the new oil seal lip and press the seal into its location. Ensure the seal is fully "home" and coat the outer surface of the seal with a sealing compound (General Motors L000 167/4). Fit the crankshaft pulley and tighten it to a torque of 54 lb.ft., fit the fan belt and tension it correctly as detailed in section "COOLING".

Technical Data

		1.5 ltrs.	1.7 ltrs.	1.7 ltr. - S	1.9 ltr. - S	Remarks
Cylinder block		"15"	"17"	"17"	"19"	Embossed on left-and right-hand side of engine. 1.7 and 1.7 ltr.-S = equal
Bore	mm. (in)	82.5 (3.25)	88.0 (3.47)	88.0 (3.47)	93.0 (3.66)	Nominal value
Compression		8.2	8.2	8.8	9.0	Equal cylinder heads on 1.7 ltr. and 1.9 ltr.- S
Maximum brake horse poser (GMC - Test 20)		68	73	84	102	
Cylinder head gasket		Eliptical cutouts	Circular cutouts	Circular cutouts	Circular cutouts	Equal gaskets on 1.7, 1.7-S and 1.9-S
Cylinder head		"15"	"19"	"17"	"19"	Identification numbers stamped into land between 1st and 2nd valve lifter bore. Ribs at face mean: without rib = 1.5 ltr. one rib = 1.7 ltr.-S two ribs = 1.9 ltr.-S and 1.7 ltrs.
Camshaft		equal		equal		Identification between 1.5 and 1.7 ltr. engines: Bead between 2nd and 3rd exhaust cam or red paint marking
"Roto Caps"		no	yes	yes	yes	
Intake valve head diameter	mm (in)	38 (1.50)	40 (1.57)	40 (1.57)	40 (1.57)	Face alumetized
Exhaust valve head diameter		32 (1.30)	34 (1.34)	34 (1.34)	34 (1.34)	Face armored, head surface alumetized
Piston diameter	mm (in)	82.47 (3.247)	87.97 (3.463)	87.97 (3.463)	92.96 (3.66)	Nominal values, solid skirt "Autothermic" piston, recesses in piston head
Piston pin length	mm (in)	71.0 (2.795)	74.0 (2.913)	74.0 (2.913)	82.0 (3.228

	1.5 litrs.	1.7 litrs.	1.7 litrs - S	1.9 litrs. - S	Remarks
Piston clearance in bore mm(in)	0.03 (.0012)	0.03 (.0012)	0.03 (.0012)	0.04 (.0016)	Nominal value
Intake manifold	Two-channel system	Two-channel system	Two-channel system	Four-channel system	
Exhaust manifold	single	single	double	double	
Carburetor, choke	Manual (Opel)	Manual (Opel)	Automatic (Solex)	Double barrel with automatic (Solex)	
calibration	different				See table in group 8

Nomenclature		Technical Specifications				Check with:
Type of engine		1.5 ltrs.	1.7 ltrs.	1.7 ltr.-S	1.9 ltr.-S	

Cylinder, Crankcase, Pistons, Cylinder Head, Valves

Nomenclature	units	1.5 ltrs.	1.7 ltrs.	1.7 ltr.-S	1.9 ltr.-S	Check with:
Cylinder bore limits for standard-size pistons, size 1	mm (in.)	82.45-47 mm 3.245-3.246 in	87.95-97 mm 3.462-3.463 in	87.95-87.97 mm 3.462-3.463 in	92.95-97 mm 3.659-3.660 in	Dial gauge
Cylinder bore limits for standard-size pistons, size 2	mm. (in.)	82.48-82.53 (3.247-3.249)	87.98-88.03 (3.464-3.466)	87.98-88.03 (3.464-3.466)	92.98-93.03 (3.661-3.663)	Dial gauge
Cylinder bore limits for standard-size pistons, size 3	mm. (in.)	82.54-82.59 (3.250-3.252)	88.04-88.09 (3.467-3.469)	88.04-88.09 (3.467-3.469)	93.04-93.09 (3.664-3.668)	Dial gauge
Cylinder bore limits for oversize pistons (0.5 mm) .02 in. oversize	mm. (in.)	82.97-83.00 (3.266-3.268)	88.47-88.50 (3.483-3.485)	88.48-88.50 (3.483-3.485)	93.47-93.50 (3.679-3.681)	Dial gauge
Cylinder bore limits for oversize pistons 1mm (.04in.) oversize	mm. (in.)	83.47-83.50 (3.268-3.288)	88.97-89.00 (3.502-3.504)	88.97-89.00 (3.502-3.504)	-------	Dial gauge
Max permissible cylinder bore out-of-roundness	mm. (in.)	0.013 (.0005)				Dial gauge
Max. permissible cylinder bore typer	mm. (in.)	0.013 (.0005)				Dial gauge
Piston clearance, nominal		0.03 (.0012)	0.03 (.0012)	0.03 (.0012)	0.04 (.0016)	Dial gauge
No. 1 compression ring side clearance in piston groove	mm (in.)	0.060 - 0.087 .0024 - 0034				
No. 2 compression ring side clearance in piston groove	mm. (in.)	0.035 - 0.062 .0013 - .0024				Feeler gauge, roll ring in groove
Oil control ring side clearance in piston groove	mm. (in.)	0.035 - 0.062 .0013 - .0024				
No. 1 compression ring		0.30-0.45 (.0118-.0177	0.30-0.45 (0118-.0177	0.30-0.45 (.0118-.0177)	0.30-0.55 (.0118-.0216)	
No. 2 compression ring		0.30 - 0.45 (.0118-.0177)	0.30-0.45 (.0118-.0177)	0.30-0.45 (.0118-.0177)	0.30-0.55 (.0118-.0216)	Feeler gauge, ring installed in groove
Oil control ring		0.25-0.40 (.0098-.0157)	0.25-0.40 (.0098-.0157)	0.25-0.40 (.0098-.0157)	0.25-0.40 (.0098-.0157)	
Piston pin in piston		Selective fit according to paint marks yellow, blue and green				
Assembling piston to connecting rod		Heating connecting rod to 608° F (320° C) in electric over MW 101				

Valve spring pressure		Intake	Exhaust		
Valve closed	mm. (in)	41.5 = 33 kg (1.634 = 72.75 lbs.)	35 = 31 kg (1.378 = 68.34 lbs.)		Spring Scale
Valve open	mm. (in)	33.5 = 57 kg (1.319 = 125.66 lbs.)	27 = 59.7 kg (1.063 = 131.61 lbs.)		

		Technical Specifications				Check with:
Type of engine		1.5 ltrs.	1.7 ltrs.	1.7 ltr.-S	1.9 ltr.-S	
Valve dimensions		Intake		Exhaust		
Stem diameter, standard size		8.987-9.000mm (.3538-.3543in)		8.952-965mm(.3524-3528 in.)		
Stem diameter, 0.075 mm (.004 in.) oversize		9.062-9.075 (.3567-.3572in)		9.027-9.040 (.3553-.3559in)		Micrometer Vernier caliper
Stem diameter, 0.150 mm (.0059 in) oversize		9.137-9.150 (.3597-.3602in)		9.102-9.115 (.3583-.3588in.)		
Stem diameter, 0.300 mm (.0118 in.)		9.287-9.300 (.3656-.3661in)		9.252-9.265 (.3642-.3647in.)		
Total length, nominal		123 mm (4.843 in)		125 mm (5.021 in.)		
Valve head diameter						
intake	mm. (in.)	38 (1.496)	40 (1.574)	40 (1.574)	40 (1.574)	
exhaust		32 (1.259)	34 (1.338)	34 1.338)	34 (1.338)	
Valve guide bore in cylinder head (Intake and Exhaust)						
Standard size	mm (in.)	9.025-9.050 (.3553-.3562)				
0.075 mm (.004 in.) oversize		9.100-9.125 (.3582-.3592)				Dial gauge
0.150 mm (.006 in.) oversize		9.125-9.200 (.3615-.3622)				
0.30 mm (.0118 in.) oversize		9.325-9.350 (.3671-.3681)				
Valve stem clearance in guide Intake	mm. (in.)	0.025-0.063 (.001-.0025)				Micrometer
Exhaust		0.050-0.088 (.002-.0035)				Dial gauge
Max. permissible head to stem runout Intake	mm. (in.)	0.08 (.0032)				Valve checking gauge
Exhaust		0.05 (.0019)				
Valve seat and correction angle in cylinder head Intake and Exhaust		Valve seat angle 45° Correction angle 30°				
Valve face angle		44°				
Valve seat width in cylinder head Intake	mm. (in.)	1.25-1.50 (.049-.059)				Vernier caliper
Exhaust		1.60-1.85 (.063-.073)				
Valve head contact area		Aim at centricity				
Valve cleanance at 176° F(80°C) coolant and 140° F - 176° F (60° C - 80°C oil temperature Intake and Exhaust		0.30 (.012)				Feeler gauge
Cranking Mechanism						
Max. permissible out-of-roundness of connecting rod bearing journals		0.006 (.0002)				Micrometer
Max. permissible taper of connecting rod and crankshaft bearing journals		0.01 (.0004)				Micrometer
Max. permissible radial runout of crankshaft main bearing journals		0.03 (.0012)				Dial gauge
Max. permissible unparallelism of connecting rod bearing journals when crankshaft is placed in V-blocks so that main bearing journals next to each other are supported		0.012 (.0005)				Dial gauge
Max. permissible runout at crankshaft to flywheel contact area		0.02 (.0008)				Dial gauge
Crankshaft end play		0.043-0.156 (.0017-.0061)				Dial gauge
Main bearing clearance		0.023-0.064 (.0009-.0025)				Dial gauge Micrometer
Connecting rod bearing clearance		0.015-0.058 (.0006-.0023)				Dial gauge Micrometer
Connecting rod length play on bearing journal		0.110-0.242 (.0043-.0095				Feeler gauge

		Technical Specifications			Check with:
Type of engine		1.5 ltrs.	1.7 ltrs.	1.7 ltr.-S	1.9 ltr.-S

Max. permissible lateral runout of installed flywheel (reading taken on clutch friction area at 200 mm (8 in.) diameter)	mm (in.)	0.1 (.004)	Dial gauge

Valve mechanism

Camshaft bearing clearance	mm (in.)	0.025-0.065 (.001-.003)	Micrometer Dial gauge
Camshaft end play	mm(in.)	0.1-1.0 (.004-.04)	Feeler gauge
Max. permissible radial runout of camshaft center bearing (camshaft supported on outer bearings)	mm (in.)	0.025 (.001)	Dial gauge
Max. permissible radial runout of camshaft sprocket journal (camshaft supported on outer bearings)	mm (in.)	0.025 (.001)	Dial gauge
Valve lifter clearance in bore in cylinder head	mm (in.)	0.007-0.032 (.0003-.0013)	Micrometer Dial gauge
Weight difference of connecting rods without piston and bearing sheels, within one engine		max. 28 oz. (8g)	Scales
Fitting ring gear on flywheel		Heat ring gear to 356° F - 446°F (180° C - 230° C)	
Max. permissible lateral runout of ring gear		0.5 (.0197)	Dial gauge

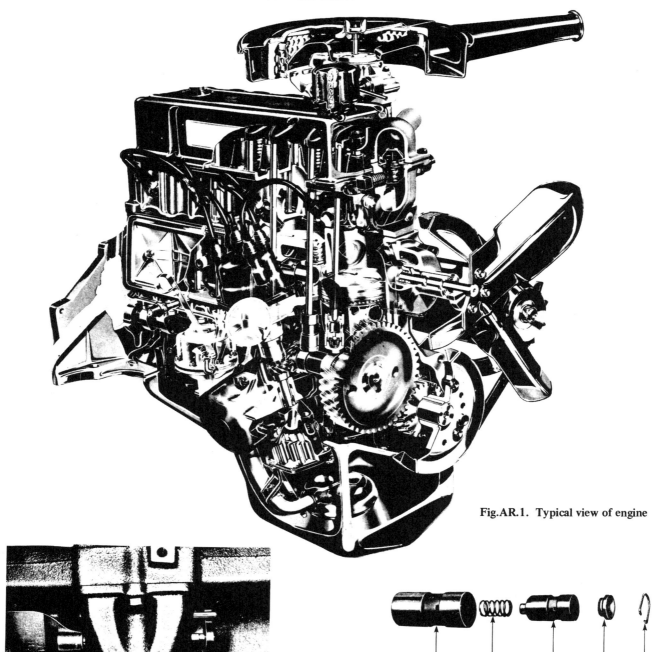

Fig.AR.1. Typical view of engine

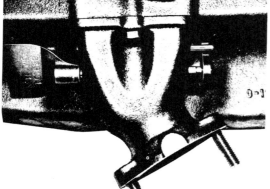

Fig.AR.2. Manifold heat control valve

Fig.AR.3. Valve lifter - exploded diagram

1. *Body*
2. *Spring*
3. *Plunger and ball check valve*
4. *Push rod seat*
5. *Retainer*

Engine -Ranger

DESCRIPTION

Two engines are fitted into the Ranger series car, these are the 130 HC cubic inch (2131 cc) and the 153 cubic inch (2508 cc). Both engines are in-line valve-in-head engines with five main bearings.

The engines use hydraulic valve lifters and hollow push rods to operate the individually mounted rocker arms. An oil pump, driven from the distributor shaft provides pressure lubrication.

ENGINE - Removal and Installation

Jack the car up and place it on stands which will adequately take the weight. Open the drain taps on the crankcase and the radiator and drain the cooling system into suitable containers. Lightly scribe alignment marks on the bonnet and the bonnet hinges and remove the bonnet.

Disconnect the heater hoses and the top and bottom radiator hoses at the engine attachment points. Remove the battery connections and then remove the radiator and the air cleaner. Disconnect the coil, the ground strap, the oil pressure, engine temperature, generator and starter cables. Disconnect and plug all fuel lines at the fuel pump and carburettor and also disconnect the accelerator control linkages and the choke.

Remove the exhaust pipe from the manifold and disconnect the clutch push rod, spring and relay lever engine link or bowden control cable. Remove the rocker arm cover and the vent valve and fit lifting eyes into two cylinder head bolt holes. Secure an engine hoist to the lifting eyes. Remove the propeller shaft and plug the end of the transmission extension housing.

Disconnect the steering idler arm bracket at the suspension crossmember and remove the mounting bolts from the rear of the engine. Unscrew the speedo cable and disconnect the transmission control rod linkage. Loosen the mounting bolts at the front of the engine and raise the engine to take the weight. Remove the engine mounting bolts and the transmission cross member and remove the transmission rear mounting. WARNING: stand clear of the cross member during removal as it is possible that the transmission extension and/or the cross member will swing suddenly downwards when released.

Check that no connections will prevent the engine from being removed and slowly lift the engine and the transmission from the car.

To install the engine use a hoist to lift the engine from the bench or frame and lower the engine and transmission unit slowly into its approximate installed position. Support the transmission and fit the rear cross member under the transmission mounting points. Lift the engine slightly and fit the front cross member. Lower the engine and position the front mountings over the cross member so that the securing bolts can be inserted. Fit the rear mounting bolts and disconnect the hoist and remove the lifting eyes.

Fit the propeller shaft and the U-bolts and join and secure the transmission. Fit the relay lever engine link, connect the clutch pedal and fork push rods and install the return spring. Connect the rods controlling the transmission. Connect the speeds drive cable and check, and if necessary refill, the transmission with oil. Make the connections to the carburettor and to the choke cable.

Fit the exhaust pipe to the manifold, using a new gasket and make all the necessary electrical connections to the engine including reconnecting the ground strap. Connect the fuel lines and fit the radiator and the hoses. Refill the radiator and check that the engine oil is at the correct level. Fit the bonnet assembly to the lines scribed at removal. Adjust the valve lash as necessary and fit the rocker arm cover gasket, the cover and rocker cover vent valve. Road test the car to ensure correct operation of all moving parts then check for leaks in the cooling system and the lubrication system.

MANIFOLDS - Removal, Inspection and Installation

Remove the wing nut securing the air cleaner and withdraw if from its location. Disconnect both of the throttle rods at the bell crank and remove the throttle return spring. Disconnect the fuel and the vacuum lines from the carburettor and remove the carburettor as an assembly. Remove the bolts securing the exhaust pipe at the manifold flange and then remove the manifold securing bolts and clamps and remove the manifold assembly.

Clean the connection flanges and check for cracks in the casting. The intake and exhaust manifolds can be disassembled by removing the attaching bolt and nuts. If this operation is carried out, ensure that the bolt is not tightened until after the manifolds are connected to the cylinder head. Use a new gasket and tighten the bolt to a torque of 15 to 30 lb.ft.

The installation of the manifold assembly is the reverse of the removal procedure taking note of the following instructions:- Use new gaskets for the manifold and a new packing seal at the connection of the exhaust pipe and manifold. The centre clamp bolts should be tightened to a torque of 25-30 lb.ft. and the end bolts to 15-20 lb.ft.

Check the manifold heat control valve for correct operation (it should be free). If it is sticking use a solvent to free it. An illustration of the valve is given in Fig. AR.2.

VALVE LIFTERS - Removal

Remove the rocker arm cover, loosen the rocker arm nuts and pivot the rocker arms to clear the push rods. Remove the plug leads and the high tension lead on the coil and the distributor. Remove the push rod cover and the gasket and withdraw the push rods and lifters. Identify the lifters and rods so that on installation they are fitted into the same location as they were removed from.

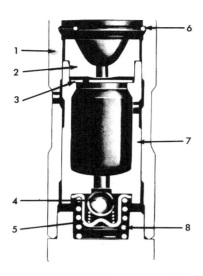

Fig.AR.4. Valve lifter - cross section

1. *Lifter body*
2. *Push rod seat*
3. *Metering valve*
4. *Check ball*
5. *Ball retainer*
6. *Push rod seat retainer*
7. *Plunger*
8. *Plunger spring*

Fig.AR.5. Adjusting valve lash

Fig.AR.7. Typical vacuum cup

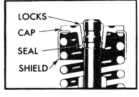

LOCKS
CAP
SEAL
SHIELD

Fig.AR.8. Valve installation

Fig.AR.6. Compressing the valve springs

1²¹⁄₃₂''
TO
1²³⁄₃₂''

Fig.AR.9. Valve spring installed height

VALVE LIFTERS - Dismantling and Assembly

Hold the plunger down with a push rod and remove the plunger and the push rod seat retainer. Remove the seat (Fig.AR. 3), plunger, check valve and the spring, it is necessary to remove the check valve from the plunger for the purpose of cleaning. A cross section of the valve lifter is shown in Fig.AR.4.

Clean all parts with a solvent and inspect them for damage or wear. If any parts require replacement then the assembly must be replaced.

To assemble, insert the lifter spring into the body and then the plunger and check valve: align the holes in the body and the plunger. Fill the assembly with SAE 10 and insert the push rod into the plunger and press it down until it is solid; the holes in the lifter body and the plunger assembly should be aligned. Insert a pin through the holes, to hold the plunger down against the spring tension, and remove the tool from the top of the lifter.

Fill the assembly with SAE 10 and install the push rod seat and the spring retainer. Depress the push rod seat and remove the pin.

VALVE LIFTERS - Installation and Adjustment

Install the lifters into the cylinder block, fit the push rods into the lifters and locate and fit the push rod cover with a new gasket. Insert the distributor, according to the position marked on the rotor housing during removal, and screw in the spark plugs and connect the cables.

Pivot the rocker arms in place and turn the adjusting nut until the lash is eliminated. Adjust the valve lash when the lifter is on the base circle of the cam as follows: - Remove the distributor cap and crank the engine until the rotor is at No.1 cylinder terminal with the contacts open: the piston of No.1 is at T.D.C. on compression and both valves can be adjusted. Turn the nut until all lash is eliminated from the valve train: check push rod side play by hand (Fig.AR.5) while adjusting. When there is no lash, turn the adjusting nut one more turn to bring the plunger to the centre of travel, then tighten to 14 lb.ft.

Continue the adjustment to cylinders 3 - 4 - 2 in that order until complete. Fit the rocker cover gasket, then the cover, check the engine oil level prior to starting the engine to check correct operation. Check for oil leaks and switch off.

CYLINDER HEAD - Removal

Drain the coolant from the system, remove the carburettor air cleaner, disconnect the choke cable and disconnect the accelerator pedal rod at the bell crank on the manifold. Remove the vacuum line and the fuel pipes at the carburettor.

Disconnect the exhaust pipe and remove the manifold complete. Remove the radiator hose at the water outlet housing, remove the plug leads and the spark plugs. Disconnect the battery and remove the battery ground lead from the cylinder head. Remove the pipe clip from the water outlet and disconnect the temperature sending unit and the coil.

Remove the bolts securing the rocker cover and lift off the rocker cover. Slacken the rocker arm nuts, pivot the rocker arms to clear the push rods and remove the push rods. Undo the cylinder head and the gasket and place it on two blocks of wood so that the valves are not damaged. Cover the exposed cylinders and pistons with a length of clean lint free cloth.

CYLINDER HEAD - Dismantling and Inspection

Remove the rocker arm nuts, the ball seats and the rocker arms. Compress the valve springs (Fig.AR.6) and remove the valve keys. Release the compressing tool and withdraw the spring caps, oil seals, spring seats, springs and the spring dampers. Push the valves down and remove them from the bottom of the cylinder head; identify them so that they can be replaced into their original positions. Remove the water outlet and the thermostat and then its housing.

Decarbonise the combustion chambers and the valve parts using a rotary wire brush. Clean the carbon from the push rods, guides and rocker arms and buff the valve stems and heads. Clean the head gasket mating surfaces.

Check the head for cracks or distortion and valves for burning or damage. Slide the valve stems into their respective bores and check to ensure that the bore clearance is not excessive. The intake valve stem to bore clearance should be 0.001 - 0.002 in. and the exhaust valve stem clearance 0.002 - 0.004 in. If the clearance is not within these limits the the guides should be reamed and oversize valves used.

If a valve spring tester is obtainable, test the springs at a compressed height of 1.21/32 in: the compression should be 84 to 92 lbs, if it is below 70 pounds it must be replaced. If no tester is available and the engine is low in power or has poor economy then it is recommended that new springs be fitted.

Check the valve lifters for a free fit in the block and check that the camshaft contacting surface end is smooth. If the surface is well worn or very rough then the lifter should be replaced.

Valves with oversize stems are available for both inlet and outlet in sizes 0.003 in, 0.015 in. and 0.03 in. Rocker arm studs with damaged threads can be replaced by standards studs but loose studs require oversizes of either 0.003 in. or 0.013 in.

Regrind the valve seats, if necessary, by cleaning the valve guides to ensure they are free of carbon or dirt then fitting a valve reseating tool. Insert the expanding pilot of the tool into the valve guide bore and tighten it into its correct position. Place the 46° forming stone over the pilot and clean the valve seat. Fit a finishing stone and smooth off. Narrow the valve seats down to the correct width of 1/16 to 3/32 in. for the intake and exhaust.

Remove the pilot tool and thoroughly clean all material from the cylinder head. Valves can be ground but not to a knife edge. If the edge of the valve head is less than 1/32 in. after grinding then the valve must be replaced. Use a refacing machine with the chuck set at 45°. Reface the valve until it is true and smooth all round, then remove any pitting from the rocker arm end of the stem.

To check good contact area make pencil marks approximately a quarter of an inch apart around the valve, across the

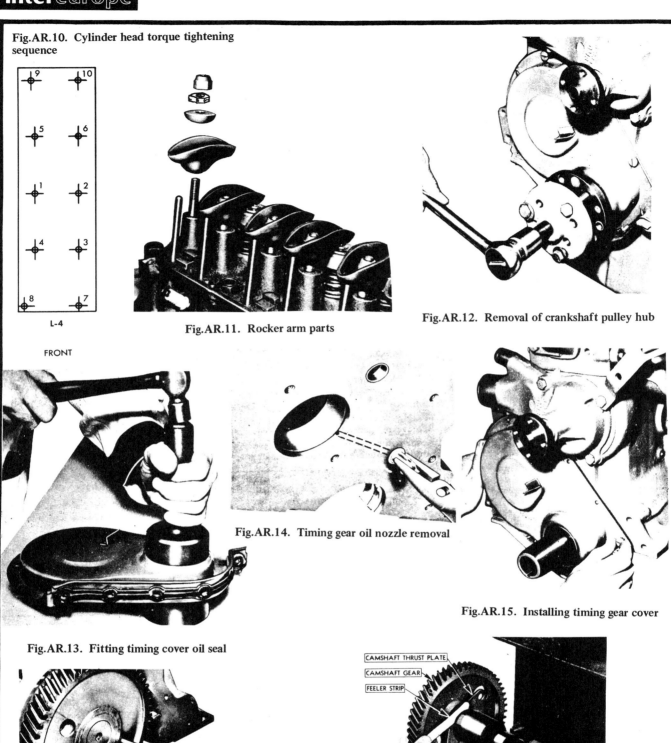

Fig.AR.10. Cylinder head torque tightening sequence

L-4

FRONT

Fig.AR.11. Rocker arm parts

Fig.AR.12. Removal of crankshaft pulley hub

Fig.AR.14. Timing gear oil nozzle removal

Fig.AR.15. Installing timing gear cover

Fig.AR.13. Fitting timing cover oil seal

CAMSHAFT THRUST PLATE
CAMSHAFT GEAR
FEELER STRIP

Fig.AR.16. Removing camshaft thrust plate screws

Fig.AR.17. Crankshaft end play

seating area; place the valve in the cylinder head and give it a half turn in each direction under pressure. If the pencil marks are not removed, regrind.

CYLINDER HEAD - Assembly

Commencing with No.1 cylinder, fit the exhaust valve into the head and secure it with the spring and cap. Place the spring and the rotator on to the exhaust valves, compress the spring and fit the seal and the valve keys. Note, the valve springs must be positioned with the closed coil end toward the cylinder head.

Assemble the remaining valves, springs etc. and check the seals by placing a vacuum cup over the stem and cap and squeezing the cup to ensure that no oil leaks past the seal. The valve installation is shown in Fig.AR.8 and a typical vacuum cup in Fig.AR.7.

Check the installed height of the valve springs; the measurement should be as shown in Fig.AR.9. If the measurement is in excess of that shown, fit a 1/16 in.spring seat shim.

CYLINDER HEAD - Installation

Fit a new gasket over the cylinder block dowel pins and check that the bores and the piston heads are clean and free from foreign particles. Carefully guide the head into place and after oiling the head bolts fit them finger tight. With reference to Fig. AR.10, tighten the bolts a little at a time in the sequence shown until all bolts are torqued to 95 lb.ft.

Insert the valve push rods down through the openings in the head and seat them in the lifter sockets. Fit the rocker arms, balls and nuts and tighten the rocker arm nuts until all the push rod play is eliminated (Fig.AR.11).

Fit thermostat and housing and the water outlet with a new gasket and then connect the radiator hose. Fit the temperature sending unit and tighten it to a torque of 20 lb.ft. Clean the spark plugs, check the gap at 0.028 - 0.032 in, and fit them. Clean the manifold gasket surfaces, fit a new gasket and then slide the manifold into place and secure it as detailed earlier within this section.

Connect all fuel lines, vacuum pipes, linkages etc. and fill the cooling system. Adjust the valve lash as previously detailed, fit the rocker arm cover, clean the air cleaner or change the filter as required. Run the engine and check for correct operation and also for leaks at all jointing surfaces.

TIMING GEAR COVER - Removal and Installation

Drain the radiator of coolant and remove it. Remove the crankshaft pulley and the hub (Fig.AR.12) and drain the engine oil and remove the sump. Unscrew the timing cover securing screws and remove the cover and its gasket.

After removing the timing gear cover it may be necessary to remove the oil seal by prying it out from the front with a screwdriver. Fit a new seal (with the lip inside the cover) and drive or press it into its location (Fig.AR.13). The timing gear oil nozzle can be removed using pliers (Fig.AR.14) and a new nozzle driven into place with a rubber hammer.

To install the cover, clean the gasket surfaces of both the cover and the block and fit a centering tool over the end of the crankshaft. Obtain a new gasket and coat it with light grease prior to sticking it into position on the block. Fit the cover and secure it with the screws to a torque of 7 lb.ft. Remove the centering tool, fit the crankshaft hub and pulley and fit the oil sump with new gaskets and seals.

Fit the radiator, connect the hoses and fill the cooling system. Fill the engine with the correct oil and then check all new gaskets for leaks. Run the engine and re-check.

CAMSHAFT - Removal, Inspection and Installation

Drain the oil from the engine and the water from the radiator. Disconnect all items from the engine assembly and with care remove it from the chassis. Remove the valve cover and the gasket, loosen the valve rocker arm nuts and pivot the rocker arms clear of the push rods.

Remove the distributor, noting its rotor position. Remove the coil, side cover and gasket and remove the push rods and valve lifters. Remove the crankshaft pulley and hub and the oil sump and timing gear cover. Remove the two camshaft thrust plate screws as shown in Fig.AR.16 and remove the camshaft and gear assembly by pulling it through the front of the block. Support the shaft carefully as it is removed so as to avoid damage to the camshaft bearings.

The cast iron alloy camshaft has three bearing journals with a dimension of 1.8682 - 1.8692 in. This dimension should be checked for an ovality which must not exceed 0.001 inch. If the camshaft exceeds this it should be replaced.

Check the camshaft end play as shown in Fig.AR.17, the clearance should be 0.001 to 0.005 inch and examine the camshaft bearings to see if they need replacing. If the inspection of the camshaft indicates that the shaft, gear or plate be replaced, then they must be removed from the shaft using tool J - 0971 (camshaft gear remover).

Place the camshaft through the gear remover and put the end of the remover on a press table and press the shaft out of the gear as shown in Fig.AR.18, Position the thrust plate so that no damage is caused by the Woodruff key and support the hub of the gear to prevent damage to the gear.

Assemble the camshaft by supporting the shaft at the back of the front journal in an arbor press. Fit the gear spacer ring and the thrust plate over the end of the shaft and insert the Woodruff key. Locate the camshaft gear and press it on to the shaft until it contacts the gear spacer ring. Check that the clearance of the thrust plate is between 0.001 and 0.005 in.

Install camshaft assembly into the engine block taking care not to damage the bearings or the cams. Turn the crankshaft and the camshaft until the valve timing marks on the gear teeth align then push the camshaft into mesh. Fit the camshaft thrust plate and tighten the screws to a torque of 7 lb.ft.

Check the camshaft and the crankshaft gear runout with a dial indicator (Fig.AR.19). The camshaft gear runout should not exceed 0.004 in.and the crankshaft gear runout 0.003 in. If these measurements are exceeded the gears must be removed and any burrs cleaned from the shaft; if this does not bring the runout within the tolerance then the gear must be replaced.

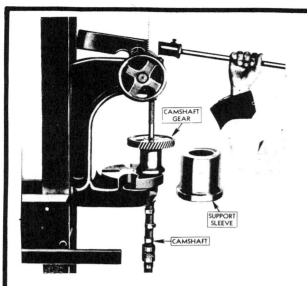

Fig.AR.18. Removing the camshaft gear

Fig.AR.19. Camshaft gear runout dial check

Fig.AR.20. Checking timing gear backlash

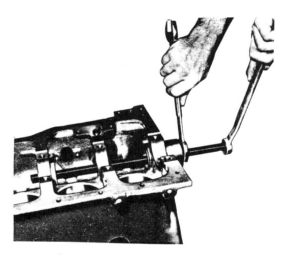

Fig.AR.21. Removing the camshaft bearings

Fig.AR.22. Driving in front and rear bearings

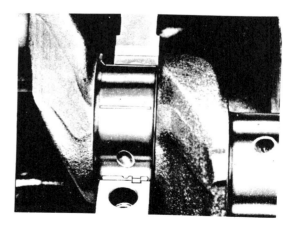

Fig.AR.23. Plastigage fitted on the journal

Check the backlash (Fig.AR.20) with a dial feeler gauge; the measurement should not be less than 0.004 in. and not more than 0.006 in.

Fit the timing cover, the gasket, the oil sump cover (with new gaskets) and install the crankshaft pulley, using a harmonic balancer installer tool J - 8782. Align the keyway in the crankshaft pulley hub with the key on the crankshaft and drive the hub on to the shaft until it contacts the crankshaft gear. Fit the valve lifters and push rods and the side cover with a new gasket. Install the distributor, positioning the rotor according to the marks made during removal. Pivot rocker arms over the push rods and lash the valves as previously detailed in this section.

Lower the engine assembly into the chassis and connect and secure it as required. Fit the fan belt and adjust the tension by moving the generator. Install the radiator and connect the hoses. Fill the cooling system with water and the engine with correct oil. Start the engine and check for leaks. If necessary check and adjust the timing.

CAMSHAFT BEARINGS - Removal and Installation

The bearings can be replaced while the engine is dismantled or after the camshaft and flywheel have been removed. The operation is eased if the crankshaft is also removed.

Drive out the expansion plug from the rear cam bearing, working from the inside. Position a bearing pilot in the inner bearing and fit a nut on the puller screw so that the screw can be threaded into the pilot while the nut extends from the front of the block. Fit the remover section on to the puller screw, fit the screw through the cam bore and thread it into the pilot.

Hold the screw shaft and turn the puller nut (Fig.AR.21) to remove the bearing. Remove the pilot from the shaft and fit it on to a driver handle (ensure that the shoulder is against the handle). Drive out the front and rear bearings from the outside to the inside of the block.

Upon installation, fit the inner bearings first. Remove the handle from the pilot and fit the inner bearing on to the pilot. Position the inner bearing and the pilot to the rear of the inner bearing bore and install the screwshaft (complete with remover adapter) through the block, from the front of the engine, into the pilot. Align the oil holes on the bearing and gallery and tighten the nut against the adapter. Hold the screwshaft and turn the puller nut to pull the bearing into position. Note: The oil hole is on top of the bearing shell and is not visible, it is therefore necessary to align the bearing shell oil hole with the oil hole in the bore and mark the opposite side of the bearing and the block at the bore. This allows easy positioning during installation.

Fit the new number one bearing on the pilot with the drive handle attached. Align the bearing and the gallery oil holes and drive the bearing in from the front of the engine as shown in Fig.AR.22. The front bearing must be driven in until the oil hole to the timing gear oil nozzle (Fig.AR.14). is uncovered.

Repeat the previous operations to drive the rear bearing into position from the rear of the block. The rear bearing is positioned flush with the inner edge of the rear cam bearing bore. On completion of assembly fit a new expansion plug at the rear bearing.

MAIN BEARINGS - Replacement

The main bearings are precision insert types and do not use shims for adjustment pruposes. If the clearances are excessive then new standard or oversize bearing inserts are required. Shimming may be necessary if the main bearing caps are replaced, laminated shims are available and will be determined by the bearing clearance.

With the crankshaft already removed, remove the main bearing caps and the connecting rod caps and lift the crankshaft out of the cylinder block. Inspect and measure the crankshaft, the journals are ground to 2.2978 - 2.2988 in. and the crankpin journals to 1.999 - 2.000 in. If the journals exceed 0.001 in. out-of- round or the crankshaft is tapered it should be replaced or reground to an undersize figure.

Remove the old bearing shells from the cylinder block and from the caps. Remove the rear main bearing oil seal and install the new bearing shells in the cylinder block and caps. Note: the shells with oil holes are the upper halves of the bearing shells and must be inserted between the crankshaft and the cylinder block. Place the crankshaft in the bearings and fit the bearing caps (the caps are identified with an arrow which must point to the front of the engine).

Check the crankshaft end clearance and the main bearing clearance. Fit a new rear bearing oil seal and fit the connecting rod bearings and caps.

MAIN BEARING - Clearance

Use Plastigage to check the clearance. Plastigage consists of a wax-like material which compresses evenly between the bearing and journal surfaces without damage to either.

To assure proper seating of the crankshaft, remove the rear main bearing oil seal and torque all bearing cap bolts to the specified figure. Wipe the surface of the crankshaft journal and bearing to clean off all oil. Start at the rear main bearing and remove the cap; wipe the oil from the journal and bearing cap.

Place a piece of Plastigage the full width of the bearing (parallel to the crankshaft) on the journal (Fig.AR.23). Do not rotate the crankshaft. Fit the bearing cap and evenly tighten the bolts to 65 lb.ft. Remove the bearing cap and note that the Plastigage is adhering to either the shell or journal. Without removing the Plastigage check its compressed width, at the widest point, with the graduations on the Plastigage envelope (Fig.AR.24). If the clearance is not over 0.004 in.(worn) or 0.003 in.(new) or is not less than 0.001 in. then the insert is satisfactory. If the clearance is not within these limits then the insert must be replaced.

If a new bearing cap clearance is less than 0.001 in. check it for burrs or nicks and if none is found insert shims as required. Note: bearings are available in standard sizes and 0.002 in, 0.01 in, 0.02 in. and 0.03 in. undersize.

Proceed to the next bearing and after all have been checked rotate the crankshaft to ensure that no excessive drag exists. Check the end play by forcing the crankshaft to the extreme front position and checking at the front side of the rear main bearing with a feeler gauge: the clearance should be between 0.002 and 0.006 in. (Fig.AR.25).

Fig.AR.24. Measuring the Plastigage in one thousandths of an inch

Fig.AR.25. Checking crankshaft end play

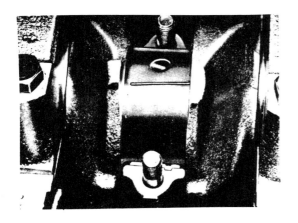

Fig.AR.26. Plastigage fitted on crankpin

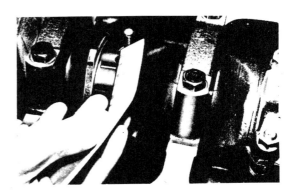

Fig.AR.27. Measuring the Plastigage on the crankpin

Fig.AR.28. Checking the connecting rod side clearance

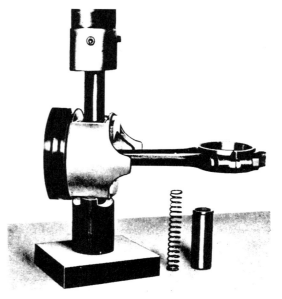

Fig.AR.29. Removing the piston pin

Fit a new rear main bearing oil seal in the cylinder block and main bearing cap.

CONNECTING ROD BEARINGS - Clearance

Connecting rod bearing inserts are available in standard sizes in undersizes of 0.001, 0.002, 0.01 and 0.02 inches. These bearings are not shimmed, excessive clearances need the next undersize bearing inserts. Do not file the rod or the rod caps.

Drain the engine oil and remove the engine. Remove the oil sump and the connecting rod bearing cap then wipe the bearing insert shell and the crankpin clean of oil. Place a piece of Pastigage the full width of the bearing on the crankpin (Fig.AR.26) so that it is parallel to the crankshaft, fit the bearing cap and evenly tighten the nuts to a torque of 35 lb.ft. Do not turn the crankshaft.

Remove the bearing cap and without removing the Plastigage check its width at the widest point with the gauge supplied on the envelope (Fig.AR.27). If the measure is not over 0.004 in or not less than 0.001 in.then the fit is satisfactory. If the clearance is not within these limits then the bearing must be replaced. Do not file the bearing caps. A new bearing shell insert clearance should be 0.003 in.maximum and 0.001 in. minimum.

Rotate the crankshaft after the bearing adjustment to ensure that the bearings are not too tight. Check the connecting rod end clearance between the connecting rod cap and the side of the crankpin as shown in Fig.AR.28.

Fit the oil sump complete with new gaskets and seals. Install the engine and fill it with the correct engine oil. Start the engine and check for oil leaks. With new bearings fitted the engine must be run in to ensure good performance.

PISTON AND CONNECTING ROD - Removal and Dismantling

Drain the engine oil and the cooling system and remove the engine. Remove the cylinder head and the sump and remove any ridge or any deposits from the upper end of the cylinder bores with a reamer. Prior to reaming, push the piston to the bottom of its travel and place a cloth on the piston to catch any of the deposits or cuttings. When the reaming is completed, turn crankshaft until the piston is at the top of its stroke and carefully remove the cloth and the deposits.

Check the connecting rods and pistons for cylinder identification and mark them on the side nearest the camshaft. Remove the connecting rod caps and push the rods away from the crankshaft; refit the caps and nuts loosely. Remove the piston and rod assemblies from the top of the cylinder block.

To dismantle, remove the piston pin as shown in Fig. AR. 29. Piston pins are matched to the piston and are not available separately. To assemble the piston and connecting rod, lubricate the piston pin and the rod and position the rod so that when assembled with the cast depression in the piston crown to the front of the engine, the marking on the rod is towards the camshaft.

Insert the piston pin on the installer and the pilot spring and the pilot in the support. Install the piston and the rod on the support, indexing pilot through the piston and rod.

Place the support on the arbor press and start the pin into the piston; press on the installer until the pin pilot bottoms.

Remove the installer and support assembly from the piston and connecting rod assembly. Check the piston pin for freedom of movement in the piston bore (Fig.AR.31).

Piston Rings

The piston rings are supplied in standard sizes and oversizes of 0.02 in, 0.03 in.and 0.04 in. The oil control rings consist of two segments and a spacer and the compression rings are the deep section twist type. Compression rings are marked with a cast number, this number should always be towards the top of the piston.

Remove the piston rings by expanding them and sliding them off the piston. Clean out the piston grooves and check them for signs of damage. Select the rings to be fitted and note that each ring should be fitted to its individual cylinder for correct gap spacing and to its individual piston and groove for correct groove clearance.

Push the ring into the cylinder bore and, using the head of the piston for that cylinder, press the ring down the bore until it is approximately two inches from the top of the bore. Check the gap between the ring ends with a feeler gauge (Fig.AR.32). The compression ring gap and the oil control ring gap are given in Engine Specification at the end of this section. If the ring does not meet its specific requirement remove it and try another.

Fit the rings to the pistons. Install the oil ring spacer in the oil ring groove and position the gap in line with the piston hole. Hold the spacer ends together and fit the steel rail on the top side of the spacer; position the gap at least one inch to the left of the spacer gap. Fit the second rail on the lower side, with the gap at least one inch to the right of the spacer gap. Check the clearance, as shown in Fig. AR.33, and refer to the Engine Specification at the end of this section. The compression ring clearance is between 0.002 and 0.0035 in. Ensure that the expander ends do not align with the ring gap.

PISTON AND CONNECTING ROD - Installation

Lightly coat the pistons, the rings, the cylinder walls with light engine oil and with bearing caps removed install tool J - 5239 on the bearing cap bolts. Use a clamp round the piston to hold in the rings then fit each piston (Fig.AR.34) into its correct bore: the side of the piston with the cast depression in the head should be to the front of the block.

Guide the connecting rod bearing into place and fit the bearing caps. Check the bearing clearance as previously described within this section. Fit the sump with new gaskets and seals. Fit the cylinder head with new gasket and install the engine into the chassis. Fill the engine with its correct oil and the cooling system with water and check for leaks.

CYLINDER BLOCK - Inspection

With the engine dismantled, check the cylinder block for cracks in the wall, or in the water jacket or on the main bearing webs. Check the cylinders for ovality and for taper, using a dial gauge as shown in Fig. AR.35. Set the gauge so that the thrust pin must be pushed in approx. 0.3 in. to fit the gauge in the bore

C

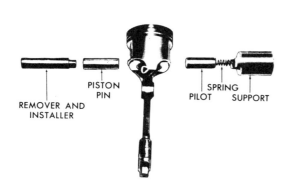

Fig.AR.30. Piston pin replacement

REMOVER AND INSTALLER

PISTON PIN

SPRING

PILOT SUPPORT

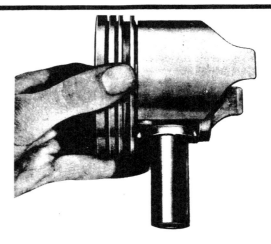

Fig.AR.31. Checking piston pin fit

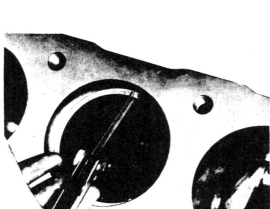

Fig.AR.32. Using feeler gauge to check ring gap

Fig.AR.33. Checking piston ring to groove clearance

Fig.AR.34. Fitting a piston

Fig.AR.35. Checking cylinder for out-of-round and taper

then turn the dial to zero. Determine the taper and out-of-round by moving the gauge to cover all parts of the cylinder wall. If the cylinder exceeds 0.002 in. out-of-round, it must be rebored or honed and oversize pistons fitted.

Technical Data

General Data:	130 cu.in.	153 cu.in.
Horsepower @ rpm	85 @ 4400	90 @ 4000
Torque @ rpm	128.4 @ 2800	152 @ 2400
Type	Valve-in-head	Valve-in-head
Number of Cylinders	4	4
Bore	3.563	3.875
Stroke	3.25	3.250
Displacement (cu.in.)	130 cu.in.	153 cu.in.
Taxable Horsepower (A.M.A.)	20.3	24
No. System (Front to Rear)	1 - 2 - 3 - 4	1 - 2 - 3 - 4
Firing Order	1 - 3 - 4 - 2	1 - 3 - 4 - 2
Compression Ratio	8.5 : 1	8.5 : 1
Compression Pressure*	140 PSI	140 PSI
Idle Speed		
Manual	550 RPM	550 RPM
Recommended Fuel	Premium	Premium
Cylinder Head Material	Cast Alloy Iron	Cast Alloy Iron

* At cranking speed with throttle open.

Cylinder Bore:		
Out-of-Round (max.)	.002	.002
Taper (max.)	.005	.005
Diameter (base)	3.563	3.875

Pistons:	
Material	Cast Aluminium Alloy
Type	Flat-Notched Head
	Auto Thermic Slipper Skirt
Clearance Limits	
Top Land	.033—.044
Skirt	.0006—.0010
Ring Groove Depth	
Compression Top	.1755—.1845
2nd	.1755—.1845
Oil	.183—.192

Piston Rings:	
Compression	
Material	Cast Alloy Iron
Type	One Piece Inside Bevel
Coating	Flash Chrome Plate
Width	.0770—.0780
Bevel Direction Upper	To Top of Ring
Lower	To Bottom of Ring
Gap	.010—.020
Oil Ring	
Material	Steel
Type	Multi-Piece—
	Rail Expander and Spacer
Coating (Rail)	Chrome
Width	.184—.188
Gap	.015—.055
Wall Thickness	.150—.156
Expanders	Yes

Piston Pins:	
Material	Chromium Steel
Length	2.990—3.010
Diameter	.9270—.9273
Clearance	
In Piston	.00015—.00025
In Rod	Press Fit
Wear Limit	.001
Offset Direction in Piston	.055—.060 To Camshaft
	(Right) Side

Connecting Rods:	
Material	Drop Forged Steel
Length (C/L to C/L)	5.700

Connecting Rods (Continued):	
Bearing	
Material	Durex (M-100)
Effective Length	.797—.807
Clearance	
New	.0007—.0028
Wear Limit	.0004
End Play	.008—.014

Crankshaft	
Material	Forged Steel
End Play	.002—.006
End Thrust Taken by	Rear Main Bearing
Main Bearing	
Journal Diameter and Bearing	
Overall Length	
No. 1	2.2983 x .802
No. 2	2.2983 x .802
No. 3	2.2983 x .802
No. 4	2.2983 x .802
No. 5	2.2983 x 1.008
Material	Durex (M-100)
Type	Precision Removable
Clearance (Min.—Max.)	.0008 — .0040
Crankpin Journal	
Diameter	1.999 — 2.000
Taper	.001
Runout	.001

Camshaft:	
Material	Cast Alloy Iron
Lobe Lift*	.22170
Cam Bearings	
Journal Diameter and Bearing	
Length	
No. 1	1.8692 x .90
No. 2	1.8692 x .90
No. 3	1.8692 x .90
Bearing	
O.D.	1 and 2—1.999—2.001
	3—2.009—2.011
Material	Extra-Life Steel Backed Babbit
Type of Drive	Gear
Crankshaft Gear Material	Helical Cut Steel
Camshaft Gear Material	Helical Cut Fibre

* Measured at Push Rod

Valve Systems:	
Lifters Type	Hydraulic
Rocker Arm Ratio	1.75:1
Valve Lash Adj.	
Intake (Hot)	1 Turn Down From No. Lash
Exhaust (Hot)	1 Turn Down From No. Lash
Timing Marks Location	Timing Gear
Valve Timing	
Inl.	
Opens (^{o}BTC)	61°
Closes (^{o}ABC)	84°
Exh.	
Opens (^{o}BBC)	84°
Closes (^{o}ATC)	61°
Intake	
Material	Carbon Steel
Overall Length	4.9024—4.9324
Head Diameter	1.715 — 1.725
Face Angle	45°
Seat Angle	46°
Stem Diameter	.3410 — .3417

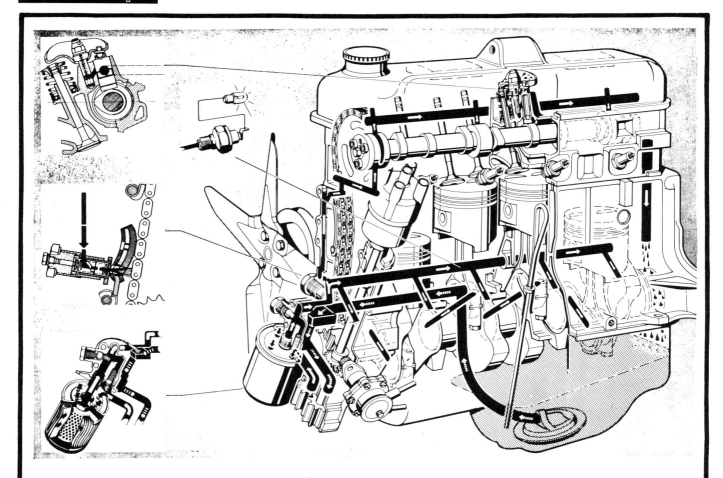

Fig.B.1. Engine lubrication system

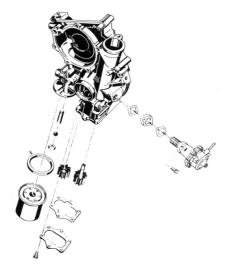

Fig.B.2. Oil pump and filter location

Fig.B.3. Position of oversize stamping

Fig.B.4. Oil pump - exploded

Lubrication System

DESCRIPTION

The engine is lubricated by a forced feed system incorporating a gear type pump driven by the distributor shaft. The pump body forms part of the timing case and a passage in the cylinder block, with a suction pipe, connects the pump to the screen cover assembly in the sump. The timing case also contains the pump pressure relief valve and the oil filter by-pass valve.

The filter is a full flow type with a by-pass system controlled by a valve to ensure direct oil circulation if the filter element becomes blocked. The valve is normally closed if the element is not restricted.

A diagram of the oil flow through the engine is given in Fig.B.1. The pump draws oil from the sump through the screen and then passes it through the timing case to the filter element. It then passes to the cylinder block main oil gallery, with a branch off to the No. 1 camshaft bearing. From the main gallery it flows to the main bearings of the crankshaft then to the connecting rod bearings.

The camshaft front journal controls the supply of oil to the cylinder head from where oil is forced, under pressure, to all the valve lifters, No. 2 and 3 camshaft bearings and the rocker arm seats. An additional passage connects the valve lifter and the rocker arm seat. All other lubrication within the engine is provided by splashed oil, or by gravity feed.

The engine has a positive crankcase ventilating system which is connected to the clean side of the intake system.

OIL PUMP - Overhaul

Note that some timing cases are installed, in production, with gear and shaft bores 0.008 in. oversize. This may apply to one or both gears but is anyway identified by an 0.2 stamped on the straight web of the pump housing. (The 0.2 refers to the oversize measurement in millimetres). Fig.B.3 shows the position with a white arrow.

Remove the oil pump housing cover and remove the oil pump parts (Fig.B.4). Check the oil pump pressure regulator valve for correct operation and install the new oil pump gears into a dry oil pump housing. Use a straight edge and feeler gauge (Fig.B.5) to check the end clearance of the gears. The gears must not protrude by more than 0.004 in. beyond the oil pump housing.

Refer to Fig.B.6 and using a feeler gauge, check the backlash of the gears. The gauge should show a measure between 0.004 and 0.008 in. Liberally oil the gears and insert them with the cover and a new gasket. Fit a new pump cover, the old one will be scored by the gear action. Remove the plug from the oil pump housing and prior to starting the engine fill the oil pump with engine oil.

OIL FILTER ELEMENT - Replacement

The filter element on a new, or on an overhauled engine, should be replaced after the first 600 miles, then after 3,000 miles and after every further 6,000 miles. It is not possible to clean the element, it must be disposed of.

Unscrew the filter element from the timing case using a strap wrench. Obtain a new filter element and lightly oil the rubber gasket (Fig.B.8) before screwing the filter element in by hand. Ensure that the gasket is correctly seated then tighten the element.

Start the engine and check around the filter for any leaks Stop the engine and check the oil level on the dipstick, replenish with the correct engine oil as required.

OIL FILTER PRESSURE RELIEF VALVE - Replacement

Remove the oil filter element as previously described and using a suitable drift, remove the valve sleeve which is located below the attaching flange (Fig.B.8). Do not, under any circumstances, damage the sealing area for the filter element. Remove the valve ball and spring.

Use a compressed air supply to clean the bore and the channel and insert the new spring and the valve ball. Locate the valve sleeve with the open sleeve side facing outward and using a drift, drive the sleeve into its correct position. Refit the filter element with reference to the description in this Section.

OIL SUMP GASKET - Replacement

To change the oil sump gasket it is necessary to remove the fan belt and place a cable around the groove of the water pump pulley. Connect each end of the cable to the hook of an engine lifting device (Fig.B.9 shows short cable S - 1220 and engine lifter S - 1244). Lift the engine until the engine mountings are not taking any weight.

Press the steering relay rod ball stud out of the Pitman arm and disconnect the front suspension cross member from the frame and the engine from the engine mountings. Note the heat deflector on the right-hand side engine mounting. Detach the brake hoses from the support and from the lower cross member and move the hoses only so far as to be clear without straining the hose or connections. Detach the left and right tie rod ball joints.

Remove the oil sump cover and thoroughly clean it and the oil pump screen. Clean the contact area around the bottom of the crankcase and remove the old gasket.

Prior to installing the oil sump cover and the gasket, coat the crankcase contact area with sealer and carefully line up and fit the new gasket parts. Fill the four gasket ends with sealing compound (General Motors recommend L 000 402/4) and coat the front and rear groove for the rubber gaskets with the same sealer as used for the crankcase contact area (General Motors recommend L 000 161/3). Install the gasket and the oil sump cover.

Carefully clean the outside of the sump cover to aid in checking for oil leaks. Refit the items removed and lower the engine until it is correctly located on its mountings. Replace the

Fig.B.5. Checking pump gear end clearance with straight edge and feeler gauge

Fig.B.6. Checking pump gear backlash with feeler gauge

Fig.B.7. Filter element location

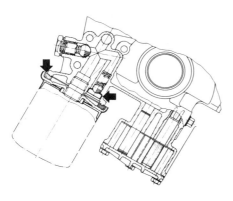

Fig.B.8. Cross section of filter showing gasket and valves

Fig.B.9. Lifting engine for sump removal

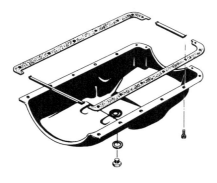

Fig.B.10. Oil sump and gasket assembly

Fig.B.11. Applying sealing compound

fan belt and check its tension and fill the engine to the maximum
mark on the dipstick with the correct engine oil. Start the
engine and check the sump contact area for leaks.

Technical Data

Oil pump gear backlash	mm (in.)	0.10-0.20 (.004-.008)	Feeler gauge
Oil pump gear end play in housing		Gears protruding over edge of housing: not more than 0.10 (.004)	Straight edge Feeler gauge
Clearance in spindle in bore of oil pump driven gear	mm (in.)	0.008-0.039 (.0003-.0015)	Micrometer Dial gauge
Clearance between oil pump drive gear and bushing	mm (in.)	0.009-0.038 (.00035-.0015)	Micrometer Dial gauge
Oil pump relief valve spring pressure at a spring length of 20mm (.8 in)	mm (in.)	7.05-10.58 oz. (0.20-0.30 kg)	Spring scale

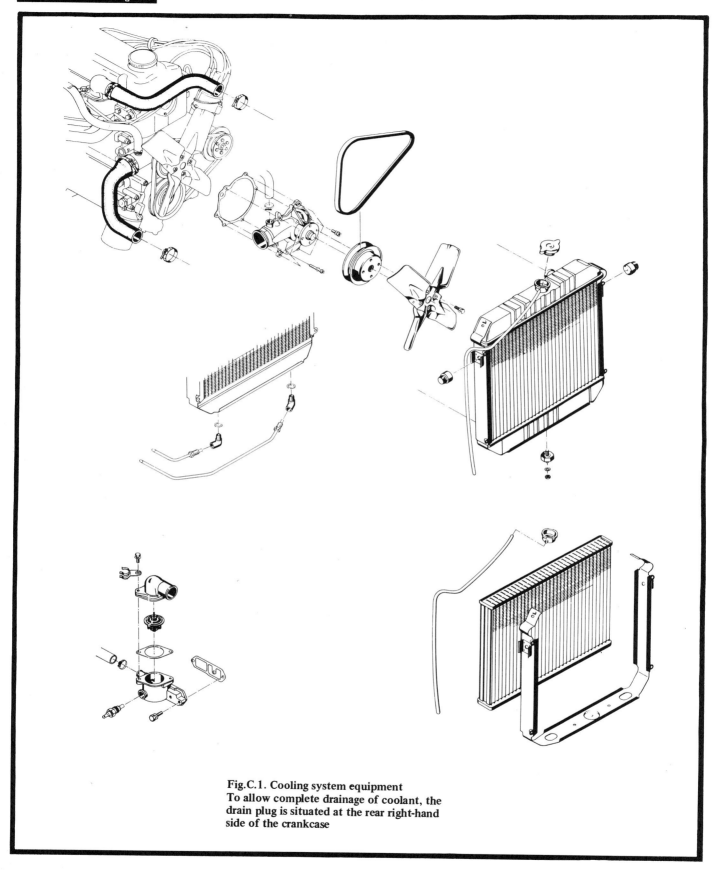

Fig.C.1. Cooling system equipment
To allow complete drainage of coolant, the
drain plug is situated at the rear right-hand
side of the crankcase

Cooling System

DESCRIPTION

The cooling system is of the pressure circulation type complete with a circulating pump and a temperature control thermostat. The radiator is of the fin and tube type with a pressure cap filler in the header tank. The water pump is driven by a belt via a pulley mounted directly to the face of the pump. A four - bladed fan is mounted on the water pump pulley.

The high pressure relief valve fitted into the radiator filler cap maintains a pressure of 11.4 lb./in^2 (0.8 kg/cm^2) this raises the boiling point of the coolant to approx. 241ºF (116ºC). The cap is identified with a number 800. In order to avoid contraction of the coolant hoses as the temperature drops, a low pressure valve is incorporated in the filler cap which opens at a vacuum of 0.9 to 1.4 lb./in^2 (0.06 to 0.1 kg/cm^2) and so admits air into the cooling system.

A pellet type thermostat is fitted at the front right - hand side of the engine and incorporates a temperature feeler. The thermostat remains closed below a temperature of approx. 188º F (87ºc) and the coolant is drawn from the cylinder head through a by - pass channel into the crankcase. The thermostat is fully open at 216ºF (102ºC). If there is a defect in the thermostat it will remain closed and therefore cause an excessive temperature rise which will be noticed on the temperature gauge.

To allow complete drainage of the cooling system a drain plug is fitted in the underside of the radiator and also at the lowest part-rear right-hand side of the crankcase. General Motors advise the use of the articulated wrench MW 113 to remove the crankcase drain plug.

Arranged in parallel with the coolant circulation is the preheating of the automatic choke and the carburettor. (1.7 s and 1.9 S engines) and of course the heater. On cars with automatic transmission a heat exchanger is incorporated in the radiator bottom tank.

NOTE: When filling the cooling system always use an anti-corrosion, anti-freeze mixture which will not freeze down to a temperature of - 22ºF (-30ºC). A test should be made at the beginning of the cold season to ensure that the coolant is up to this standard.

WATER PUMP - Removal

Drain the coolant from the radiator, disconnect the radiator hoses at top and bottom. If you are using an anti-freeze mixture which has not become too contaminated it should be drained into a suitable container and re-used.

NOTE: On vehicles with automatic transmission the oil lines should be unscrewed from their angled connectors at the lower radiator tank and the tank connectors and oil lines suitably plugged (it is essential that no dirt is allowed to enter the oil system).

Unscrew the hexagon nuts securing the radiator and lift the radiator out of the engine compartment. Loosen the bolts securing the generator and swing the generator in towards the engine to allow the fan belt to slacken, remove the fan belt.

Unscrew and remove the four bolts securing the fan and remove the fan and the fan belt pulley. Release and remove the hoses from the water pump then unscrew the bolts and withdraw the water pump from the timing case. Remove the gasket from between the water pump and the timing case and throw it away.

No individual spare parts are supplied for the water pump. therefore, a defective water pump cannot be satisfactorily overhauled but must be replaced with a new unit.

WATER PUMP - Installation

Ensure that the surface between the water pump and the timing case is clean, then locate the water pump, fitted with its new gasket, correctly on the timing case and partially tighten the securing bolts. With a torque wrench (or tool MW 82) tighten the bolts to a reading of 11 lb.ft.

Fit the fan pulley and the four - bladed fan and secure them with the necessary bolts. Check that both hoses to be fitted to the water pump are not perished or cracked in any way then push them firmly on before securing with clips. Fit the fan belt and adjust it by swinging the generator away from the engine until the fan belt can only be depressed by 0.3 to 0.5 inches and then tighten the generator securing bolts. After tightening always check that no movement has been allowed which will cause the belt to be either too slack or too tight.

Check the radiator for leaks prior to installing (see RADIATOR - Removal and Installation), then position the radiator and secure it with its nuts. Push on the upper and the lower radiator hoses and secure them with their clips. Fit the automatic transmission oil lines then partially fill the radiator and then position the heater control on the facia to warm and start and run the engine at idling speed. Now continue to fill the radiator until it is 2 inches below the bottom of the filler neck, Fit the radiator cap, check for leaks and then switch off.

NOTE: After running the engine for a few minutes check the water level and top up as necessary. Always take care to allow the pressure to escape slowly. Complete removal of the cap prior to release of pressure will cause a gush of hot water with subsequent scalding.

THERMOSTAT - Removal, Inspection and Installation

Drain the coolant from the radiator into a suitable container and disconnect the water outlet of the top hose on the radiator from the thermostat housing by removing the two securing bolts. Remove the gasket and withdraw the peller type thermostat.

To check the valve opening temperature, submerge the thermostat together with a thermometer into water and then heat the water. Ensure that neither the thermostat or the thermometer are allowed to touch the side or the bottom of the water container as this will give incorrect readings.

The thermostat valve will start to open at approx. 188ºF (87ºc). At approx. 203ºF (95ºc) the thermostat will have opened (if it is in proper working condition) by 0.18 in (4.5 mm) and will be fully opened to 0.28 (7 mm) at 216ºF (102ºc). If the

Fig.C.2. Engine crankcase drain plug

Fig.C.3. Water pump, showing ratchet tool for removal

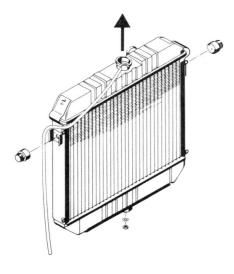

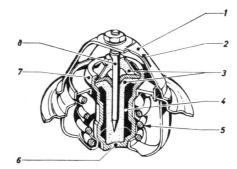

1. Thermostat shell
2. Arrow
3. Diaphragm
4. Wax
5. Closing spring
6. Pressure casing
7. Wax elememt
8. Actuating pin

Fig.C.5. Pellet type thermostat

Fig.C.4. Radiator and securing rubbers

Fig.C.6. Thermostat location

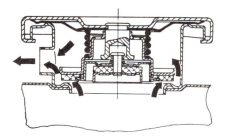
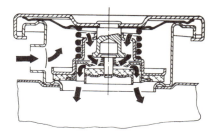

Fig.C.7. Radiator pressure cap
Left - At excessive pressure the relief valve opens
Right - At vacuum the low pressure valve opens

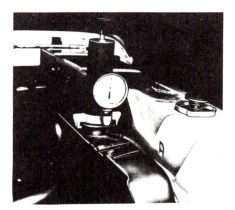

Fig.C.8. Checking radiator for leaks in - situ

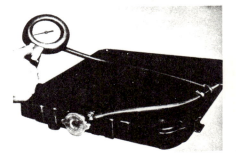

Fig. C.9. Checking radiator when removed

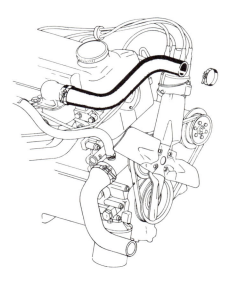

Fig. C.10 Radiator top hose

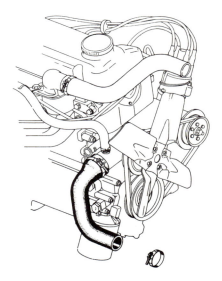

Fig.C.11 Radiator bottom hose

thermostat does not meet these requirements it should be replaced.

Install the thermostat in the housing, ensuring that the arrow on the side of the thermostat points upwards. Fit a new gasket and then secure the water outlet to the housing by the two bolts. Close the radiator drain tap and fill the radiator with coolant. During this filling operation move the heater control knob on the facia to the warm position and run the engine at idling speed. Top up the radiator as necessary and check for leaks.

RADIATOR - Removal. Inspection and Installation

Drain the coolant from the radiator into a suitable container. Release the clips securing the upper and lower hoses and withdraw them from the radiator. On vehicles with automatic transmission hold the angled connectors on the lower radiator tank with pliers, and unscrew the oil lines (plug the angled connectors and the oil lines to prevent undue oil loss).

NOTE: It is essential that no dirt is allowed to enter the automatic oil system.

Unscrew the nuts securing the radiator, including the one on the lower rubber radiator bumper and lift the radiator out of the engine compartment. Flush the radiator out with clean water.

To pressure test the radiator close off the top and bottom hose connection tubes so that they are air tight. Ensure that the plugs fitted to the oil line connectors (automatic transmission) are air and water tight. Remove the overflow hose and connect a 0.28 in. inside diameter pressure resistant hose to the overflow hose tube: secure it with a hose clamp. On the other end of the hose slide in a short length of 0.3 in. tube and secure it with a hose clamp. Attach a suitable pressure supply to the tube. Fit the radiator cap.

Place the radiator in a container filled with water until it is completely immersed and then slowly apply a pressure up to 14.2 lb./in^2 (1 kg/cm^2)' Do not exceed this pressure or damage to the radiator will result. Check that no air bubbles are escaping. If air bubbles are detected then carry out the necessary soldered repair.

Always ensure that the contact areas to be soldered are clean and that the solder contains 40% tin.

Position the radiator and secure it with its nuts. Push on the upper and lower radiator hoses and secure them with their clips. Fit the automatic transmission oil lines and partially fill the radiator with coolant. Position the facia heater control at warm and start up and run the engine at idling speed. Continue to fill the radiator until the level is 2 inches below the top of the filler cap neck. Fit the radiator cap, check for leaks, then switch off.

RADIATOR - Leak Test In-Situ

Check the level of coolant in the radiator and ensure that it is 2 inches below the top of the filler neck. Remove the filler cap and install a radiator pressure tester. Apply a pressure of approx. 14.2 lb/in^2 (1 kg/cm^2) and check the radiator, hoses, water pump gasket and engine block for leaks: bleeding coolant indicates the leaky spot. If the pressure decreases and no bleeding of coolant is noticed then internal coolant loss is indicated. An example of this is a defective cylinder head gasket.

Release the pressure, remove the pressure tester and check the coolant level. Top up as necessary and replace the radiator cap.

FLUSHING THE COOLANT SYSTEM

Approximately once yearly the cooling system can be flushed to avoid a build up of residue. Remove the radiator cap and insert a hose connected to a water supply, turn the water supply on after first releasing both the radiator drain tap and the cylinder block drain plug. Start the engine and allow to run at idling speed and position the facia heater control at warm. Allow the water to run until the water emerging from both drain points is clean: shut both drain points and refit the radiator cap.

Fuel System

DESCRIPTION

The fuel system incorporates a mechanically operated fuel pump, carburettor, fuel tank, accelerator control, choke control and air cleaner. The fuel tank is situated under the rear of the car and the fuel pump at the forward part of the engine.

FUEL PUMP - Removal

Pull the fuel line connecting hoses from the fuel pump fittings and plug the delivery hose. Remove the two bolts at the pump flange and withdraw the pump and the two paper and one asbestos gasket. Dispose of the paper gasket and retain the asbestos gasket.

FUEL PUMP - Dismantling and Assembly

Unscrew the bolt from the centre of the cover and lift off the cover and withdraw the fuel filter screen. Mark the upper and lower part of the pump, across the join, with a scraper to facilitate re-installation and then remove the bolts securing the two halves. With reference to Fig.D.5 unscrew the inlet valve and then remove the retainer from the push rod groove. Dismantle the lower part of the pump.

Check the sealing area for the inlet valve in the upper part of the pump and also the valve for correct operation. If on inspection, either of them are found to be damaged discard the upper part of the pump and replace with a new part. On the lower part of the pump check the outlet valve for correct operation and the oil seal ring, if either are defective replace with a new part.

Lightly oil the push rod and insert it into the pump body, together with the thrust springs. Fit the push rod retainer to the push rod groove and attach the upper and lower parts of the pump together: position the parts with reference to the markings previously made. Replace the fuel screen and bolt the cover to the pump body.

NOTE: Always use new cover gaskets.

FUEL PUMP - Installation

Fit the asbestos gasket between new paper gaskets and locate the pump into its position. Fit and tighten down the two fixing bolts. Remove the plug from the fuel delivery line and push the connecting hoses on to their fittings. Start the engine and check that the pump is delivering its correct amount of fuel and that there are no oil or fuel leaks.

CARBURETTOR - Removal

OPEL CARBURETTOR - 1.5 and 1.7 litre

Remove the air cleaner and pull the vacuum and fuel connecting lines from the carburettor fittings. Plug the lines to prevent the ingress of dirt and the loss of fuel. Disconnect and remove the bowden control wire from the carburettor and then remove the throttle control rod attaching parts. Remove the heater hose support and the bolts securing the carburettor to the inlet manifold and remove the carburettor. Place a clean cloth over the manifold opening to prevent dust or dirt or other foreign matter from entering the engine.

SOLEX CARBURETTOR - 1.7 S - and 1.9 litre - S

Open the radiator drain tap and partially drain the cooling system into a suitable clean container. Close the drain tap and remove the water hoses from the throttle valve body and from the automatic choke. On 1.7 litre S engines, remove the throttle control rod attaching parts. On 1.9 litre S engines, remove the retaining spring and then detach the throttle control rod from the throttle valve lever ball nut. With both carburettor types remove the heater hose support and the bolts securing the carburettor to the inlet manifold and remove the carburettor. Place a clean cloth over the manifold opening to prevent dust or dirt or other foreign matter from entering the engine.

CARBURETTOR - Dismantling

OPEL CARBURETTOR - 1.5 and 1.7 litre

Remove the two screws and remove the air intake from the carburettor housing. Unhook the metering rod spring and turn the metering rod a quarter of a turn to the left and then withdraw it. Remove the screws securing the carburettor cover and lift the cover off. Withdraw the carburettor pump plunger. With reference to Fig.D.15 screw out the nozzle jet end plug and the nozzle jet (identified A).

NOTE: Do not remove the emulsion tube. Screw out the idle passage end plug and the idling jet (identified B). Refer to Figs. D.16 to D.17 and unscrew the pump jet channel end plug and the pump jet. Screw out the pump inlet and the outlet check valve end plug, then unscrew the check valve. Withdraw the float spindle and remove the float and then the float valve. Unscrew the float needle valve seat and then remove the cap from the carburettor cover: the screen can now be removed. Screw out and remove the idle mixture screw.

CARBURETTOR - Inspection and Assembly

OPEL CARBURETTOR - 1.5 and 1.7 litre

Clean all parts of the carburettor with clean petrol (gasoline) using a soft-hair brush. Dry the parts and clean out all passage ways with compressed air. On no account should jets be cleaned with wire. Check all parts for signs of wear and renew them as necessary. Obtain a complete set of seal rings and gaskets and fit these as the carburettor is assembled. Locate the float valve and the float lever gauge (Opel tool S-601/6) - carry out this operation with the gasket removed. If it is necessary for the float level to be reset, bend the float lip. With reference to Fig.D.20, if the float lip (A) contacts the float needle and the float (B) contacts the gauge when the float is lightly depressed then resetting is not necessary.

Insert the mixture screw and screw down lightly, then

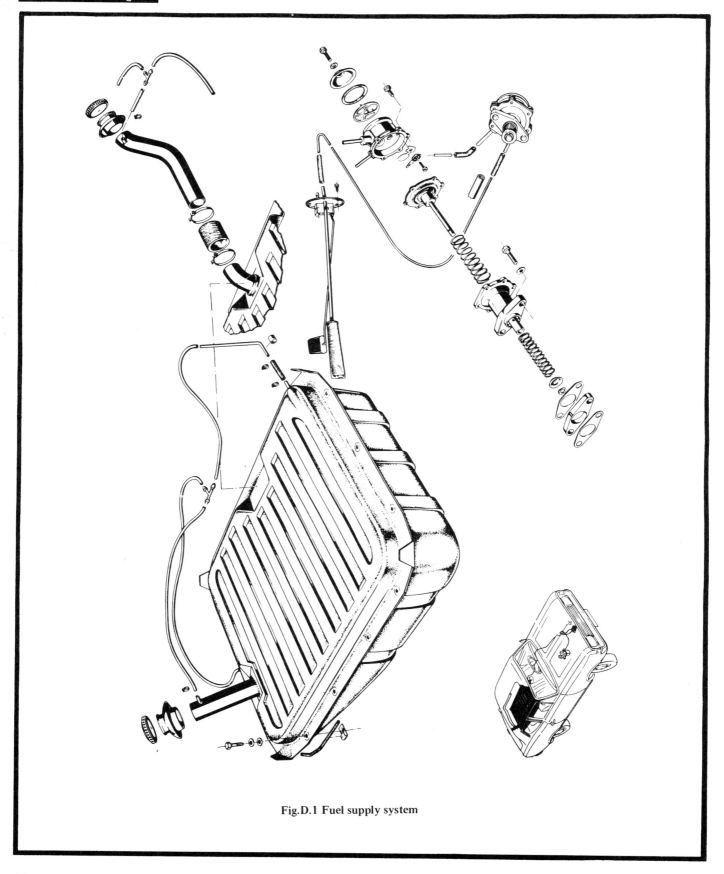

Fig.D.1 Fuel supply system

Fig.D.2.Fuel pump, showing securing bolts and hoses

Fig.D.3. Fuel pump and gaskets

Fig.D.4. Fuel pump cover and screen

Fig.D.5. Unscrewing inlet valve of pump

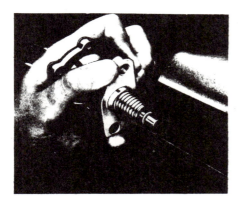

Fig.D.6. Lower part of pump

Fig.D.7. Pump upper part

Fig.D.8. Pump outlet valve

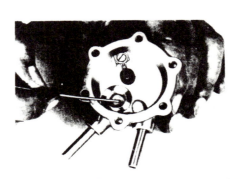

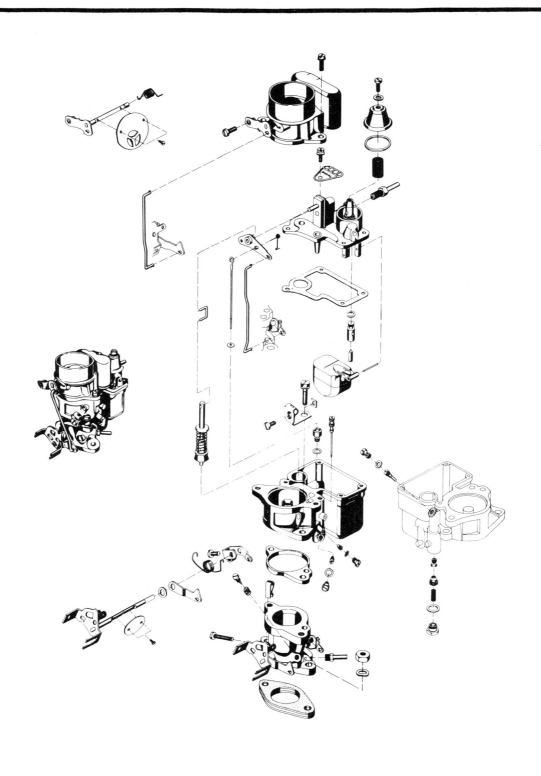

Fig.D.9. Opel carburettor - 1.5 and 1.7 litre

open by between 1.1/4 and 1.3/4 turns. Fit the screen and the cap into the carburettor cover then screw in the pump inlet and outlet check valve. Locate and screw in the inlet and outlet check valve end plug and the pump jet and its channel end plug. Refer to Fig.D.15 and fit and screw in the idle well jet (B) and its end plug. Locate the nozzle jet (A) and screw in its end plug. Refer to Fig.D.14 and screw in the idle jet (A) and the main jet (B).

Insert the accelerator pump plunger and check the clearance of the accelerator pump lever bushing on its shaft. If the clearance is excessive then the pump lever must be replaced. Fit the carburettor cover and secure it with the screws.

Fit the metering rod and then check as shown in Figs. D.22 and D.23 with a metering rod gauge 200: ensure that the throttle valve is fully closed. There must be no play between the throttle connecting rod and the accelerator pump lever (A) and if the gauge just touches the metering rod pivot pin (B) then the adjustment is correct. If adjustment is necessary, bend the throttle connector link at the throttle valve end (remember to remove the gauge before attempting adjustment).

CARBURETTOR - Dismantling

SOLEX CARBURETTOR - 1.7 litre - S

With reference to Figs. D.25 to D.27 remove the clamp ring and unhook the rod . Unscrew and remove the screws securing the carburettor cover, remove the cover and unscrew the float needle valve. Withdraw the copper sealing ring and remove the float, the float spindle and the leaf spring from the float chamber.

With reference to Figs. D.28 to D.31 screw out the idle jet (identified A) and the air correction jet (identified B). Unscrew and remove the end plug with its sealing ring and withdraw the main jet. Remove the clamp ring securing the accelerator pump connecting rod and remove the screw securing the pump to the valve body: remove the accelerator pump and spring. Remove the screws securing the upper and lower part of the throttle valve body and remove one from the other. Discard the gasket and unscrew and remove the idling mixture adjustment screw.

With reference to Figs. D.32 to D.36 loosen the locknut securing the main venturi retaining screw and withdraw the main venturi. Screw out the enrichment valve and then remove the fillister head screw and the filler pin from the carburettor cover. Remove the screws from around the automatic choke body pull off the retaining ring, then unscrew the bolt securing the automatic choke cover and remove the cover. Remove the three screws retaining the vacuum choke valve, carefully remove the cover in order that the spring is not lost.

CARBURETTOR - Inspection and Assembly

SOLEX CARBURETTOR - 1.7 litre S

Clean all parts of the carburettor with clean petrol (gasoline) using a soft - hair brush. Dry the parts and clean out all passage ways, including the vacuum and compensating bores, with compressed air. On no account should jets be cleaned with wire. Check all parts for signs of wear and renew them as necessary. Obtain a complete set of new seal rings and gaskets. relevant to this carburettor and fit them as the carburettor is assembled.

The assembly of the carburettor is the reverse of the dis-

mantling procedure but reference should be made to particular items which ensure satisfactory carburettor operation. Inspect the vacuum and compensating bores and check the vacuum plunger for free operation (Fig.D.37), check the moving parts on the automatic choke body including the diaphragm for wear and the actuating rod for free movement (Fig.D.38). Inspect the accelerator pump injector channel and the suction channel to ensure that they are perfectly clean and check the needle of the enrichment valve for any sign of wear. If the needle is worn, replace the complete valve assembly. Locate and install the venturi ensuring that both lugs rest in the cut-outs in the face of the housing.

Check the float for leaks prior to installation and do not bend the float arm to effect adjustment. With reference to Fig. D.40, fit the leaf spring so that the spring end rests upon the float spindle. Fit a copper sealing ring, which has a thickness of 0.08 in.(2 mm), to the float needle valve before inserting it into position. Check that the bi-metalic spring on the automatic choke cover is positioned on the bent end of the lever during installation and ensure that a new gasket is fitted to the cover prior to locating. After securing the automatic choke cover fit the clamping rings so that they have a lateral play of between 0.01 and 0.02 in. Fit the idling adjusting screw and screw fully down, back off the screw between 2 and 2.1/2 full turns to set at optimum setting. Slacken the throttle valve stop screw by 3/4 of a turn and check that the lever rests firmly against the diaphragm of the pump: use the brass nut to affect adjustment. When adjustment is considered to have correctly effected, caulk the pump connecting rod thread. At final assembly, close the choke valve and adjust the throttle valve gap to a measurement of 0.03 in.(0.85 mm) using the nut on the automatic choke connecting rod.

CARBURETTOR - Dismantling

SOLEX CARBURETTOR - 1.9 litre S

With reference to Figs. D.45 to D.47 remove the clamp ring and push the intermediate lever off the throttle valve lever pin. Remove the vent valve rod cotter pin and withdraw the clamp ring from its location: remove the carburettor cover. Refer to Figs. D.48 and D,49 and unscrew and remove the retaining ring prior to removing the cover from the automatic choke body. Unscrew the unloader cover of the vacuumatic choke valve, then unscrew the vacuum case as an assembly prior to dismantling it. Take care to retain the spring during dismantling.

Use a spanner to unscrew and remove the float needle from the cover and then withdraw the injection tube, the ball valve and the spring from the float chamber followed by the float, the float spindle and the leaf spring.

Refer to Fig.D.50 before removing the idle jet and the air correction jet from the primary and secondary carburettor barrels. They are identified as follows:-

A II	Secondary idle jet
B II	Secondary air correction jet
B I	Primary air correction jet
A I	Primary idle jet

With reference to Fig.D.51 screw out and remove the primary main jet AI and the secondary main jet AII. Screw out and remove the end plug B together with the ball valve and then remove both primary venturis. Remove the clamp ring

Fig.D.10. Opel carburettor attaching parts

Fig.D.11. Air horn removed from housing

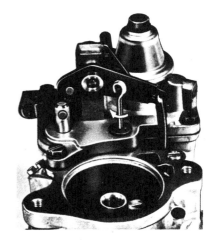

Fig.D.12. Carburettor metering rod

Fig.D.13 Opel carburettor cover and pump plunger

Fig.D.14. (A) idle jet, (B) main jet

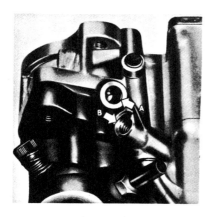

Fig.D.15. (A) nozzle jet, (B) idle jet

Fig.D.16. Pump jet channel end plug

Fig.D.17. Check valve

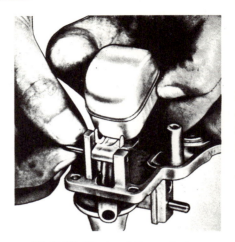

Fig.D.18. Float and float spindle

Fig.D.19. Cap and screen

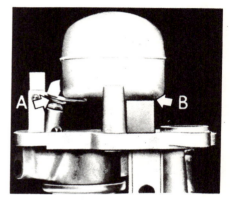

Fig.D.20. Float lip (A), float (B)

Fig.D.22. Metering rod and gauge

Fig.D.21. Accelerator pump plunger

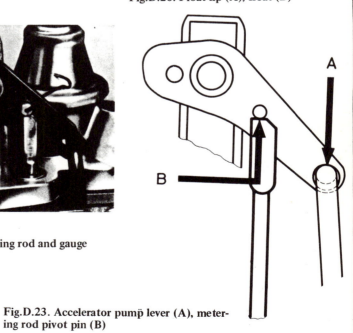

Fig.D.23. Accelerator pump lever (A), metering rod pivot pin (B)

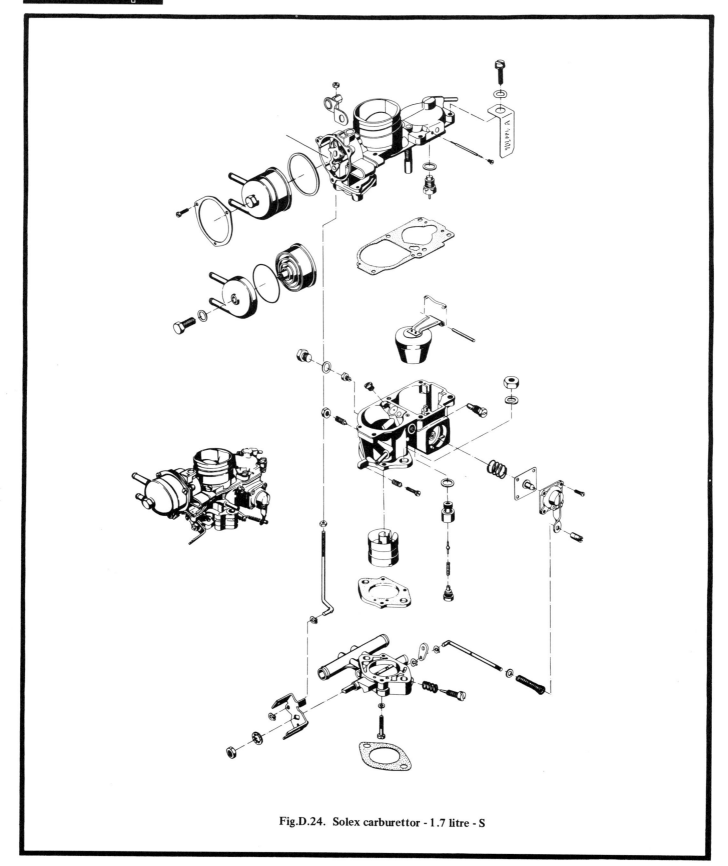

Fig.D.24. Solex carburettor - 1.7 litre - S

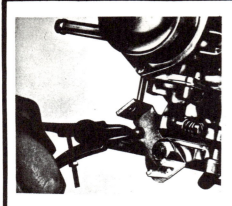

Fig.D.25 Removing clamp ring from Solex carburettor

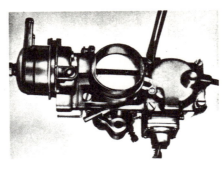

Fig.D.26 Carburettor cover

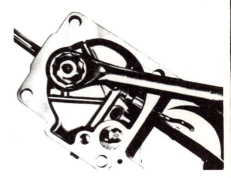

Fig.D.27. Removing the float needle valve

Fig.D28. Idle jet (A), air correction jet (B)

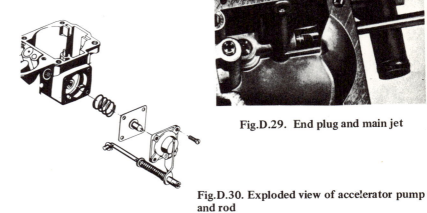

Fig.D.32. Main venturi and lock nut

Fig.D.29. End plug and main jet

Fig.D.30. Exploded view of accelerator pump and rod

Fig.D.33. Enrichment valve

Fig.D.31. Throttle valve body showing idle mixture screw

Fig.D.34. Filler pin

Fig.D.35. Automatic choke body and cover

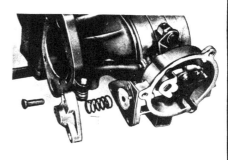

Fig.D.36. Vacuumatic choke valve

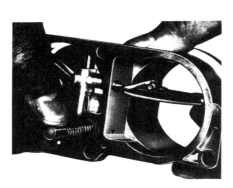

Fig.D.37. Vacuum plunger

Fig.D.38. Checking rod for free motion

Fig.D.39. Location of venturi lugs in housing

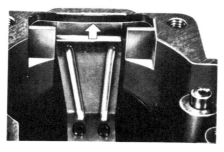

Fig.D.40. Installation of leaf spring

Fig.D.41. Automatic choke cover showing bi-metalic spring and lever

from the accelerator pump connecting rod, remove the screws securing the pump and withdraw the pump from the main body. Detach the throttle valve body as shown in Fig.D.52 and unscrew both the hot idle compensator and the idle mixture adjustment screws.

CARBURETTOR - Inspection and Assembly

SOLEX CARBURETTOR - 1.9 litre S

Clean all parts of the carburettor with clean petrol (gasoline) using a soft - hair brush. Dry all the parts and clean out all passage ways and jets, with particular attention to the fuel and vacuum passages, with compressed air. On no account should jets be cleaned with wire. Check all parts for signs of wear and renew them as necessary. Obtain a complete set of new seal rings and gaskets, relevant to the carburettor and fit them as the carburettor is assembled.

The assembly of the carburettor is the reverse of the dismantling procedure but reference should be made to the following items: - check that the operation of the push rod within the automatic choke body is free and positive. If the bushes in the vacuum case show signs of wear then fit a new vacuum case. Fit a copper sealing ring, with a thickness of 0.08 in.(2 mm), to the float needle valve before inserting it into position. Check that the bi-metalic spring on the automatic choke cover is positioned on the bent end of the lever during installation and ensure that a new gasket is fitted to the cover prior to locating. Locate and fit the automatic choke cover.

Check that the vent valve (Fig.D.54) is not bent and that it operates freely and note the cotter pin and washer position. Install the jets and the primary venturi:- refer to Technical Data at the end of this section. Locate and install the primary venturi, ensuring that the outlet arm fits into the bore. Check that the radial play on the throttle valve spindles is not excessive. Refer to Fig;D.55 and adjust the throttle valve of the secondary barrel to 0.002 in (0.05 mm); when the measure is correct, lock the screw. Refer to Fig.D.56 for connection of rod to intermediate lever - washer thickness should be 0.04 in.(1 mm).

Check the float for leaks prior to installation and do not bend the float arm to effect adjustment. With reference to Fig. D.57 fit the leaf spring with the spring end resting on the float spindle. Insert the injection tube with the bent end towards the primary barrel suction channel. Fit the outer clamp rings on to the connecting rods so that there is a lateral play of 0.012 to 0.02 in.(0.3 to 0.5 mm). Fit the idling adjusting screw and screw fully down, back off the screw 2.1/2 turns to set at optimum setting. Adjust the throttle gap to 0.04 in.(0.95 mm) by turning the nuts on the throttle connecting link (the choke valve must be closed). Refer to Fig.D.58 and check the play on the vent valve between the lever and the washer with the throttle valve closed; the play should be 0.24 in.(6 mm) and the correct measurement can be obtained by bending the intermediate lever.

Adjustment of Automatic Choke

Start the engine and run it until normal operating temperature is reached. Check the alignment of the markings on the automatic choke body and the cover (Figs. D.60). With the engine running, actuate the throttle linkage to approximately the half open position and then close the choke valve. Release the linkage and the choke valve simultaneously and do not touch the linkage

as the engine will immediately return to the normal idle speed. The engine speed should be 2400 r.p.m. on 1.7 litre engines and 2700 r.p.m. on 1.9 litre engines. If the correct engine speed is not shown then adjust by turning the nuts on the throttle connecting link (see Fig.D.61).

CARBURETTOR - Installation

Remove the cloth from the manifold opening, locate the carburettor (use a new gasket between the carburettor and the manifold) and secure it with the bolts to the manifold. Fit the heater hose support and then reconnect all linkages, hoses and bowden control wires. Refill the radiator with coolant as necessary and fit the air cleaner. Adjust the engine idling speed after the engine reaches its normal operating temperature by adjusting the throttle valve stop screw, now turn the idle mixture adjustment screw to obtain the highest engine revolutions. Reset the throttle valve stop screw to obtain the correct speed setting with reference to the following list:-

1.5 and 1.7	Manual Transmission	600-650 rpm
1.7 S and 1.9 - S	Manual Transmission	700-750 rpm
1.9 - S	Automatic Transmission	550-600 rpm

NOTE: the speed setting with automatic transmission should be obtained with the transmission selector at "D".

CARBURETTOR - Dash Pot - (Automatic Transmission)

To remove the dash pot unscrew the outer rear carburettor attaching nut and remove the dash pot and its bracket. When installing the dash pot ensure that the bracket is attached so that the dash pot pin is positioned at the centre of the throttle valve lever.

Adjust the dash pot by turning it in its bracket so that the dash pot pin is positioned 0.14 in.(3.5 mm) into the pot with the carburettor in the idle condition. Tighten the lock nut to prevent any change to this adjustment.

FUEL TANK - Removal

Disconnect the battery. Remove the drain plug from the fuel tank and collect the fuel in a suitable clean container. When the tank is empty screw in the drain plug and then remove all connecting hoses. Prise up the clips securing the fuel lines and the brake lines on the floor panel and then remove the filler cap and its rubber seal. Remove the connection to the fuel gauge tank unit and then unscrew the hexagon head screws securing the tank and from its location.

Cleaning

Remove the fuel gauge tank unit after removing the securing screws. Clean the fuel filter screen in fuel and then use compressed air to clean thoroughly. Partially fill the tank with fuel and then repeatedly move it to and fro before draining via the filler tank. Fit a new gasket to the fuel gauge unit and smear it with sealing compound prior to locating the unit into position in the tank. Secure the unit with screws.

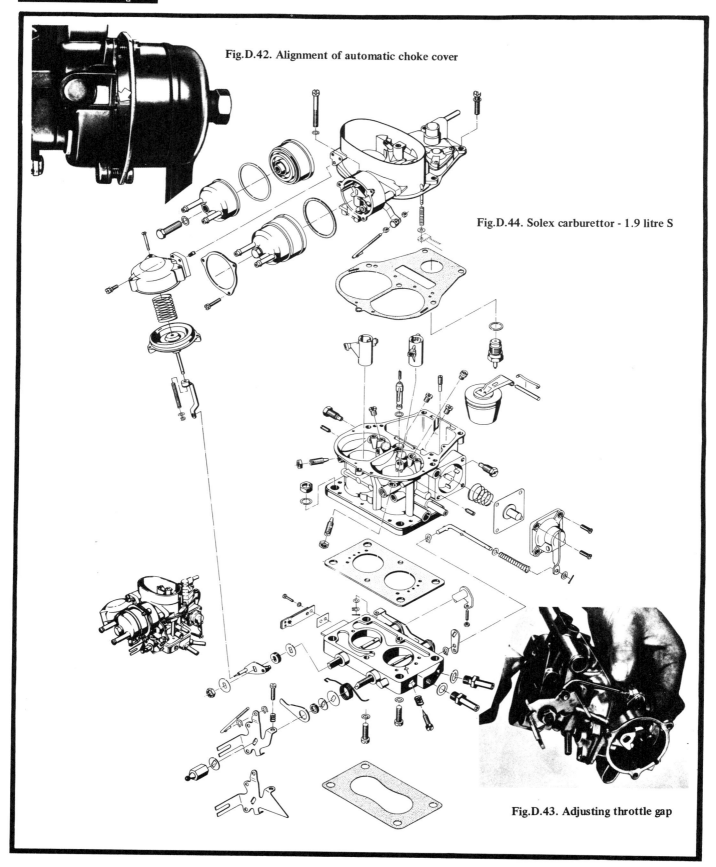

Fig.D.42. Alignment of automatic choke cover

Fig.D.44. Solex carburettor - 1.9 litre S

Fig.D.43. Adjusting throttle gap

Fig.D.45. Removing clamp ring

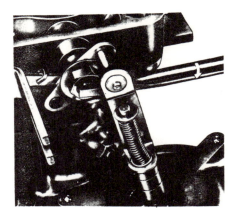

Fig.D.46. Intermediate lever and throttle valve lever pin

Fig.D.47. Removing vent valve cotter pin with pliers

Fig.D.48. Vacuumatic choke valve

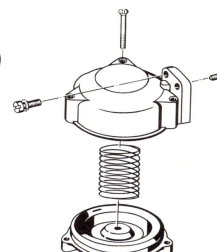

Fig.D.49. Exploded view of vacuum case

Fig.D.50. Identification of idle jets and air correction jets

Fig.D.51. Main jets (A1) primary, (A11) secondary, end plug (B)

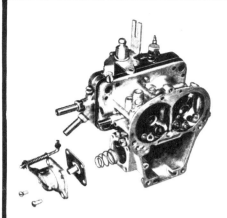

Fig.D.52. Accelerator pump parts

Fig.D.53 Throttle valve body and gasket

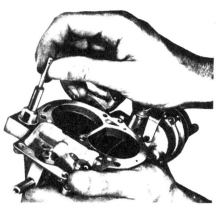

Fig.D.54. Vent valve and rod

Fig.D.55. Adjusting the secondary barrel throttle valve

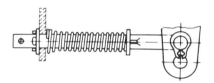

Fig.D.56. Connection of rod to intermediate lever

Fig.D.57. Installation of leaf spring

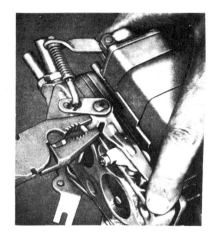

Fig.D.59. Correction of play by use of pliers

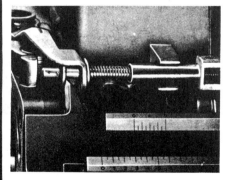

Fig.D.58. Area for checking play between vent valve lever and washer

Fig.D.60a. Alignment marks on choke body and cover - 1.7 litre S

Shorten linkage:

Slackening lower nut and tightening upper nut results in a decrease of engine rpm.

Fig.D.61a. Shortening throttle connecting link

Fig.D.60b. Alignment marks on choke body and cover - 1.9 litre S

Lengthen linkage:

Slackening upper nut and tightening lower nut results in an increase of engine rpm.

Do not twist throttle connecting link.

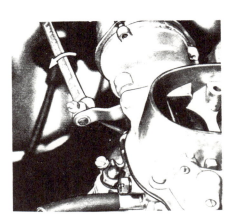

Fig.D.61b. Lengthening throttle connecting link

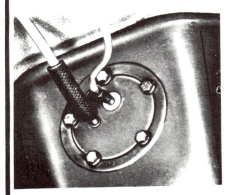

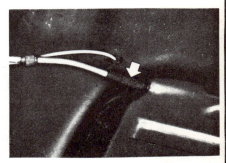

Fig.D.62. Fuel tank connections shown arrowed

FUEL TANK - Installation

Insert the drain plug into the tank and smear sealing compound on to the threads as it is screwed in. Insert sealing strip into the fuel tank well and use rubber cement to position as required. Use a plastic sealer on all areas of the tank and the tank well which contact each other then fit the tank into position. Coat the tank securing screws with sealing compound prior to securing the tank into position. Fit the rubber seal to the filler cap and then reconnect all electrical and fuel connections including the battery. Tip the fuel collected in the container into the tank using a clean funnel.

Technical Data

FUEL TANK

Capacity	14.5 galls. (55 litres)

CARBURETTORS

Engine Type	1.5 & 1.7	1.7 - S	1.9 - S	
Calibration	A	A	F	
Identification	2898545	2891504	2891006	
automatic clutch	2898546	2891505*	-	
automatic transmission	-	-	2891612	
Main Venturi diameter	25.5	28.0	24.0	28.0
Primary Venturi	-	-	2.8	3.2
Main jet	75	X140	X120	X155
Nozzle jet	200	-	-	-
Idle jet	60	g.52.5	g.50	g.75
Idle well jet	50	-	-	-
Pump jet	50	-	-	-
Air correction jet	-	110	120	80
Reduction jet	-	-	120	-
Float lever	0.47 in	-	-	-
Metering rod gauge	200	-	-	-
Float needle valve	-	1.75	2.0	-
Float needle valve seat	155	-	-	-
Float needle copper seal	-	0.08 in	0.08 in	-
Idle air passage	-	-	1.6	-

* light green paint dot near vacuum line connecting tube on float chamber - No Automatic choke.

Carburettor-Ranger

DESCRIPTION

The Ranger uses the Weber 36 DCD carburettor which is a dual barrel vertical downdraft type consisting of two single barrel carburettors with two venturis in each barrel. The carburettor has a progressive starting device which is actuated by the choke control. Fig. DR.1 shows an exploded view of the carburettor.

CARBURETTOR - Removal and Dismantling

Remove the air cleaner and the gasket fitted between the cleaner and the carburettor. Remove the throttle linkage from the throttle control lever and detach the fuel lines from the carburettor. Disconnect the choke control and remove the vacuum pipe from the carburettor connection. Remove the four retaining nuts and lift the carburettor and gasket from the manifold.

Start the dismantling by removing the fuel filter (Fig. DR. 2). Slacken the screws retaining the cover and then lift the cover off and remove the gasket. Gently push the float fulcrum pin from the cover and then lift the floats and the needle valve from the cover. Unscrew the needle valve seat and remove the sealing washer.

Remove the starting device air valve by withdrawing the circlip and the air valve plunger seat, plunger and spring. If necessary, gently tap out from the top the disc in the underside of the cover. Remove the accelerator pump as shown in Fig.DR.3; to dismantle the assembly, compress the spring, rotate the piston and withdraw it from the hooked end of the control rod followed by the spring and the split retainer.

Unscrew the accelerator pump inlet valve (Fig.DR.4) from the base of the float chamber. Shake the inlet valve to ensure that the ball inside the valve body slides freely. Remove the accelerator pump delivery valve between and on top of the barrels and lift the pump jet from the body. Note that there is a washer on both sides of the jet. Shake the delivery valve to ensure that the ball inside the body slides freely.

Unscrew the starting air corrector jet and the starting jet assembly and pull the starting jet from the carburettor jet. Remove the primary air corrector jet and emulsion tube assembly then the secondary corrector jet and emulsion tube from the top, between the barrels and the float chamber, of the carburettor.

Remove the idling jet holder from the side of the body, withdraw the jet from its holder and inspect the sealing ring. Unscrew the main jet holders from their locations on each side above the mounting flange. Remove the copper seating washer from each holder, hold the hexagon head and unscrew the main jet.

If necessary, inspect the progression hole by removing the inspection plug. Also, if it is necessary, to remove the starting device control shaft, remove the cover and remove the nut, washer, lever and spring then carefully prise out the starting device piston spring guide/retainer. Withdraw the spring and

invert the carburettor to extract the piston.

With reference to Fig.DR.5. remove the volume control screw and the throttle stop screw. With reference to Fig. DR.6 dismantle the throttle linkage by releasing the lock tab to allow removal of the outer throttle lever nut and the lever from the shaft. Remove the throttle mechanism cover from the body and remove the spacer and slotted thrust washer. Withdraw the secondary throttle actuating sector from the primary shaft.

CARBURETTOR - Inspection, Assembling and Installation

Clean the filter and the jets and examine the seating of the idling jet, starting jet and emulsion tubes. When replacing the air correction jets it should be noted that, to facilitate identification, the primary and secondary air correction jets have hexagon heads and the main jets are circular.

Fit new gaskets and also the sealing rings fitted to the idling jet holder, main jet holders, accelerator pump delivery valve, needle valve seat and filter retainer. Shake the accelerator pump inlet valve and delivery valve to ensure that the ball in each valve slides freely.

To assemble, fit the secondary throttle actuating sector over the primary throttle shaft; ensure that full throttle opening is available on both throttle valves. Replace the steel thrust washer and brass spacer. Fit the sector housing cover and then replace the accelerator lever locking tab and nut, tighten it and fit a locking nut.

Fit the starting device piston tapered end first and then the coil spring and spring guide/retainer. Refit the control shaft so that the arm is towards the bottom of the cover. Fit the return spring with its straight end in the cover hole and place the operating lever on the shaft and turn it so that it is against the stop furthest away from the clamping arm. Turn the spring counterclockwise and hook the end behind the lever; fit a washer and nut.

Locate the starting device cover by its dowels (Fig.DR.7) and secure it. Check that the piston can be raised by the lever and lowered by the spring action. Fit the progression hole inspection plug in the barrel above the mounting flange (Fig.DR.4) and then screw each main jet into its hexagonal holder and fit each holder in position above the mounting flange and below the flat chamber. Inspect the idling jet holder sealing ring and push the jet into the circular headed holder. Fit the holder on to the side of the carburettor below the top of the body (Fig.DR.5.).

Screw an air corrector jet into each emulsion tube (Fig.DR. 8). the primary jet is numbered 200 and the secondary 180. Fit the assemblies between the barrels and the float chamber. Push the starting petrol jet into the starter air jet, open end first, and screw it into the top of the carburettor between the float chamber and the barrels.

Fit the accelerator pump jet and delivery valve; locate a fibre washer in the recess (Fig.DR.8) and fit the pump jet. Fit another fibre washer then slide the delivery valve through the pump jet and screw it into the carburettor (Fig.DR.4).

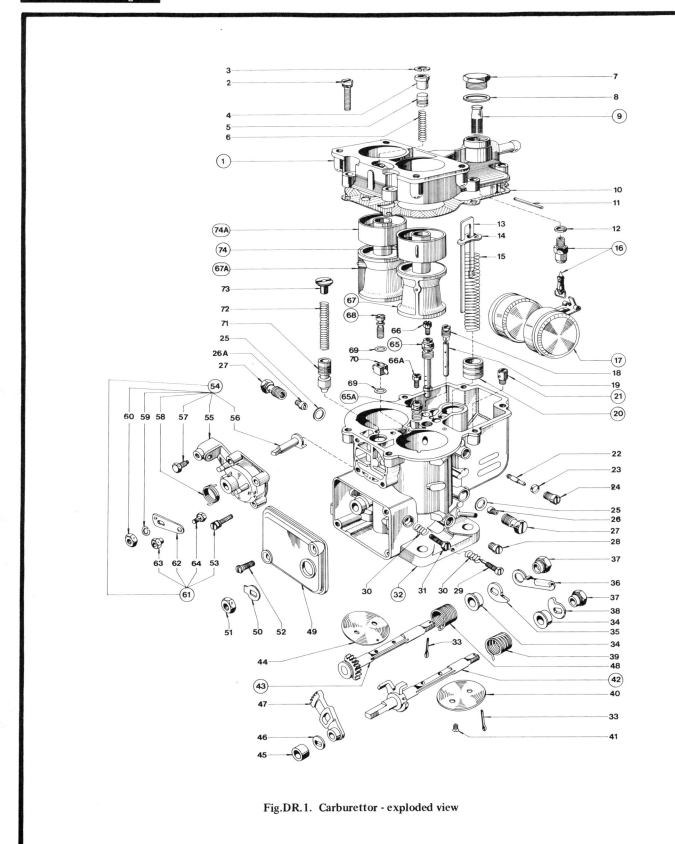

Fig.DR.1. Carburettor - exploded view

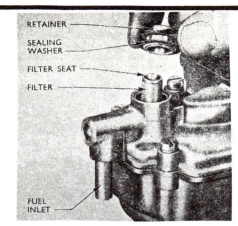

Fig.DR.2. Carburettor fuel filter

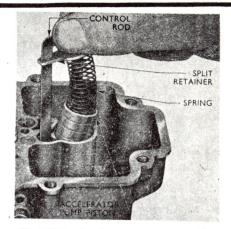

Fig.DR.3. Accelerator pump assembly

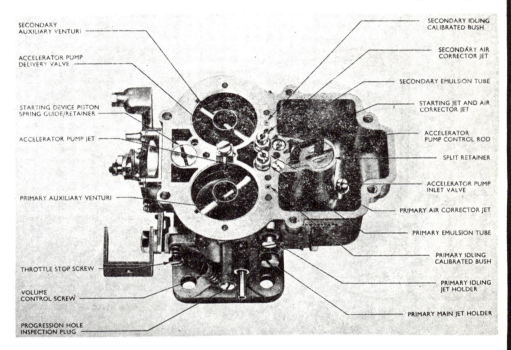

Fig.DR.4. Jet positions

Fig.DR.5. Carburettor - primary side

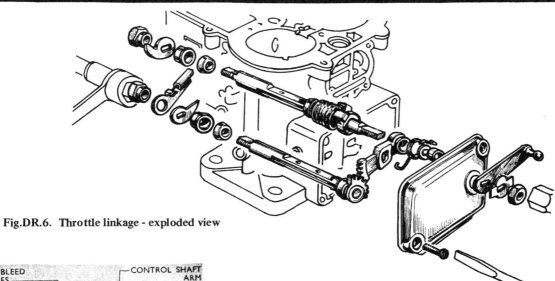

Fig.DR.6. Throttle linkage - exploded view

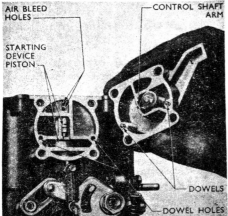

Fig.DR.7. Starting device piston and cover

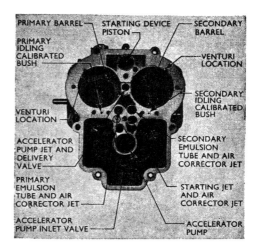

Fig.DR.8. Locations of carburettor jets

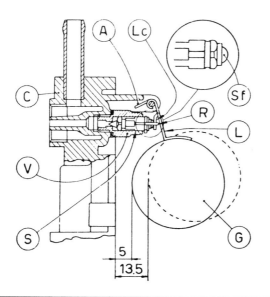

Fig.DR.9. Float level check identification

Check that the accelerator pump inlet valve ball moves freely; screw the valve into the base of the float chamber.

Reassemble and fit the accelerator pump, fit the assembly into the carburettor and press the split retainer into position. Check the operation of the pump by actuating the throttle. Invert the carburettor top and place the starting device air valve plunger into the bore. Fit the spring and retainer.

Screw the needle valve seat into the cover and refit the needle valve and floats. Slide the tab float under the needle valve hook and push the float fulcrum pin through the cover "legs" and float hinge.

With reference to Fig. DR.9, check that the float G does not leak and slides freely on its shaft and ensure that the needle valve V is screwed in tightly. Check that the ball Sf moves freely then hold the cover C so that the floats G hang down and the tab Le is in tight contact with the ball Sf. The distance between the floats G and the cover mounting face should be ˙5 mm. If necessary, bend the arms L to obtain this dimension.

Fit a new gasket on the carburettor and fit and secure the cover. Locate the filter in the top cover and screw the retainer, with a sealing washer, into the cover. Carefully screw in the volume control screw until it contacts its seat and then unscrew it two turns. Fit the throttle stop screw until it contacts the throttle stop lever then screw it in a further half-turn.

Install the carburettor assembly to the manifold ensuring that the gasket is in good condition. Tighten the nuts evenly. Connect the throttle linkage and fit the fuel supply pipe. Connect the choke control ensuring that the choke control on the facia is pushed fully in. Fit the distributor vacuum pipe and then fit and secure the air cleaner complete with a new gasket.

Adjust the slow running after running the engine until it is at its normal operating temperature.

CARBURETTOR - Adjustment

Screw in the throttle stop screw until the engine idles at a fast speed. Turn the volume control screw to obtain maximum vacuum (use a vacuum gauge connected to the inlet manifold). Readjust the idling speed until the maximum vacuum reading is gained consistent with a reasonable slow running speed.

Without a vacuum gauge, screw the throttle stop screw in to obtain a fast idling speed then screw the volume control screw until the engine runs evenly. Readjust the stop screw as necessary then adjust the volume control screw again. Repeat the operations until a satisfactory result is obtained.

Technical Data

Model		Weber 36 DCD	
Part No.		3422661	
Needle valve and seat	1.75 mm	Primary air correction jet	2.0 mm
Float weight	18 Grams	Secondary air correction jet	1.8 mm
Starting air corrector jet	1.5 mm	Primary venturi	27 mm
Starting Petrol jet	F 1/100	Secondary venturi	28 mm
Accelerator pump inlet valve	5 mm	Pump jet	.5 mm
Primary idling jet	5 mm	Primary auxiliary venturi	4.5 mm
Primary main jet	1.45 mm	Secondary auxiliary venturi	4.5 mm
Secondary main jet	1.45 mm	Float level	5.0 mm
Primary Emulsion tube	F 23	Float stroke	8.5 mm
Secondary Emulsion tube	F 23	Progression hole	1.95 mm

E

Fig.E.1. Throttle control rod spring

Fig.E.2. Transmission mounting positions

Fig.E.3. Dished washer on seal ring assembly

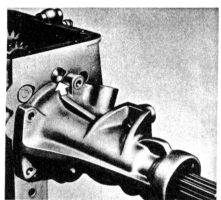

Fig.E.4. Arrow shows end of countergear shaft

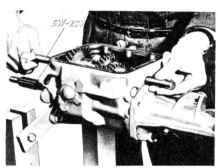

Fig.E.5. Driving out the countergear shaft

Fig.E.6. Countergear with thrust washers shown as (A)

Fig.E.7. Driving out pivot pin of reverse intermediate lever

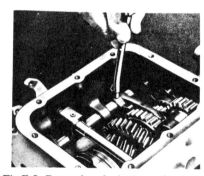

Fig.E.8. Securing bolts of selector shaft link and support

Fig.E.9. Removing the lock pin from the shifter fork for first and reverse gear

Fig.E.10. Pulling back the selector shaft to seat the intermediate lever

Gearbox

DESCRIPTION

A three or four speed synchromesh transmission is fitted and is actuated by either a gearshift lever on the steering column or by a console-located gearshift lever. All the forward speeds are fully synchronized and the mechanism is based upon friction clutches which equalize the speed of the gears to be engaged.

A locking mechanism prevents the engagement of the gears until synchronization of the gears has been achieved.

TRANSMISSION - Removal and Installation

Refer to Fig.E.1 and remove the spring clip to allow the release of the throttle control rod. Remove the propeller shaft as detailed in "Rear Axle and Suspension" and seal the rear of the transmission to avoid loss of oil (General Motors recommend sleeve SW -191). Remove the bolts securing the mounting points at the rear of the engine (see Fig.E.2). Support the engine at a position below the clutch housing.

Remove the bolts attaching the transmission to the clutch housing and carefully withdraw the transmission from its location. Clean all contact areas in readiness for re-assembly.

The installation of the transmission is a reversal of the removal procedure but prior to installation ensure that the following jobs are carried out:-

Ensure that the convex side of the seal ring assembly dished washer (Fig.E.3) rests against the ball bearing and that the oil return hole in the transmission case is not restricted. The hole is below the clutch gear ball bearing. Fill the hollow space behind the seal ring with protective grease (B 040 881/4).

Clean off the clutch gear journal and the splines and then coat them with molybdenum disulfide paste. Obtain a new clutch housing gasket and smear it with sealer prior to locating into its correct position. When the transmission is located, insert the bolts into the clutch housing and tighten them in a diagonal and crosswise pattern to ensure even pressure all round.

Rub the inside of the selector shaft bushing with molybdenum disulphide paste and then check the level of oil after having removed the special seal and attached the propeller shaft. Top up the oil level until it reaches the lower edge of the filler hole.

TRANSMISSION - Dismantling

With reference to the details given in the remainder of this section, remove the gear shift linkage, the transmission case cover (draining the oil into a suitable container prior to disposal), the speedometer gear and the seal ring in the transmission case extension. These actions obviously assume that the transmission has been removed from the car.

Countergear

To remove and disassemble the countergear, unscrew and remove the bolts securing the transmission case extension. Turn the extension case until the end of the countergear shaft is exposed (Fig.E.4.). Carefully drive out the shaft, from the front towards the rear, using a suitable drift (Fig.E.5). Leave the drift in place and ensure that the lock ball is not lost. The three-speed transmission requires a long drift.

The drift used for the four-speed transmission can be made in your own workshop to the following measurements: - length 6.7 inches, diameter 0.64 inches. The steel should be SAE 1045 and the edges at each end should be chamfered to ease insertion into the shaft aperture.

With the drift inserted, withdraw the countergear from the transmission case and with reference to Fig.E.6 remove the two thrust washers and then disassemble the countergear parts. Check all parts for signs of wear.

When assembling, install the 24 needles in the front and in the rear of the countergear by greasing each one with bearing grease and then using a long drift.

Selector Shaft and Levers

To remove the selector shaft and the intermediate levers from the three-speed and from the four-speed transmission, refer to Figs.E.7 to E.18.

Remove the four-speed transmission selector shaft and intermediate levers by driving out the reverse intermediate lever pivot pin (Fig.E.7) and withdrawing the lever from its position. Remove the plug from the reversing light switch threaded sleeve. Unscrew the selector shaft link support from the transmission case (Fig.E.8) and remove the selector shaft.

Remove the three-speed transmission selector shaft by firstly driving the lock pin out of the shifter fork for the first and reverse gear (Fig.E.9). It is recommended that you use tool SW - 203 and a drift. Place the first and reverse shaft into the neutral position and push the shifter fork towards the wall of the transmission case.

Pull back the selector shaft (Fig.E.10) so that the second and third gear intermediate lever is seated in the notch of the second and third speed shifter shaft. Turn the first and reverse shifter shaft approx. 20 to 30º towards the inside. Use tool SW - 203 and completely drive the lock pin out of the first and reverse speed intermediate lever. Push the selector shaft towards the cover plug and drive out the lock pin (Fig.E.11) from the second and third speed intermediate lever.

On the four-speed transmission, turn the selector shaft so that the lock pins are in a vertical position (Fig.E.12). Drive the lock pin out of the third and fourth speed intermediate lever and then out of the first and second speed intermediate lever.

Use a screwdriver to pry out the seal ring (seal rings on transmission operated by a console type gearshift lever). Remove the two lock ball plugs as shown in Fig.E.13 and withdraw the thrust springs and the balls.

Fig.E.11. Driving the lock pin out of first and reverse gear

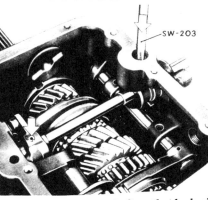

Fig.E.12. Turning the shaft so that lock pins are vertical

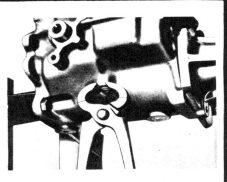

Fig.E.13. Removing the lock ball plugs (four speed trans.)

Fig.E.14. Spacer plate fitted between the second and third speed shifter fork and the casing

Fig.E.15. Driving locking pins out of shifter forks and selector dogs

Fig.E.16. Driving out shifter shafts

Fig.E.17. Driving out reverse shifter shaft (four speed trans.)

Fig.E.18. Removing the lock ball plugs (three speed trans.)

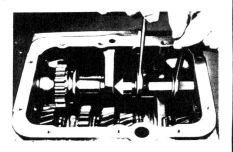

Fig.E.19. Removing the reverse idler gear

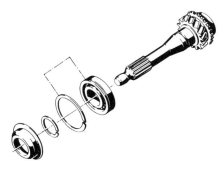

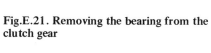

Fig.E.20. Clutch gear - exploded diagram

Fig.E.21. Removing the bearing from the clutch gear

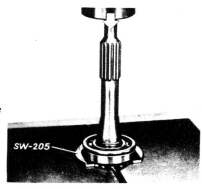

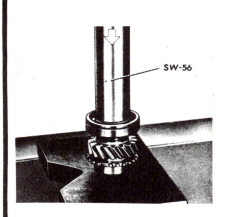

Fig.E.22. Fitting new bearing to clutch gear

Fig.E.23. Removing the securing snap ring from the extension case mainshaft assembly

Fig.E.24. Vent valve in case extension

Fig.E.25. Disassembled mainshaft assembly

Fig.E.26. Removing snap ring from clutch hubs

Fig.E.27. Removing snap ring from speedo drive gear

Fig.E.28. Drive gear locking ball

Fig.E.29. Mainshaft and removable parts

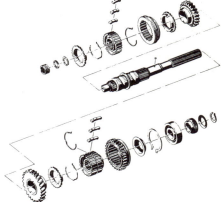

Fig.E.30. Mainshaft assembly - exploded diagram (three speed trans.)

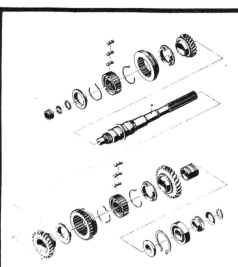

Fig.E.31. Mainshaft assembly - exploded diagram (four speed trans.)

Fig.E.32. Small clutch hub keys are arrowed towards the shifter fork groove

Fig.E.33. Inserting keys into large clutch hub (three speed trans.)

Fig.E.34. Securing speedo drive

Fig.E.35. Fitting the mainshaft assembly snap ring

Fig.E.36. Synchronizer ring, spacer and keys

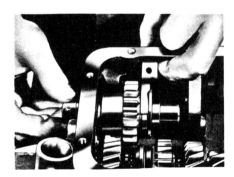

Fig.E.37. Installing reverse idle gear and shifter fork

Fig.E.38. Selector shaft and levers (three speed trans.)

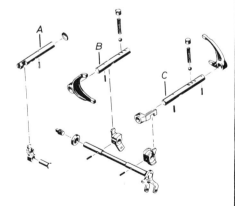

Fig.E.39. Selector shaft and levers (four speed trans.)

For the three-speed transmission, refer to Fig.E.14 and engage the second speed and place a spacer plate between the shifter fork for the second and third speed and the transmission case. The spacer plate can be made up in the form of a letter "U" from sheet steel 1 mm (0.04 in) thick. The distance between the two uprights is 0.6 inches and the height from bottom to top is 1 inch. The spacer depth is 0.94 in.

Refer to Fig.E.15 and drive the lock pins out of the shifter forks and selector dogs. On four-speed transmissions it is necessary to engage first speed prior to this action.

Turn the transmission case extension to expose each shifter shaft in turn and, working from the rear towards the front, drive out both foward speed shifter shafts (Fig.E.16). Note that on three-speed transmissions attention must be paid to the lock balls.

With the four-speed transmission refer to Fig.E.17 and drive out the reverse shifter shaft working from the front towards the rear. Note that the shifter fork remains in the transmission case.

With the three-speed transmission refer to Fig. E.18 and using a suitable size of drift drive out both the lock ball plugs and remove the thrust springs.

Reverse Idler Gear

Turn the transmission case extension until the shaft of the reverse idler gear is exposed and then push out the shaft, from the front towards the rear. Continue to push the shaft until the press-fit slackens and pay attention to the lock ball. Remove the shaft, the reverse idler gear and (on the four-speed transmission) the shifter fork from the transmission case (Fig.E.19).

Clutch Gear

Fig.E.20 shows an exploded view of the clutch gear. Shift the front clutch sleeve into the neutral position then remove the seal ring and then the snap ring from in front of the ball bearing. If tool SW-205 is available refer to Fig.E.21 and press the ball bearing off the clutch gear shaft.

Fig.E.22 shows the ball bearing being pressed onto the clutch gear, using tool SW-56. When locating the bearing ensure that the annular groove faces the journal. Secure the bearing with the snap ring, fit the seal ring and fill the hollow space behind the seal ring lip with protective grease.

Mainshaft Assembly

Withdraw the transmission case extension together with the mainshaft assembly from the transmission case. Refer to Fig.E.23 and using long-nose pliers remove the snap ring from the groove in the extension. The mainshaft assembly can now be removed from the extension case.

Refer to Fig.E24 and remove the vent valve cap. Check that the ball in the valve moves freely and replace if necessary. Refit the cap. Check the transmission case extension bushing, or the bushing in the selector shaft intermediate lever (console gearshift lever). If the bushing is worn then replace it as detailed later within this section.

Disassemble the mainshaft assembly (Fig.E.25) and remove and inspect the needle bearings, spacer ring, synchronizer ring, clutch sleeve, keys and the front clutch key spring at the journal side.

Remove the snap ring in front of the clutch hub and the snap ring behind the speedometer drive gear (Figs. E26 and E.27). Refer to Flg.E.28 and remove the drive gear locking ball from the mainshaft.

For three-speed transmission press out the large clutch hub and ball bearing. Remove the clutch sleeve, synchronizer rings, keys and clutch key springs from the clutch hub.

For four-speed transmissions press out the ball bearing and, by hand, remove the spacer plate, the extension case snap ring, the first speed gear, the needle bearing, the synchronizer ring, the clutch sleeve, the keys and the rear clutch key spring (Fig. E.29).

Press out the large clutch hub as well as the needle bearing inner sleeve. Press out the small clutch hub.

TRANSMISSION - Assembling

When assembling the mainshaft always use new synchronizer rings, clutch key springs and keys. Refer to Fig.E.30 for an exploded diagram of the three-speed transmission mainshaft assembly and to Fig.E.31 for a diagram of the four-speed transmission.

When assembling, coat all parts (especially the seats of clutch hubs and the needle bearing inner sleeve on the mainshaft) with transmission oil. Complement the small clutch hub (3-speed transmission) and both clutch hubs (4-speed transmission). To achieve this, place the clutch sleeve on to the respective clutch hub. Note that the groove on the small clutch hub shifter fork faces the clutch hub splines.

Place the keys into the grooves. Note that the arrow on the keys (Fig.E.32) on the small clutch hub point towards the shifter fork groove. Secure the keys with two clutch key springs on both sides. Insert the springs opposite to each other with their hooks into the same hub groove.

For three-speed transmissions refer to Fig.E.33 and complement the large clutch hub. To achieve this, insert both clutch key springs opposite to each other with their hooks into the same hub groove. Place the keys into the grooves so that the hump of each key is toward the front clutch key spring.

Place the clutch sleeve on to the clutch hub, with the shifter fork groove opposite the front clutch key spring. From the journal side, slide the second speed gear (three speed transmission) or third speed gear (four-speed transmission) on to the mainshaft. Slide the synchronizer ring on to the gear cone. Press on the complemented small clutch so that the shifter fork groove points towards the mainshaft journal. Note that the keys must be in the synchronizer ring recesses.

For three-speed transmissions slide the first speed gear, the synchronizer ring, the complemented large clutch hub, the retaining plate, the extension case snap ring and its relevant ball bearing on to the mainshaft. Note that the shifter fork groove of the large clutch hub points towards the rear.

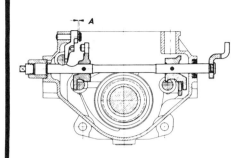

Fig.E.40. Axial play shown at (A)

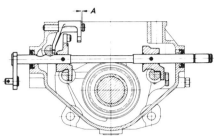

Fig.E.41. Axial play shown at (A)

Fig.E.42. Bolt and seal ring on console type gear lever box

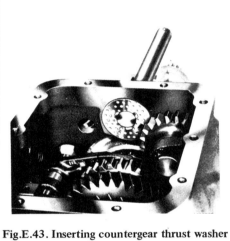

Fig.E.43. Inserting countergear thrust washer

Fig.E.44. Extension case and bushing

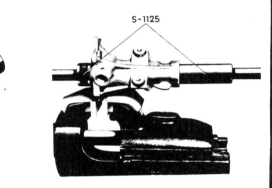

Fig.E.45. Reaming the extension case bushing

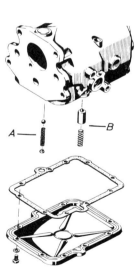

Fig.E.46. Extension case and oil seal

Fig.E.47. Transmission case gasket (parts A and B are locking parts on four - speed transmissions)

For four-speed transmission slide the second speed gear, the synchronizer ring, the complemented large clutch hub and the needle bearing inner sleeve on to the mainshaft. Note that the shifter fork of the large clutch hub points towards the rear and that the keys must be in the synchronizer ring recesses.

All the parts which have been slid on to the mainshaft should now be pressed into position.

Referring to the four-speed transmission, slide the needle bearing, the synchronizer ring, the first speed gear, the spacer plate (with its chamfer towards the rear), the extension case snap ring and its ball bearing on to the mainshaft. Ensure that the keys are in the synchronizer ring recesses and then press the parts into position on the mainshaft. Note that all gears must rotate freely on the mainshaft.

Insert the lock ball, for the speedometer drive gear, into the mainshaft. Fit the drive gear and the dished washer and secure it with a snap ring (Fig.E.34). On the journal side, secure the clutch hub with a snap ring.

When installing the mainshaft assembly, place the assembly into the transmission case up to its stop and then fit the snap ring as shown in Fig.E.35. Use a sealer to glue a new gasket on to the transmission case extension and then slide the mainshaft assembly into the transmission case. Refer to Fig.E.36 and place the synchronizer ring into the small clutch hub. The keys must rest in the recesses of the synchronizer ring. Slide the spacer ring and the needle bearing on to the journal and secure the assembly. Coat the needle bearing with bearing grease.

Install the clutch gear into the transmission up to its snap ring stop. Turn the transmission case extension until the bore for the reverse idler gear shaft is exposed and place the lock ball into the shaft. Insert the shaft from the rear towards the front. 3-speed transmission - simultaneously install the reverse idler gear, with the oil bore towards the rear. 4-speed transmission - simultaneously install the reverse idler gear and shifter fork, with the shifter fork groove of the reverse idler gear and the shoulder of the shifter fork towards the front (Fig.E.37). Snugly drive in the reverse idler gear giving attention to the lock ball.

Refer to Fig.E.38 and install the selector shaft and intermediate levers of the three-speed transmission. Refer to Fig.E.39 and install the selector shaft and intermediate levers of the four-speed transmission.

Install the shifter shafts for the forward speeds from the front towards the rear. With reference to three-speed transmissions, insert the shifter shaft for the second and third speed (Fig.E.38A) with the notches first. Insert the shifter shaft for the first and reverse speed (B) with the notches last. Turn them so that the intermediate groove on the selector shaft is towards the transmission case wall. Slide the shifter forks on to the shifter shafts.

With reference to four-speed transmission, and to Fig.E.39, insert both the shifter shafts (B) and (C) with the notches first and showing upwards. Slide the shifter forks and selector dog on to the shifter shafts. Insert the reverse speed shifter shaft (A) with its notches first and showing downwards. Insert it from the rear towards the front, into the transmission case and the shifter fork.

Fit a new shifter shaft bore plug using a sealer. Drive the lock pins into the shifter forks and the selector dog; the pins

should protrude 0.08 in. Insert the lock balls and thrust springs into the bores in the transmission case and then drive in the plugs.

Prior to installing the new seal ring or rings(console type gearshift lever) place it/them into transmission oil for approximately three minutes. Drive in the seal ring on the oil filter plug side or, on console type gearshift lever, on both sides.

From the oil filler plug side, install the selector shaft, with its lever pointing downwards, and fit both intermediate levers. On three-speed transmissions drive the lock pins into the intermediate levers until the pins protrude by 0.08 in. On four-speed transmissions drive the lock pin firstly into the first and second speed intermediate lever and then into the third and fourth speed intermediate lever. The pins should protrude by 0.08 in. Engage the reverse speed intermediate lever into the lever of the third and fourth speed selector shaft and with the pivot install the assembly into the transmission case. Note that the axial play should be between 0.004 and 0.012 inches (Fig.E.40 "A").

Insert the selector shaft bore plug with sealer for three-speed transmissions or screw in the square head plug for four-speed transmissions. Fit the selector shaft link and its support. On console-type gearshift levers insert the selector shaft opposite to the oil filler plug side and point the lever upwards.

As on console-type gearshift levers a four-speed transmission for RHD is installed, the selector shaft, intermediate levers first and second speed, third and fourth speed as well as reverse speed, pivot pin and third and fourth speed shifter shaft are in comparison with a LHD transmission changed in shape and also in their arrangement. Note that the axial play (A), shown in Fig.E.41, should be between 0.004 and 0.012 inches.

With reference to Fig.E.42 (console type gearshift lever) fit a bolt and seal ring into the threaded bore on the oil filter plug side.

To install the countergear, coat the thrust washers with bearing grease and stick them to the transmission case. The lugs of the thrust washers must fit into the transmission case slots.

Turn the transmission case extension until the countergear shaft bore is exposed. Place the lock ball into the shaft and insert the shaft so that the thrust washer is held in position (insert from the rear towards the front). Hold the opposite thrust washer (Fig.E.43) with a short drift.

With the drift inserted through the countershaft, place the countershaft into position in the transmission case. Insert the shaft into the countergear and ensure that it fits snugly into the transmission case. Note the lock ball. Align the transmission case extension and bolt it to the transmission case. The bolts for the through holes should be coated with sealer.

EXTENSION CASE BUSHING - Replacement

With the transmission case extension removed and the seal ring detached, as described later in this section, use a drift to press out the bushing (press out side). Insert the new bushing so that the joint of the rolled bushing is opposite the oil return passage in the extension case. Use a drift to press the bushing in up to the stop.

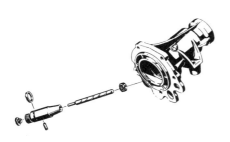

Fig.E.48. Extension case and speedometer drive

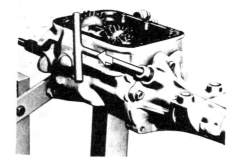

Fig.E.49. Removing speedometer gear housing

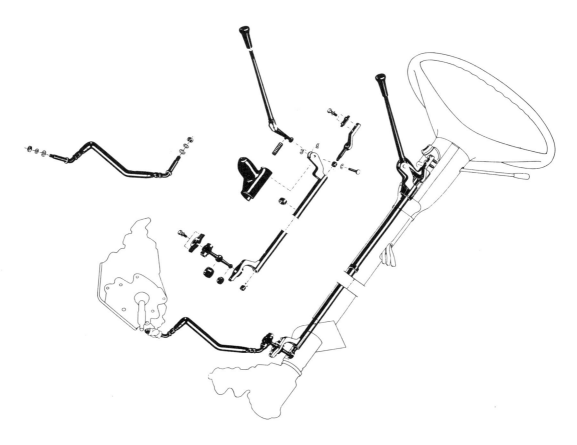

Fig.E.50. Steering column gearshift lever assembly

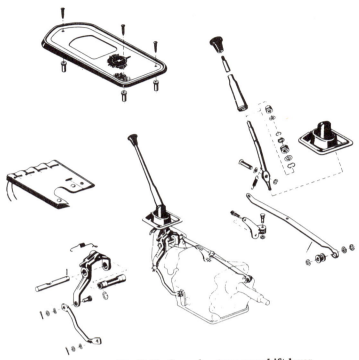

Fig.E.51. Console - type gearshift lever assembly

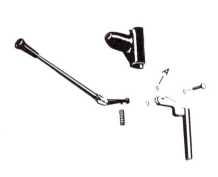

Fig.E.52. Steering column gearshift lever

Fig.E.53. Console gearshift lever

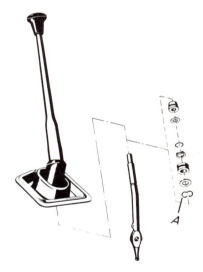

Fig.E.54. Console type gearshift lever dampening parts

With reference to Fig. E.45 insert the guide bushing of the tool S - 1125 into the extension case. Use the adjusting ring of the tool to adjust a reamer to an undersize of 1 - 2 graduations and ream the bushing. Remove any burrs with a scraper.

Adjust the reamer to the specified size and again ream the bushing. Use the checking pin of the tool S - 1125 and check the bushing bore for the correct tolerance. Removal all cuttings from the case and thoroughly clean it.

EXTENSION CASE OIL SEAL - Replacement

Remove the propeller shaft as detailed in "Rear Axle and Suspension". Use a puller tool and withdraw the oil seal (shown in Fig. E.46). Obtain a new oil seal, locate it in position and drive it in up to its stop, Fill the hollow space between the sealing lips of the seal with protective grease.

TRANSMISSION CASE COVER GASKET - Replacement

Unscrew and remove the bolts securing the transmission case cover and withdraw the cover and the gasket. On four-speed transmissions withdraw the transmission case carefully and take care not to lose the locking parts for the reverse shifter shaft (A) and the first and second speed intermediate lever (B). These items are shown in Fig. E.47.

Fit a new gasket by smearing it with a sealer and sticking it to the transmission case. On four-speed tranmissions fit items (A) and (B) in Fig. E.47 and locate and secure the transmission cover with the bolts. Fill the transmission with oil up to the lower lip of the filler hole.

SPEEDOMETER GEAR - Replacement

Refer to Figs. E.48 and E.49 and unscrew the speedometer drive cable from the transmission. Remove the locking pin securing the speedometer gear housing and withdraw the housing with a puller (Fig. E.49 shows the withdrawal using tool SW - 204). Check the gear for wear and if necessary press the gear off the shaft and press on a new gear.

Discard the oil seal ring and place the new ring into transmission oil for approximately three minutes. Lightly coat the gear, the cable and the ring with transmission oil and, using a new lock pin, install the drive into the case. Fit the speedometer cable to the drive.

STEERING COLUMN GEARSHIFT LEVER - Removal and Installation

During the process of removing the gearshaft lever pin it is necessary to hold the gearshift lever as the thrust spring is under tension. Refer to the Fig. E.52 and ensure that the washer (A) does not drop into the steering column jacket: the washer is located between the shift control tube and the gearshift lever.

Prior to installing the lever assembly on the steering column, coat the spherical end of the gearshift lever and the sliding surface in the shift control tube with bearing grease. Refit all items and check for correct and free operation.

CONSOLE GEARSHIFT LEVER Removal and Installation

Remove the screws securing the ornamental plate on the console and remove the plate (Fig. E.51). Unhook the spring shown in Fig. E.53 and remove the shift finger bolt. Withdraw the lever from its location.

Locate the new gearshift lever ensuring that the spherical end of the shift finger is coated with protective grease. Coat the finger bolt with grease and insert it from the rear towards the front, fit the spring and prior to fitting the ornamental plate check the gearshift for correct operation. Fit the ornamental plate and secure it with the screws.

If it is necessary to check the items used for dampening the gearshift lever movements refer to Fig. E.54. Remove the circlip (A) and pull the shift finger from the gear lever; replace parts as necessary.

Clutch

CLUTCH - Removal, Inspection and Installation

Refer to Fig.F.3 and the "Electrical" section and remove the electrical connections and the bolts securing the starter motor to the clutch housing. Refer to the section covering the "Rear Suspension and Rear Axle" and remove the necessary items prior to the removal and withdrawal of the propeller shaft.

Loosen the screws securing the clutch housing, with its attached transmission assembly, to the engine block. Remove any connections which prevent the withdrawal of the clutch assembly, including the clutch bowden control cable. Refer to Fig.F.4 and ensure that the necessary assembly marks are visible at the flywheel clutch junction; if the marks are not visible, use paint or a stamping to ensure correct re-location.

Remove the clutch housing screws and remove the housing together with the clutch assembly disc. Refer to Figs. F.1 and F.2 for an exploded diagram showing the parts of the clutch assembly.

Prior to re-installing the clutch, inspect any and all of the parts that are subject to wear. Note the following paragraphs and replace any defective parts.

Check the release bearing for free operation and also ensure that it is "rattle - free". The bearing is permanently packed with grease and therefore must not be washed out with a cleanser. Check the hollow space behind the bushing in the crankshaft, wipe it clean and then partly fill it with clean grease.

Inspect the retaining spring of the clutch release lever to ensure that it is correctly seated and that its tension is adequate, replace the spring if necessary. Check the thrust pins in the clutch lever to ensure that they are firmly seated. Reseat the rivets or replace the release lever as required.

Inspect the flywheel and the clutch pressure plate friction areas. If there is any indication of scoring on the pressure plate then the clutch assembly should be replaced. Note that if it is required, the flywheel may be refaced and reference should be made to the information given within this section.

On installation of the clutch, coat the clutch disc hub internal splines with clutch oil (General Motors B 040 992/0). When bolting the clutch assembly to the flywheel, centre the clutch disc (with the long side of the clutch disc hub facing the flywheel) with an aligning arbor. Note the assembly marks previously described and install the clutch assembly into its correct location. Installation is the reversal of the removal procedure.

Coat all sliding and bearing surfaces, with the exception of the clutch disc hub splines, with a molybdenum disulfide paste. Upon completion of the clutch assembly installation, adjust the clutch pedal (as detailed within this section) and road test the car.

CLUTCH LININGS - Replacement

Check the clutch disc dampening effect (Fig.F.8) by obtaining a discarded clutch gear. Clamp the clutch gear into a vice and slide the clutch disc, with the long end of the hub downwards, over the splines. Turn the clutch disc to both left and right and note that the dampening effect is more pronounced in the clockwise direction (coasting) than it is in the counter-clockwise direction (driving). The clutch disc should always return to the starting position and it should be noted that the damper springs are slightly pre-loaded when the disc is not twisted.

Replace the clutch linings with reference to Fig.F.9. Use a drill to remove the clutch linings rivets and remove the linings from the clutch disc. Obtain the correct replacement linings, locate them on the clutch disc and diagonally rivet the new linings to the disc.

Refer to Fig.F.10 and check the disc with a dial gauge as shown. The runout on the disc should not exceed 0.016 in. when measured at the circumference of the disc. Make the corrections necessary to bring the runout within this figure.

Measure the disc thickness at serveral places and ensure that the thickness does not exceed the permissible maximum of 0.37 in.

Balance the clutch disc prior to assembly by obtaining a balancing support and placing it on a flat table. Use a spirit level both longitudinally and transversely to ensure that the balancing support is both level and upright. Use a suitable arbor through the clutch disc and as shown in Fig.F.11 determine the unbalance. Mark the point which stops at the bottom (shown arrowed in the illustration) and repeat two or three times to ensure that the unbalance point is determined accurately.

As shown in Fig.F.12, insert lead rivets as necessary to eliminate the unbalance. Always insert the rivets at the opposite side to the mark previously made. Repeat the operation of balancing the clutch disc until all unbalance has been eliminated.

CLUTCH RELEASE BEARING - Removal and Installation

Loosen the lock nut and with a screwdriver screw the ball stud out of the clutch housing. Free the slot, for the screwdriver. in the ball stud head by pushing off the release lever. Pull the clutch release bearing from the clutch release lever (Fig.F.13) and the clutch release lever from the ball stud.

Refer to Fig.F.14 and soak the new felt ring in oil and locate it into the release bearing. Coat the sliding area with molybdenum disulfide paste.

Check the retaining spring of the clutch release lever for proper seating and tension and replace it if necessary. Check that the thrust pins in the lever are firmly seated, if they are not then reseat the rivets or replace the complete clutch release lever. Coat the clutch release lever ball stud with molybdenum disulfide paste and adjust the dimension X in Fig.F.15 to 0.7 inches.

Coat the clutch gear splines with clutch oil and when the clutch assembly is fitted into the car, adjust the clutch pedal free travel and road test the car.

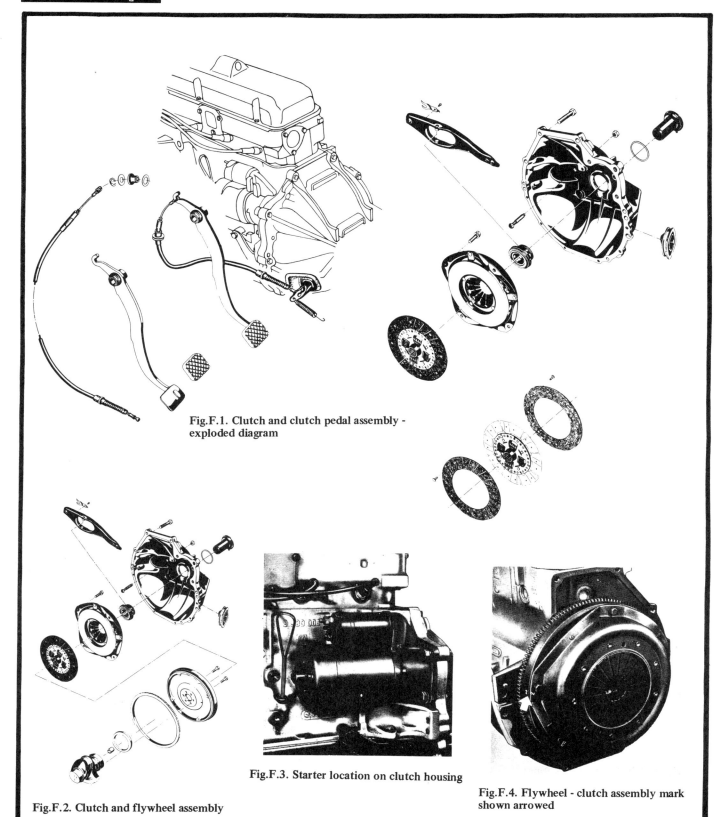

Fig.F.1. Clutch and clutch pedal assembly - exploded diagram

Fig.F.3. Starter location on clutch housing

Fig.F.4. Flywheel - clutch assembly mark shown arrowed

Fig.F.2. Clutch and flywheel assembly

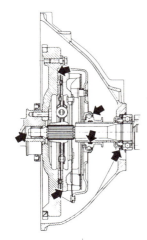

Fig.F.6. Flywheel - clutch assembly, showing aligning arbor

Fig.F.7. Clutch linings

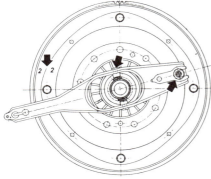

Fig.F.5. Points to inspect prior to clutch assembly

Fig.F.8. Checking clutch disc dampening effect

Fig.F.9. Drilling out clutch lining rivets

Fig.F.10. Checking clutch disc runout

Fig.F.11. Balancing the clutch disc prior to assembly

Fig.F.12. Inserting lead rivets to balance clutch disc

Fig.F.13. Clutch release lever arrowed

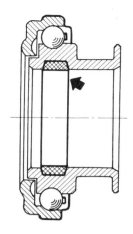

Fig.F.14. Felt ring in clutch release bearing

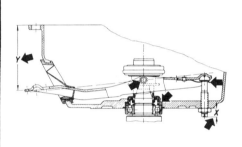

Fig.F.15. Clutch release lever adjustment dimension

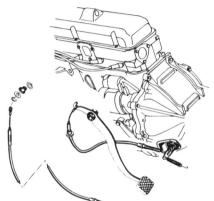

Fig.F.16. Clutch cable and pedal assembly

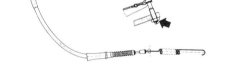

Fig.F.17. Clutch cable and pedal adjustment

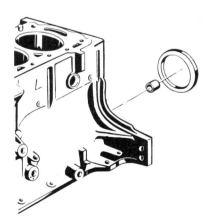

Fig.F.18. Clutch gear pilot bushing

Fig.F.19. Removing the pilot bushing using Kukko puller

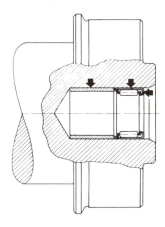

Fig.F.20. Needle sleeve and spacer bushing (service replacement)

Fig.F.21. Bolt hole on flywheel marked " P "

Fig.F.22. Checking flywheel axial runout

Fig.F.23. Splitting the flywheel ring gear with a chisel

Fig.F.24. Driving a new ring gear on to fly-wheel

Fig.F.25. Refacing the flywheel in a lathe

F

CLUTCH CONTROL CABLE -
Replacement and Adjustment

If a new clutch cable is to be fitted or the cable adjustment has been disturbed during a removal operation then the cable must be re-adjusted. Note that the clutch pedal free travel can only be adjusted by the ball stud.

To facilitate the task of disconnecting the cable, withdraw the E - ring from its groove in the bowden control cable and pedal rubber stop. Unhook the clutch return spring and the cable from the clutch release lever and from the clutch pedal. Discard the cable if a new one is to be fitted.

Fit the new bowden control cable and carry out the following adjustments with reference to Fig.F.15:-

Adjust the ball stud so that the outer end protrudes 0.7 inches out from the face of the clutch housing. Allow the clutch release bearing, together with the clutch release lever, to rest against the diaphragm springs. Turn the ball stud so that the dimension shown at Y is approximately 4.2 inches. Check the measure at X to ensure it has not been disturbed.

Pull the bowden control cable until the clutch pedal rests against the rubber stop and then release the bearing against the diaphragm springs. With reference to Fig.F.17, install the E-ring two grooves ahead of the washer.

Fit the return spring and using the ball stud adjust the clutch pedal free travel to a measurement between 0.6 and 1.0 inch.

CLUTCH GEAR PILOT BUSHING - Replacement

Remove the clutch assembly as previously detailed and, using a Kukko puller 22 - 1 and a Kukko adaptor 21 - 2, remove the clutch gear pilot sinter bronze bushing.

Note that the replacement for the sinter bronze bushing, inserted in production, is a needle sleeve with a spacer bushing. Use a drift to drive both parts into position and ensure that the face with the stamped letters is positioned on the outside (Fig. F.20).

The needle sleeve is supplied with lubricant ready for installation. Dry bearings must be lubricated with ball and roller bearing grease.

For crankshafts with 0.04 in. oversize bore, a letter A is stamped on the face of the flywheel centering shoulder. No needle sleeves are supplied for these crankshafts and an oversize sinter bronze bushing must be used.

FLYWHEEL - Replacement

Remove the clutch assembly as previously detailed and remove the securing screws and withdraw the flywheel from the crankshaft.

Refer to Fig.F.21 and install the new flywheel together with its ring gear. Note the bolt hole marked with the letter "P" and locate as relevant. Insert the bolts and tighten to a torque of 43 lb.ft. Remove the balance of the old flywheel and transfer it to the new flywheel .

Check the axial runout of the flywheel at a point 8 inches from its centre, as shown in Fig.F.22 and ensure that it does not exceed a maximum of 0.004 inches. Fit the flywheel to the crankshaft and refit the clutch assembly.

FLYWHEEL RING GEAR - Replacement

Remove the flywheel as previously detailed and drill a quarter inch diameter hole, just below a tooth gap, approximately 8 mm (0.32 in) into the ring gear. Use gripping jaws and insert the flywheel into a vice with the drilled hole at the top point. Refer to Fig.F.23 and split the ring gear using a hammer and sharp chisel.

Use an oven to heat the new ring gear to between 360 and 450ºF and then with the inner chamfer facing the flywheel shoulder, evenly drive the ring gear on to the flywheel (Fig.F.24). Use a brass drift to perform this operation.

After re-installing the flywheel, check the lateral runout of the ring gear, using a dial gauge. The amount of runout must not exceed 0.02 inches.

FLYWHEEL FRICTION SURFACE - Refacing

Remove the flywheel from the crankshaft as previously described and, using a suitable chuck, locate the flywheel into a lathe. Adjust it within the chuck until no lateral runout is, or can be, measured with a gauge (Fig.F.25).

Cut the flywheel to obtain a smooth surface, but do not cut more than 0.012 inches from the face. If a smooth surface is not obtained after a cut of this depth, then the flywheel must be replaced with a new one.

If a smooth surface has resulted from the cut then cut also the flywheel front face (contact area for clutch assembly) to retain the original dimension. The original dimension is between 0.175 and 0.18 inches.

Use a tungsten carbide tipped tool for all cutting on the flywheel.

Technical Data

Clutch pedal free travel, measured at pad center	mm (in.)	15-25 (.59-.98)
Permissible lateral runout of friction area on installed flywheel at a diameter of 200 mm (7.87)	mm (in.)	0.1 (.004)

Max. permissible clutch disc lateral runout (reading taken near edge of disc	mm (in.)	0.4 (.016)
Max. permissible clutch disc thickness including spread (after installing new linings)	mm (in.)	9.4 (.37)

Rear Axle & Rear Suspension

DESCRIPTION

The rear suspension comprises the rear axle, control arm pairs, track rod, springs, shock absorbers, an optional stabilizer and the two - piece propeller shaft.

The rear axle consists of an axle housing, axle tubes, drive pinion, ring gear with differential and rear axle shafts. The brakes are arranged at the end of each axle tube. The drive pinion transmits the engine power to the ring gear and via the differential and axle shafts to the wheels. The ring gear and drive pinion are the hypoid type and use an oil to the high pressure resistance specification GM 4744 - M.

If the ring gear and drive pinion are renewed of if a new axle is fitted then a running-in oil to specification GM 4655 - M must be used. This oil has to be drained after approximately 600 miles and replaced with GM 4744 - M.

The rear axle housing is ventilated by a plastic valve which is installed on the upper side in the middle of the left rear axle tube. The upper side of the valve is labyrinth shaped and has a moveable cover. The rear axle springs are coil type and have lower control arms to maintain the fore and aft relationship of the axle to the car body. The springs are positioned between the control arms and the side members. Sideways movement of the rear axle is controlled by the track rod.

The maintenance - free, double-acting, hydraulic shock absorbers are arranged between the axle and the car floor panel and minimize road vibrations transmitted to the car body. Each shock absorber is attached to the floor panel at one end and to a bracket welded to the rear axle tubes at the other end.

If a stabilizer has been installed on the car, it is attached to the upper control arms.

The two-piece propeller shaft consists of the front and rear propeller shaft and the intermediate bearing. The bearing is arranged on the front propeller shaft adjacent to the rear propeller shaft attachmant. It comprises the ball bearing, rubber dampering ring in which the ball bearing is embedded and the guide sleeve which encases the dampering ring. The maintenance free intermediate bearing is secured to the car floor panel. The front propeller shaft is connected to the transmission mainshaft by a slip joint and the rear propeller shaft is attached to the drive pinion flange by two U-bolts.

PROPELLER SHAFT - Removal

Lift the rear of the car, on one side only, and support it. Loosen the bolts securing the intermediate bearing and then remove the nuts and washers from the U-bolts attaching the propeller shaft to the drive pinion flange. Remove the U-bolts and remove the intermediate bearing support bracket.

Detach the propeller shaft from the transmission mainshaft by removing the slip joint and immediately fit a sleeve (tool SW - 191) for sealing the transmission mainshaft. Remove the two - part propeller shaft downwards.

Drive Pinion Oil Seal Ring and Clamp Ring

The drive pinion oil seal ring at the differential assembly

can be removed by holding the flange to prevent it from rotating and removing the flange nut and its washer. Withdraw the flange from its location and the drive pinion oil seal ring will be exposed (see Fig.G.4). Pry out the oil seal ring with a screwdriver.

Use an inner race puller and withdraw the bearing inner race from its position on the drive pinion. With the bearing inner race now removed slide the clamp ring from the drive pinion.

To install the items removed, first fit a new clamp ring and press the bearing inner race into its position on the drive pinion. Check that the bearing is not unduly worn or scored. Grease the bearing with bearing grease and adjust the drive pinion bearing pre-load. Press in the oil seal and fill the hollow space between the sealing lips with protective grease, then locate the flange and press it into position. Fit the washer and a new self-locking flange nut and caulk the nut into the drive pinion groove.

The torque of the rear axle can now be checked if a torsionmeter is available. Ensure that one wheel is free to rotate and that the other is blocked and use a torsionmeter at the drive pinion flange to obtain a reading. The reading obtained plus 0.7 lb.ft. must not exceed 1.1 lb.ft.

PROPELLER SHAFT - Installation

Offer up the two-part propeller shaft and fit the slip joint into the transmission mainshaft after first removing the seal (tool SW - 191). Locate the intermediate bearing support and hold it in position by turning the bolts to prevent it from dropping. Carefully compress the needle bearing case at the rear end of the propeller shaft, using a small G - clamp, and place the shaft into position. Turn the shaft into the correct alignment and fit the two U-bolts so that they fit into their respective tubes in the drive pinion flange. Fit new self locking nuts and torque them to 14 lb.ft; unscrew and withdraw the G - clamp.

Lower the car to the ground and with the rear springs under load tighten the propeller shaft intermediate bearing support. Road test the car to ascertain correct function.

REAR AXLE - Removal

Remove the propeller shaft as previously described but ensure that the car is jacked up and supported at both sides. Remove the hub caps, pull on the handbrake and remove both of the rear wheels: let off the handbrake. Detach the parking brake cable on one side from its lower control arm and then support the lower control arm with a jack and loosen the bolt attaching the lower control arm to the axle. Unscrew the lower control arm from the frame and push the axle towards the front of the car, with a suitable mounting bar, so that the attaching bolt can be withdrawn. Remove the bolt, bushing and self-locking nuts securing each shock absorber to the rear axle.

Lower the jack supporting the control arm slowly until the coil spring is relieved of any load and then withdraw the spring from its position. Follow the same procedure for removing the spring from the opposite side of the car and then place a jack under and support the differential casing.

With reference to Fig.G.11, detach the track rod (A) from the rear axle and remove the parking brake cable from each rear

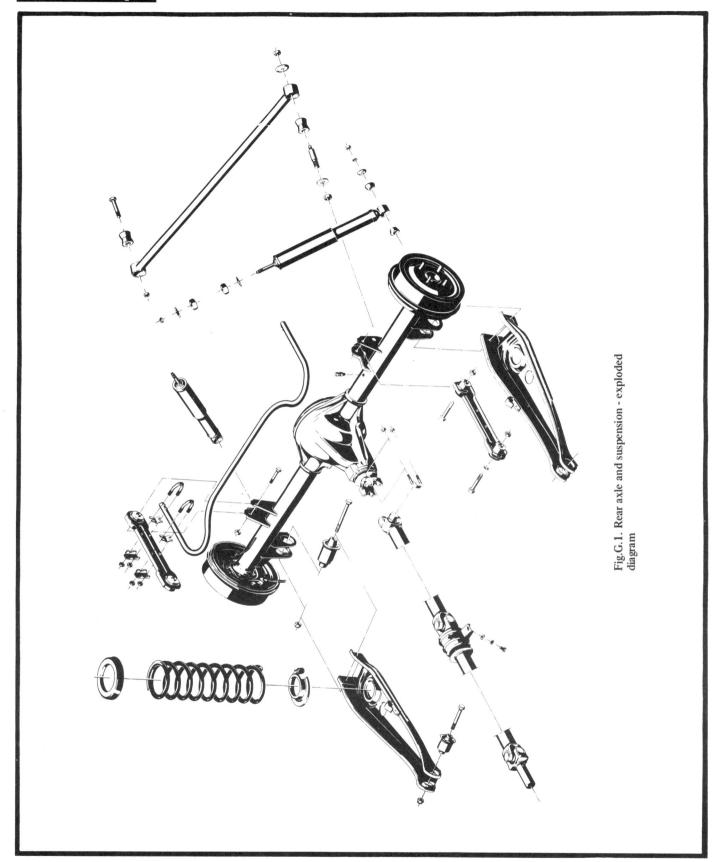

Fig.G.1. Rear axle and suspension - exploded diagram

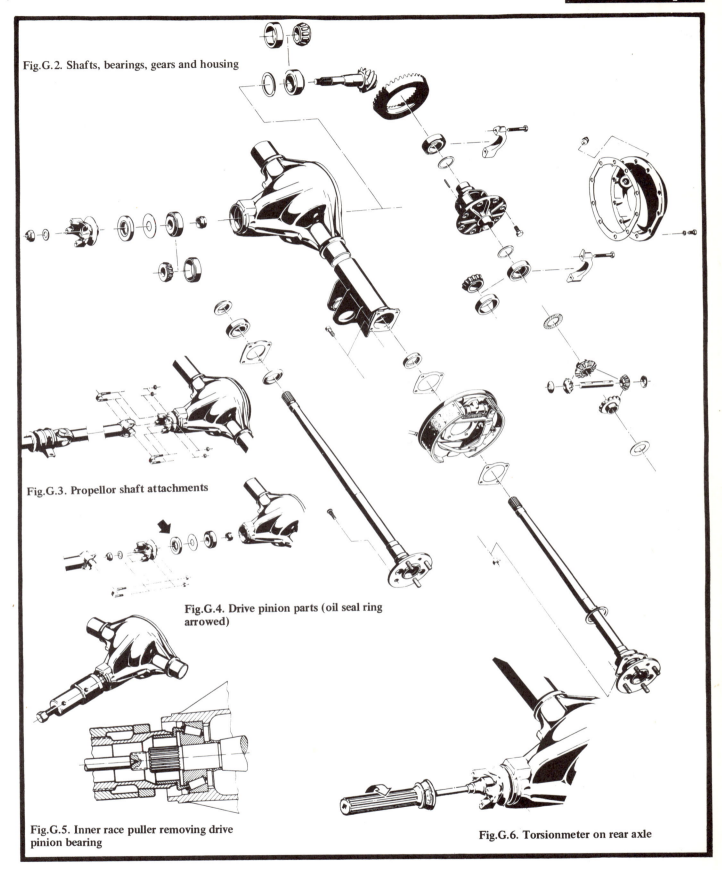

Fig.G.2. Shafts, bearings, gears and housing

Fig.G.3. Propellor shaft attachments

Fig.G.4. Drive pinion parts (oil seal ring arrowed)

Fig.G.5. Inner race puller removing drive pinion bearing

Fig.G.6. Torsionmeter on rear axle

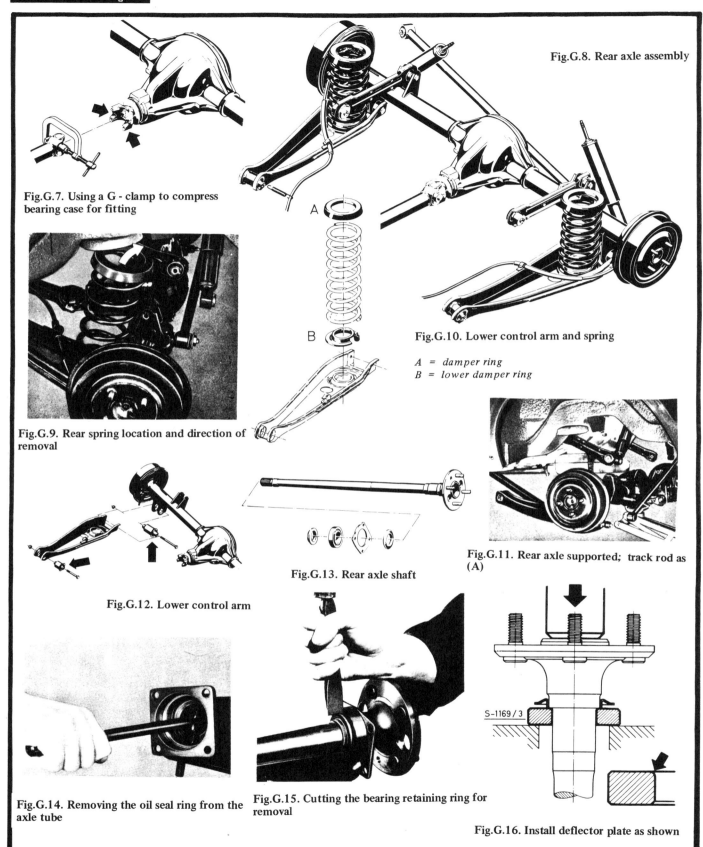

Fig.G.7. Using a G - clamp to compress bearing case for fitting

Fig.G.8. Rear axle assembly

Fig.G.9. Rear spring location and direction of removal

Fig.G.10. Lower control arm and spring

A = damper ring
B = lower damper ring

Fig.G.11. Rear axle supported; track rod as (A)

Fig.G.12. Lower control arm

Fig.G.13. Rear axle shaft

Fig.G.14. Removing the oil seal ring from the axle tube

Fig.G.15. Cutting the bearing retaining ring for removal

S-1169/3

Fig.G.16. Install deflector plate as shown

wheel brake drum. Remove the bolt securing each upper control arm to the rear axle and check that the jack supporting the rear axle is secure. Detach the stabilizer (if fitted) from the control arm and pay attention to the compensating washers installed between the stabilizer and the control arm and to their thickness.

Ensure that the lower control arms are detached from the side members and then gently lower the rear axle to a position where the axle, together with the lower control arms, can be withdrawn from under the car. Unscrew and remove the attaching bolts and remove the lower control arms from the axle.

REAR AXLE - Inspection and Overhaul

Rear Axle Half Shafts

Remove the brake drum from each wheel, as detailed in BRAKES Section. Unscrew and remove the four nuts securing the brake back plate and the half shaft to the axle tube. Withdraw the bolts and support the brake back plate and then use a puller to withdraw the rear axle shaft out of the rear axle tube.

The oil seal ring (Fig.G.14) can be removed from the rear axle tube using tool S - 1265 or similar. When a new oil seal ring is fitted it should be soaked for approximately three minutes in hypoid rear axle oil. Use an arbor to press in the ring and rotate it to ensure an even fit.

With reference to Fig.G.15 cut through the ball bearing retaining ring and prise it off the half shaft. Use a press to remove the bearing parts from the shaft. Fit a new bearing on to the axle; do not use a lubricant, the bearing must be pressed on dry. Refer to Fig.G.16 which shows the position and location of the deflector plate, with the rounded off inner edge of the installer ring facing the deflector plate.

Check the rear axle half shaft for radial and lateral run-out prior to installation. Refer to Fig.G.17 and check the shaft and shaft flange at the positions shown. Ensure that the shaft is held centrally. The maximum permissible lateral run-out value at (A) is 0.004 in. and the maximum permissible radial run-out value at (B) is 0.001 in. Note that straightening of the rear axle shaft is not permissible.

Prior to installing the half shaft, check the splines for damage and wear. Coat the splines and bearing with hypoid lubricant. Locate the brake back plate into position and using a new paper gasket push the half shaft into the axle tube and ensure that the splines engage into the differential. Secure the shaft, and the brake back plate. Fit the brake drum and secure.

DIFFERENTIAL - Removal and Dismantling

Remove the brake line from the rear axle housing cover and drain the oil from the housing into a suitable receptacle. Remove the screws and washers securing the cover and withdraw the cover and the gasket. Note that the screws arrowed in Fig. G.19 have been inserted after coating with sealing compound. Remove the rear axle half shafts as previously detailed in this section.

Turn the axle so that it is possible to lift out the differential assembly complete using two bars. Dismantle the differential assembly by using a puller to withdraw the roller bearing from the differential case. Remove the eight bolts securing the ring gear and remove it from the assembly.

Place the differential case into V-blocks and check the axial run-out of the ring gear contacting area. The permissible axial run-out is 0.001 in. If it is necessary to strip the differential further, drive out the pinion shaft lock pin and remove the axle shafts and the differential pinions together with any shims or spherical washers which may be fitted.

Thoroughly clean all parts and check for any signs of wear, damage or deformation. When it is necessary to replace one of the gear wheels, all gears that are in mesh with this gear must also be replaced.

Insert the rear axle shaft side gears and differential pinions and with the backlash at zero, check the axial play between the rear axle shaft side gears and the differential case. Use a feeler gauge as shown in Fig.G.25. The permissible axial play is 0.003 to 0.006 in. always aim to have the smallest play. If the play is larger than required, remove the side gears and install shims to your required, fit the side gears and repeat the check.

Shims with 2.44 in outside diameter

Thickness	Notches in circumference
0.0386 to 0.0402 in.	0
0.0425 to 0.0441 in.	1
0.0465 to 0.0480 in.	2
0.0504 to 0.0520 in.	3

Spherical Washer

0.0386 to 0.0402 in.	-

When a satisfactory fit is achieved, drive in the pinion shaft lock pin to secure the assembly. Check the ring gear and if satisfactory, or if it is a new part, place it into boiling water and soak it for at least one minute to allow it to heat up: it is suggested that some cord be used to allow for the ring gear to be easily retrieved from the boiling water. Locate and press the ring on to the differential case. Smear sealing compound on to the bolts, ensure that there is enough of the compound so that when the bolts are tightened compound is squeezed from beneath the bolt head. Tighten the ring gear attachment bolts to a torque of 47 lb.ft. using Fig.G.27 as a reference to the order of tightening.

Check the installed ring gear for lateral run-out which should not exceed 0.003 in. The part shown as (A) in Fig.G.28 is an adapter with cylindrical feeler. If the run-out exceeds the value shown above, check that no dirt or grit has come between the contacting areas or that the ring gear is installed in a slightly inclined position. Also check that the bolts have been tightened evenly. If these checks prove negative, renew the ring gear.

DRIVE PINION - Removal and Installation

To remove the drive pinion, hold the drive pinion flange securely and remove the nut and washer securing the pinion flange. Use a puller to withdraw the flange and then using a plastic hammer drive the pinion, towards the open end of the housing, out of the rear axle housing. Pry out the oil seal ring.

Refer to Figs. G.30 and G.31, and press out the outer race of the outer bearing using a plate and sleeve as shown. Press off the outer race of the inner bearing and then remove the roller cage from the drive pinion as shown in the illustration. Check the bearings for wear or for any roughness and replace them as necessary.

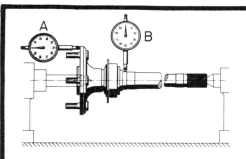

Fig.G.17. Checking rear axle shaft runout (see text)

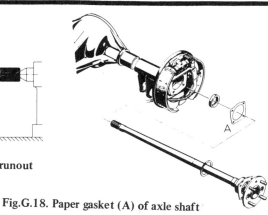

Fig.G.18. Paper gasket (A) of axle shaft

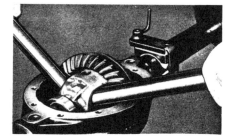

Fig.G.20. Lifting out the differential assembly

Fig.G.19. Rear axle housing cover

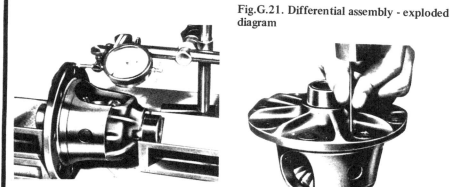

Fig.G.21. Differential assembly - exploded diagram

Fig.G.22. Removing bearing from differential case

Fig.G.23. Checking axial runout of ring gear

Fig.G.24. Pin removal (see text)

Fig.G.25. Checking axial play

Fig.G.26. Pinion shaft lock pin   Fig.G.27. Tightening order of ring gear bolts

Fig.G.28. Checking ring gear for lateral runout

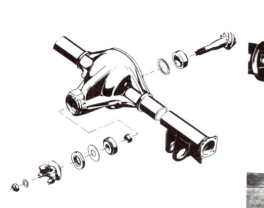

Fig.G.29. Drive pinion - exploded diagram

Fig.G.30. Pressing out outer race of outer bearing

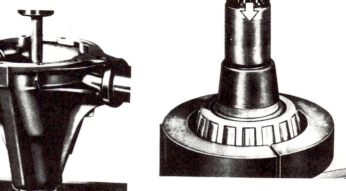

Fig.G.31. Pressing roller cage off drive pinion

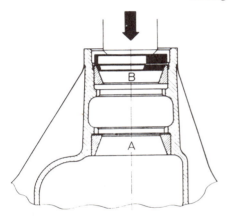

Fig.G.32. Outer race (A) and outer race (B)

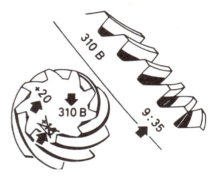

Fig.G.33. Control figures for matching pinion and ring gear

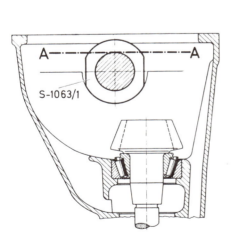

Fig.G.34. Zero line, A - A

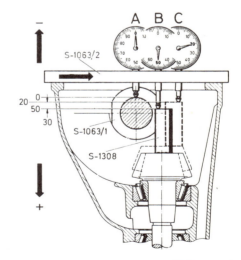

Fig.G.35. Use of dial gauge to establish correct drive pinion position

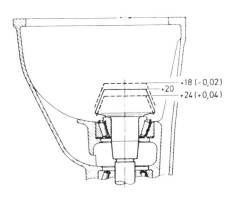

Fig.G.36. Drive pinion seat height

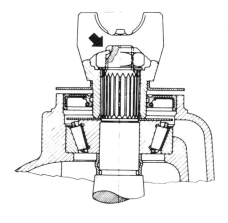

Fig.G.37. Caulked flange nut

Fig.G.38. Adjusting backlash, ring gear and drive pinion

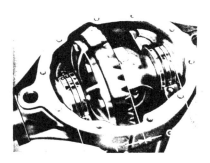

Fig.G.39. Gauge rings locked and marked

Fig.G.40. Measuring width of rings

Fig.G.41. Side bearings installed

Locate the bearings and fit them with reference to Fig.G. 32. Press in the outer race (A), do not insert shims, and the outer race (B). Use a tool to press the roller cage on to the drive pinion If the height of the drive pinion is to be measured install the roller cage on to the drive pinion without fitting the clamp ring.

Push the drive pinion into position in the rear axle housing, fit the oil seal ring and the drive pinion flange. Gradually tighten the flange nut, simultaneously checking the bearing pre-load with a torsionmeter. Note that with a new bearing the permissible pre-load is between 7 and 13 in.lb.(as near as possible to 13 in. lb) and with the used bearing the permissible pre-load is between 5 and 8 in.lb.(as near as possible to 8 in.lb). Carry out the height control of the drive pinion and adjust it with reference to the number engraved on the drive pinion head.

The following is a general explanation of the figures stamped on the pinion head and on the ring gear:-

+ 20   This is a control figure indicating the hundredths of a millimeter the pinion head face must be positioned below the zero line (Fig.G.34)

-20   A minus figure shows the same value but refers to a position above the zero line.

310B   This is a "matching" reference for the ring gear and drive pinion.

+18   The underlined figure is a factory reference only and has no significance for servicing.

9:35   Ratio of teeth on pinion to ring gear.

The reference to "zero line" is shown in Fig.G.34 as A-A and refers to the highest point of an arbor tool S - 1063.

Using a dial gauge, adjust it to its zero position on the point shown in Fig.G.35. Move the measuring rail of tool S - 1063 until the feeler of the gauge rests on arbor S - 1308. Note the reading and determine the hundredths of a millimeter the arbor is positioned above or below zero line e.g. 50/100 = 0.5 mm (B). The control figure being + 20, the drive pinion must not be more than 0.2 mm below the zero line (C), therefore shims must be added below the outer race of the inner bearing to the value of 0.3 mm.

If the figure is - 20 then this would be added to the determined reading of 0.5 to give a total of 0.7 mm. The following is a table of shim sizes and their identification:-

Shim outer diameter 2.89 in.

Shim thickness	Notch on circumference
0.05 mm	Flattened on one side
0.25 mm	0
0.275 mm	1
0.3 mm	2
0.325 mm	3
0.35 mm	4
0.375 mm	5

Remove the drive pinion, press out the inner bearing race and insert the number of shims required to obtain the correct measure. Ensure that the shims are properly centered in the bearing seat and press in the inner bearing race. Install the oil seal ring and fill the hollow space between the seal ring lips with protective grease. Lightly oil the roller bearing with hypoid oil.

Insert the drive pinion, together with a new tension ring and adjust the bearing pre-load as previously detailed. If the pre-

load has been exceeded it is necessary to fit a new tension ring and then repeat the adjustment.

With reference to Fig.G.36, the permissible tolerance in the drive pinion seat height, after the installation of the shims is + 0.0016 to - 0.008 in.(this corresponds to a measurement of + 24 up to + 18).

Fit the drive pinion flange and fit a new self-locking nut and secure the nut by caulking it into the groove of the drive pinion.

DIFFERENTIAL - Installation

Fit the differential assembly into the housing and then adjust the backlash between the ring gear and the drive pinion. Measure the backlash at the narrowest point between the ring gear and the drive pinion and adjust the measurement to between 0.004 and 0.008 in.(the most acceptable measurement is 0.005 in).

Refer to Fig.G.38 and place the gauge ring so that it is adjacent to the ring gear. The gauge ring nuts must show towards the outside. Lock the gauge rings and mark them to ensure that the adjustment is not altered. With reference to Figs. G.39 and G.40, the measure identified T = Ring gear side, and that identified G = Opposite side.

Measure the width of the gauge rings, using a micrometer, and make a note of the measurement. As an example T = 0.828; G = 0.817 in. Measure width of differential side bearing: as an example T = 0.794; G = 0.793 in. Determine shim thickness as follows: -

T	G	
21.025 mm	20.750 mm	Width gauge rings
- 20.180 mm	- 20.150 mm	Width of bearings
0.845 mm	0.600 mm	
+ 0.050 mm	+ 0.050 mm	Preload (new bearings)
0.895 mm	0.650 mm	Total

See the following table for shim selection required:-

Shims 1.96 outside diameter

Thickness	Notches in circumference
0.0059 in (0.150 mm)	0
0.0069 in (0.175 mm)	1
0.0079 in (0.200 mm)	2
0.0089 in (0.225 mm)	3
0.0098 in (0.250 mm)	4
0.0108 in (0.275 mm)	5
0.0197 in (0.500 mm)	6
0.0395 in (1.000 mm)	7

With reference to the example above; T requires shims (6 + 2 + 2) and G requires (6 + 0).

Install the side bearings (Fig.G.41) and check the bearing pre-load. The pre-load is correct if the differential case can be inserted so that the upper sides of the bearing coincide with the upper side of the axle housing. Tighten the cap bolts evenly to a torque of 32.5 lb.ft and check the backlash between the ring gear and the drive pinion.

Fit the rear axle housing cover and torque all screws to 18 lb.ft. These screws must be retightened after 600 miles of service.

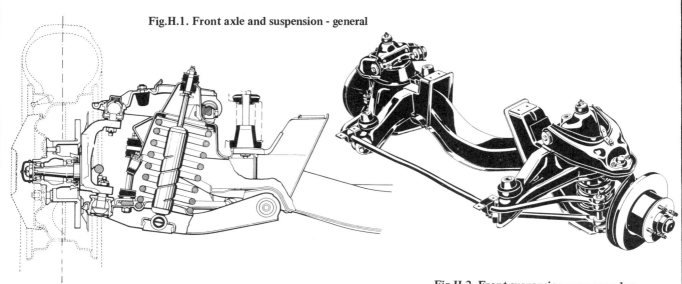

Fig.H.1. Front axle and suspension - general

Fig.H.2. Front suspension cross member

Fig.H.3. Brake caliper assembly removed from disc

Fig.H.4. Removing tie rod from steering arm (tool S- 1255 in place)

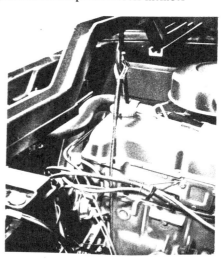

Fig.H.5. Engine sling in position

Fig.H.6. Heat deflector plate

Fig.H.7. Suspension assembly and frame (see text)

Fig.H.8. Cross member checking gauge

Front Axle & Front Suspension

The front wheel suspension has control arms of different lengths and two coil springs and tie struts. These tie struts with supporting arms permit the front suspension cross member attachment points on the front frame to be located wide apart. Noises transmitted along the front suspension cross member are effectively dampened by large pre-loaded rubber blocks at the four front frame attachment points.

The suspension is not provided with grease points: the upper and lower control arms are supported in rubber damper bushings. The bushing outer sleeve is pressed into the control arm: the inner sleeve forms the stationary control arm shaft.

The tie struts control pulling forces and dampen the movements of the lower control arms: castor corrections can be effected at the tie strut adjustment.

FRONT SUSPENSION - Removal and Assembly

Apply the handbrake, chock the rear wheels and jack up the front of the car. Remove the front wheels and remove and support the brake calliper assemblies, tape the assemblies in a position which does not interfere with the removal procedure - do not remove the brake line connections. Remove the tie rods from the steering arms using a ball stud remover and unscrew the stabilizer from the front frame. Support the front assembly in readiness for its removal with a mobile jack.

With reference to Fig.H.5 place a cable of adequate strength around the engine and then lift the engine to take the weight. Note that the cable should be placed between the cylinder block and the generator, below the oil sump and between the cylinder head and the thermostat housing. Unscrew both engine supports from the rubber damper blocks taking due regard of the heat deflector plate shown in Fig.H.6.

Refer to Fig.H.7 and unscrew the front suspension assembly from the frame: the hexagon head bolts and spacer tubes in front (A) are longer than the hexagon head bolts and spacer tubes in the rear (B). Ensure that the front suspension is now free to be removed from the front of the car and remove it by pulling it forward.

If a front suspension cross member checking gauge S-1315 is available it should be fitted, as shown in Fig.H.8, so that all four checking gauge pins enter their respective holes in the front suspension cross member. If the gauge does not fit correctly, then after checking that the gauge is not distorted, see your Opel dealer. No attempt should be made to straighten a deformed front cross member.

The installation of the front suspension assembly is the reversal of the removal procedure. Note that on installation of the suspension assembly all four hexagon head bolts can be fitted from above, new self-locking nuts must be used and they should be tightened to a torque of 51 lb.ft. When attaching the tie rods to the steering arms tighten to a torque of 29 lb.ft. and tighten the brake calliper to steering knuckle attachment to a torque of 72 lb.ft. The wheel nuts can be tightened to a torque of 65 lb.ft.

Prior to road testing the car, check the caster, and toe-in

and check the front brake system for leaks.

STEERING KNUCKLE - Removal and Installation

Apply the handbrake, chock the rear wheels, jack up the front of the car and remove the relevant front wheel. Remove the front brake calliper assembly and tape it in a position which does not interfere with the removal of the steering knuckle. Use the tool S - 1257 or lever off the grease cap on the wheel hub, remove the split pin, unscrew the castle nut and remove the washer. Pull the front wheel hub together with the brake disc off the steering knuckle.

Refer to Fig.H.9 and remove the split pin and slacken off the castle nut on the lower arm to a distance of approximately 1 mm (0.04 in). Support the steering arm and using a suitable drift loosen the lower control arm ball joint in the steering knuckle eye. Use a jack to lift up the lower control arm and support it.

Unscrew the brake disc cover plate securing screws and withdraw the plate together with the paper gasket. Swing the steering arm to the side and remove the steering knuckle from the lower control arm ball joint. Together with the upper arm ball joint unscrew it from the upper control arm. Drive the upper control arm ball joint out of the steering knuckle eye.

If it is possible to check the steering knuckle, when it has been removed, with a dial gauge then the maximum permissible radial run-out of the inner and outer wheel bearing seat is 0.001 in. Under no circumstances should a deformed steering knuckle be straightened.

On installation the high edge of the upper control arm ball joint must face towards the rear. Note the following torques when tightening nuts and bolts during the installation.

Steering knuckle to lower control arm castle nut - 40 lb.ft.
Steering knuckle to upper control arm ball joint - 29 lb.ft.
Steering arm and cover plate to steering knuckle - 51 lb.ft.
Brake calliper to steering knuckle   - 72 lb.ft.

During assembly of the brake disc cover plate to the steering arm use a new paper gasket. After fitting the front wheel hub and the brake disc to the steering knuckle, adjust the front wheel bearing clearance as detailed later in this section. After fitting the calliper brake assembly and the front wheel check the caster, camber and toe-in and check the brake lines for any sign of leaks.

FRONT SPRING - Removal and Installation

The removal of the front spring incorporates the removal of the shock absorber. Apply the handbrake, jack up the front of the car and remove the front wheel where the spring is to be removed. Remove the disc brake calliper assembly and tape it in a position which does not interfere with the removal of the front spring and shock absorber.

Remove the shock absorber by removing the nuts at the head of the shock absorber strut and withdrawing the washers

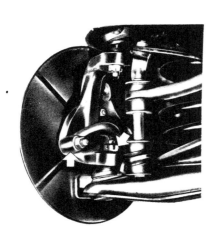

Fig.H.9. Nuts on lower control arm ball joint

Fig.H.10. Steering knuckle and upper and lower control arms

Fig.H.11. Upper control arm ball joint

Fig.H.12. Checking radial runout of steering knuckle

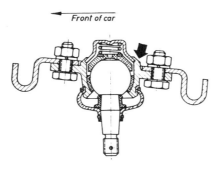

Fig.H.13. Upper control ball joint position

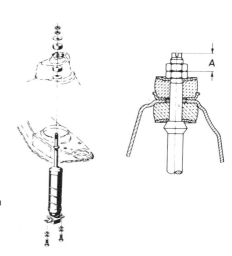

Fig.H.15. Shock absorber. (A) = 0.58 in when assembled

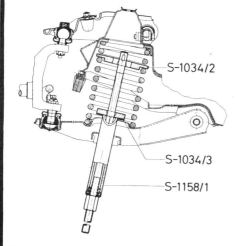

Fig.H.16. Compressing spring with tool S-1034 and spindle S-1158

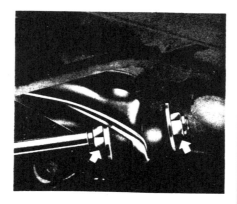

Fig.H.17. Tie strut nuts

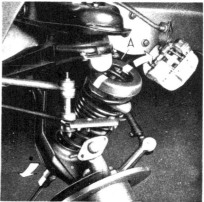

Fig.H.18. Removal of compressed spring. (A) = damper ring

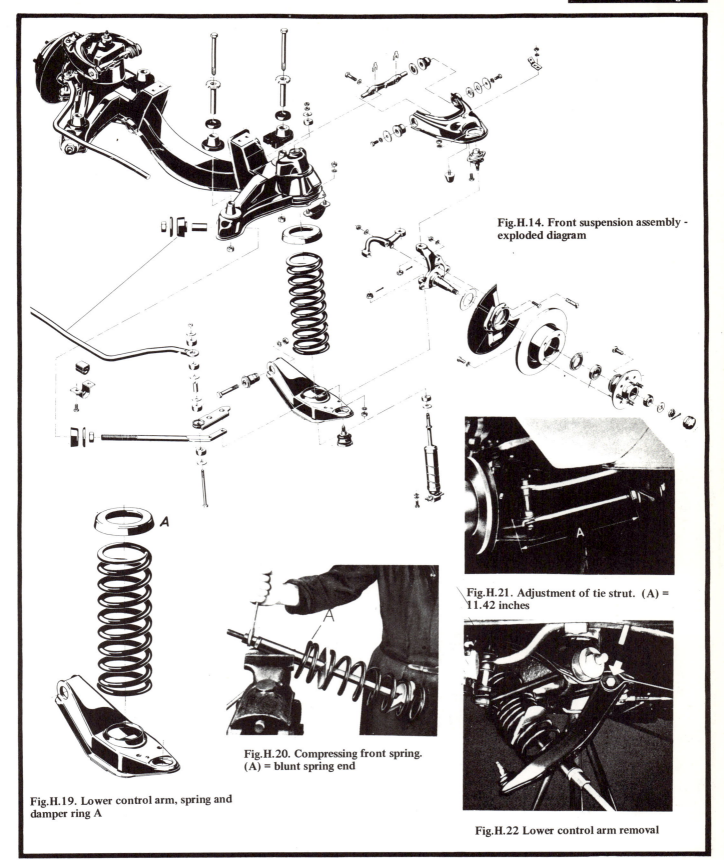

Fig.H.14. Front suspension assembly -
exploded diagram

Fig.H.21. Adjustment of tie strut. (A) =
11.42 inches

Fig.H.20. Compressing front spring.
(A) = blunt spring end

Fig.H.19. Lower control arm, spring and
damper ring A

Fig.H.22 Lower control arm removal

93

Fig.H.23. Damper bushing (A) and lower arm control

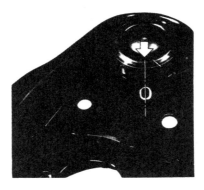

Fig.H.24. Alignment groove of lower control arm ball joint

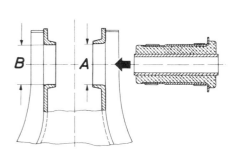

Fig.H.25. Damper bushing bores; (A) wider than (B)

Fig.H.26. Lower control arm in position

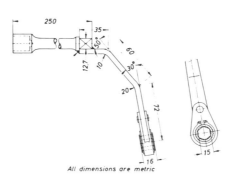

Fig.H.27. Reworked ratchets (dimensions in millimetres)

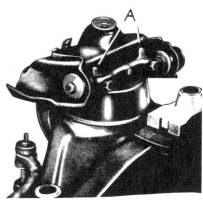

Fig.H.28. Fork - shaped shims (A)

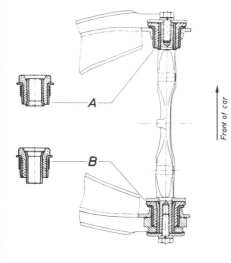

Fig.H.29. Upper control arm shaft and bushing A and B

Fig.H.20. Removing damper bushing with tool S-1249

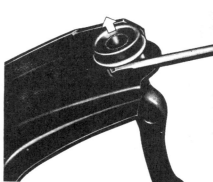

Fig.H.31. Lifting out bushing with a screw-driver

and spacers. Remove the nuts and bolts at the two attachment points at the base of the shock absorber and withdraw it from its location within the coil spring.

Refer to Fig.H.16 which shows the positioning of the tool pieces used to compress the spring. Parts S - 1034/2 and S - 1034/3 are plates and S - 1158/1 is a complete spindle. When using these tools it is necessary to locate six spring coils between the two plates as shown. Compress the spring until it is relieved of its load. Loosen the tie strut hexagon nuts (arrowed on Fig.H.17) and unscrew the tie strut together with the stabilizer support from the lower control arm.

Unscrew and release the upper control arm ball joint from the upper control arm and then push or lever the control arm downwards. There should now be adequate room to lift out the compressed front spring and the damper ring which is shown as (A) in Fig.H.19. Unscrew the spring compression tool to release the spring.

Obtain a new damper ring when replacing the spring or fitting a new spring. Attach the damper ring to the correct end of the spring using scotch tape, this action will facilitate the installation. Compress the spring to the dimension used for its removal and fit the blunt spring end into the lower control arm ensuring that it is properly seated and aligned.

Lift the lower control arm and check that the upper control arm ball joint has not been turned out of position: the high edge must be facing towards the rear. Attach and secure the tie strut and the stabilizer support to the lower control arm and tighten the securing points to a torque of 47 lb.ft. Secure the upper control arm. Unscrew the spring compressor to release the spring into its proper functioning position.

Fit the shock absorber into position, ensuring that the measurement shown at (A) in Fig.H.15, is strictly adhered to. Note that this is at the upper shock absorber attachment. Locate the securing nuts and bolts at the shock absorber locating points and secure the shock absorber into position.

With reference to Fig.H.21, carry out the basic adjustment to the tie strut: dimension (A) as shown should be 11.42 in. (290 mm). When the measurement has been achieved, tighten the outer hexagon nut. Attach the brake calliper assembly to the steering knuckle using a torque of 72 lb.ft. Replace the front wheel and lower the car to the ground. Check the caster, camber and toe - in as detailed in the "Steering" section with particular attention to the caster. Adjust as necessary. Road test the car to ascertain the correct function of the suspension and check the front brake lines and the brake calliper assembly for leaks.

Lower Control Arm and Ball Joint

The lower control arm can be completely removed during or after the removal of the front spring, however, it is unnecessary to remove the upper control arm ball joint.

Drive the lower control arm ball joint out of the lower eye of the steering knuckle. Support the steering arm from below and unscrew the lower control arm from the front suspension cross member. Withdraw the lower control arm.

Using tool S - 1250 or a tube drift of approximate diameter press out or drive out the damper bushing from the lower control arm. It is advisable to support the tool or drift with a support

plate when removing the bushing so as to avoid any distortion.

Remove the ball joint from the lower control arm by using a puller tool to withdraw it from its position. When replacing the ball joint, refer to Fig.H.24, align the groove in the lower control arm ball joint housing with the lug in the lower control arm. The maximum deviation from this position is 2º. With the ball joint correctly positioned press it into place. Press in the damper bushing ensuring that the shoulder (A) (Fig.H.23) of the damper bushing is positioned in front as viewed from the driving direction. Also note that, as shown in Fig.H.25, the bore (A) in the lower control arm is wider than the bore (B) due to the recessed damper bushing outer sleeve. The damper must be a tight fit in the control arm and no grease must be used to allow for an easier press-in fit: the bushing must be pressed in dry.

Loosely attach the lower control arm to the front suspension cross member and tighten the castle nut of the control arm ball joint to steering knuckle attachment to a torque of 40 lb.ft. During installation lift the lower control arm into a horizontal position and tighten the hexagon head bolt, attaching the control arm to the front suspension cross member , to a torque of 47 lb.ft.

Note that the damper bushing in the lower control arm must not be clamped tight when the front suspension assembly is not under load. It must be in an almost twist-free condition when the car jack is removed and the front suspension is under load.

Upper Control Arm and Ball Joint

The upper control arm can be completely removed during or after the removal of the front spring. Unscrew the steering knuckle together with the ball joint from the upper control arm.

Obtain two free-wheeling ratchets, one to be used for loosening and one for tightening, and rework the shape of them to the dimensions and shape shown in Fig.H.27. Use a ratchet to loosen the attachment of the upper control arm to the front suspension cross member. Remove the attachment bolts and use a fork wrench to remove the upper control arm. Refer to Fig.H.28 which shows the fork-shaped shims which must be re-installed in the same location and in the same numbers as removed.

Remove the damper bushing as shown in Figs.H.29 and H.31, note that the front damper bushing, identified (A) can easily be distinguished from the rear damper bushing (B) by the fact that it has a shorter inner sleeve. The illustration shows the direction of the front of the car. The front damper bushing must be pressed out until the shoulder of the bushing is above the level of the control arm and it can then be lifted out with a screwdriver. The Fig.H.30 shows the pressing out of the rear damper bushing using tool S - 1249, the guide ring (C) is always positioned in the rear.

Remove the ball joint in the upper control arm by unscrewing the nuts and washers and bolts and then removing the ball joint from its location. When replacing the ball joint ensure that the high edge is towards the rear then tighten the securing nuts and bolts.

Replace the bushings at the front and rear of the upper control arm. With reference to Fig.H.32 place the toothed washer into position and insert the control arm shaft with the longer

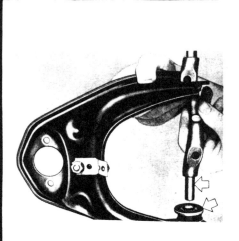

Fig.H.32. Control arm shaft and toothed washer

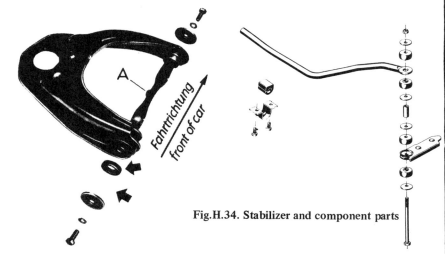

Fig.H.34. Stabilizer and component parts

Fig.H.33. Control arm shaft showing position of lug (A)

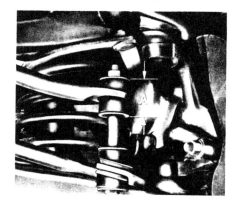

Fig.H.35 Distance (A) to be 1.46 to 1.5 inches

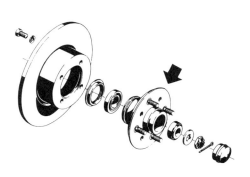

Fig.H.36. Front wheel hub and disc

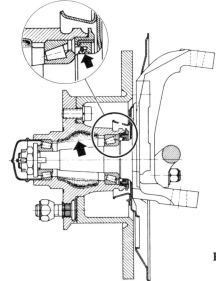

Fig.H.37. Hub cross section

Fig.H.38. Seal ring on front wheel hub

bearing journal into the rear bushing. Insert the control arm shaft and press in the front damper bushing. The control arm shaft must be fitted so that the lug, shown as (A) in Fig.H.33, is pointed in the correct direction.

Fit the rubber ring and the plastic washer and note that the shoulder of the dished washer has to face the bushing. Tighten the hexagon head bolts of the control arm shaft in the upper control arm to a torque of 22 lb.ft. Only tighten the shaft to this torque after installation of the upper control arm and if the lower control arm is in its correct position.

When installing the upper control arm to the front suspension cross member attachment tighten the bolts to 40 lb.ft and ensure that the same number of shims are installed as were removed and that they are positioned correctly.

Check the caster, camber and toe-in as detailed in the "Steering" section with particular attention to the caster. Adjust as necessary. Road test the car to ascertain the correct function of the suspension and check the front brake lines and the brake calliper assembly for leaks.

STABILIZER RUBBERS - Replacement

Jack up the front of the car, ensuring that the handbrake is on or the rear wheels are chocked. Support the car with stands under the lower control arms and then remove the nut and washer from the long bolt and withdraw the bolt from its position together with the rubber bumpers and their seatings.

When installing the end of the stabilizer into position ensure that the rubber bumpers are properly positioned with the shoulder of the rubber bumper located in the stabilizer eye and the stabilizer support. The rubber bumper seat should be installed so that the spherical side faces the rubber bumpers. Always use new self-locking nuts when installing the assembly.

Refer to Fig.H.35 which shows a measure (A) which is a dimension of between 1.46 to 1.5 in.

WHEEL HUB AND BEARING -
Removal, Adjustment and Installation

Remove the wheel hub cap and loosen the nuts securing the front wheel to be serviced. Chock the rear wheel or pull the handbrake on and jack up the front of the car. Remove the wheel and remove the brake calliper assembly as detailed in the "BRAKES" section: do not disconnect the brake lines. Pry off the grease cap and remove the split pin, castle nut and washer prior to withdrawing the front wheel hub together with the brake disc from the steering knuckle.

Use a serrated socket head wrench adaptor to detach the brake disc from the wheel hub. Press the inner wheel bearing together with its seal ring out of the front wheel hub using a large thrust plate. Using a small thrust plate and a drift, press the outer wheel bearing outer race from the front wheel hub. Inspect the bearings for wear or for score marks in the races and renew as necessary.

Press in the outer races of the inner and outer wheel bearing using a bearing installer or a pipe of appropriate diameter. Provide all the races including the roller cages of the wheel bearings with ball and roller bearing grease. Coat the contact surface of the seal ring with grease and then locate the seal ring into its correct position. Use a light hammer to tap the new seal ring evenly into the front wheel hub. Fit the wheel hub to the brake disc and secure the assembly with the bolts to a torque of 36 lb.ft.

Fit the hub and disc assembly on to the steering knuckle and slide on the washer and fit and tighten the castle nut to a torque of 18 lb.ft. Locate the brake calliper assembly and secure it to the steering knuckle to a torque of 72 lb.ft. Fit the wheel and tighten the wheel securing nuts. Rotate the wheel and slacken the castle nut until the wheel rotates jerk - free in both directions. If the hole in the steering knuckle shaft does not align with the castle nut slot then the nut must be slackened, DO NOT TIGHTEN, until the split pin can be inserted and bent over to secure. The roller bearings must under no circumstances be preloaded.

Clean the inside of the grease cap and fill it with new grease. Fill the hollow space of the front wheel hub with ball and roller bearing grease and then press on the grease cap. Lower the car to the ground and tighten the wheel nuts to a torque of 65 lb.ft. fit the wheel hub cap. Check the caster, camber and toe-in and check the brake lines and calliper assembly for leaks. Road test the car to ensure correct steering and wheel balance as necessary.

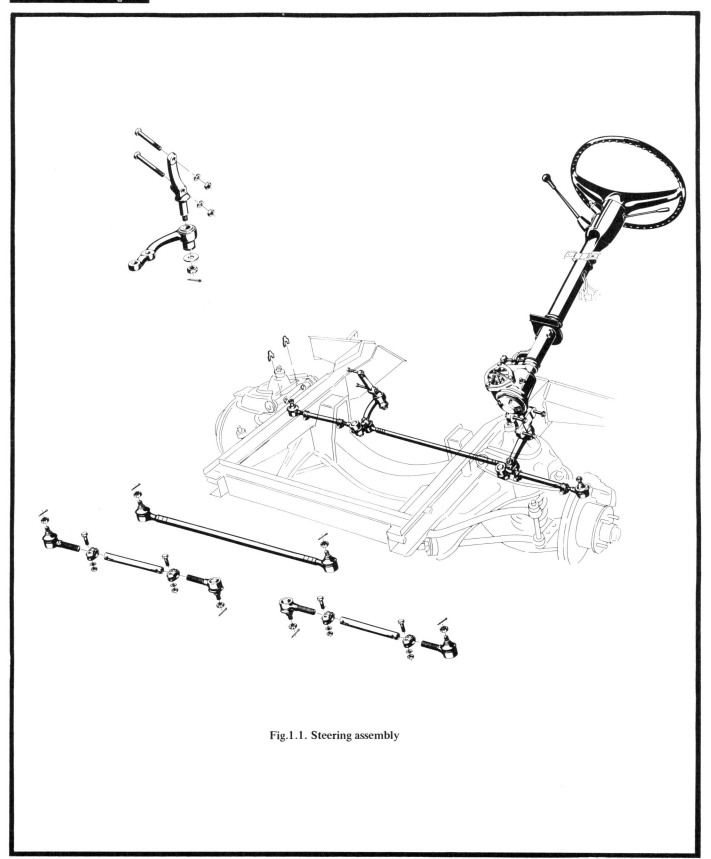

Fig.1.1. Steering assembly

Steering

DESCRIPTION

The steering is of the recirculating ball type with a self adjusting worm bearing. During production installation, fork shaped shims may be fitted between the steering gear housing and the front frame side member in order to eliminate any stress on the steering gear. If a new steering gear is fitted or the original steering gear is refitted then these shims must be re-installed at their original location.

STEERING COLUMN AND BOX - Removal

Remove the bolts securing both front seats or the front bench seat and remove the seats. With reference to Fig.1.4 remove the connections identified A,B and C from the fuse box. Refer to the Section on "Brakes" and "Clutch" and remove both the brake and the clutch pedal. Remove the screws securing the cover plate at the junction of the steering column and floorboard and remove the cover plate. Unhook the parking brake cable and then remove the gear shift control rod from the control shaft link.

Using a Pitman arm remover withdraw the Pitman arm from the Pitman shaft. Remove the bolts securing the steering gear housing to the side member and withdraw the gear noting the number and thickness of any fork shaped shims that are fitted. Remove the nuts and detach the clamp securing the column to the underside of the instrument panel and then withdraw the column and steering box through the floor aperture into the interior of the car.
NOTE: Do not place the column and box in a horizontal position and tilt it as the oil in the steering box will run into the column jacket.

STEERING BOX - Dismantling and Overhaul

Drain the oil from the steering box and then remove both the steering wheel and the signal switch (see this section). Remove the horn wire and push the housing assembly and the column bearing out of the signal switch. Remove the screws and withdraw the ignition lock.

Unscrew the backlash adjustment lock nut and then remove the steering box cover screws and lift off the cover complete with the Pitman shaft. Dismantle the Pitman shaft. Insert the column in a vice (Figs. 1.9 and 1.10) and loosen and remove the bearing adjuster locknut and the bearing adjuster from the housing: pry out the ball race from the adjuster if the bearing shows signs of wear.

Remove the ball guides and the complete ball set (54) from the ball nut. Remove the securing bolts and unscrew the control shaft link from the control shaft. Use a rod to push the felt out of the steering column jacket and then withdraw the control shaft from the top. Slide the anti-rattle rubber ring (Fig.1.14 (A) to the top of the shaft and then push the felt into position so that it is between the indentations in the column jacket. Slide the anti-rattle ring on to the control shaft using tool S-1147 with the marking on the tool coincident with the column jacket. Use a screwdriver to lever the oil seal ring from the sector shaft housing. When the oil seal is being installed it

should be soaked in steering gear oil for a few minutes. Insert the oil seal ring into position and then drive it in until it is flush with the face of the housing. Oil the ball cages of the bearings with steering box oil.

Oil the worm groove of the steering column and the ball nut with steering gear oil then slide the ball nut on the column so that the narrow taper ends (A) (see Fig.1.17) of the rack teeth are towards the side cover flange of the housing when the rack teeth are facing the sector gear teeth. Feed 18 balls into both of the ball guide holes of one circuit using a tapered wooden piece. Coat the inside of the channel of one ball guide half with vaseline and set 9 balls into the vaseline, spread vaseline into the other half, close them together and push into the ball nut: repeat the procedure with the second ball guide circuit. Rotate the nut to check that it has free movement then fit securing strap and tighten it down.

Insert the steering column and ball nut assembly into position and lightly screw in the worm bearing adjuster, ensuring that the ball cages centre with the ball races. Use grease to adhere a new paper gasket to the steering gear housing. Coat the Pitman shaft bushes with oil and feed the Pitman shaft into the housing using a screwdriver, through the oil filler hole, to tilt the ball nut and to align the centre tooth of the sector gear with the groove in the centre of the ball nut. Fit a protective sleeve (Opel No. S - 1192) into the oil seal so that it is not damaged when the Pitman shaft is fitted. Fit a new self-locking adjusting screw nut.

Fit the steering and ignition lock, the signal switch and the steering wheel.

Turn the steering until it is halfway between the stops; it is now at high point.

Turn the adjusting screw in a counter-clockwise direction to release the adjustment. As shown in Fig. 1.24 tighten the worm adjuster with, if possible, tool S - 1280 and use a torsion meter and tool SW - 503 to provide torque reading: torque should be 0.33 lb.ft. with steering at high point. Tighten locknut (Fig. 1.26) to a torque of 87 lb.ft. ensuring that the worm bearing adjuster position is not altered. Turn the adjusting nut clockwise (Fig.1.27) until resistance is felt at the steering wheel and the torsion meter shows a reading of 1.2 lb.ft.

Hold the adjusting screw and tighten the locknut to a torque of 29 lb.ft. do not alter the adjustment screw steering. Check the torque at the steering wheel.

STEERING COLUMN AND BOX - Installation

Insert the steering gear through the hole in the floorboard and then fit the bolts to the front frame side member (remember the fork shaped shims). To ensure that the steering gear is stress free do not tighten the fixing bolts of the steering gear. Loosely attach the steering column jacket by its clamp to the instrument panel. Tighten the front frame attaching bolts to 33 lb.ft. then tighten the clamp.

Fit the Pitman arm with its broad teeth coincident with the broad grooves of the Pitman shaft with the steering at high

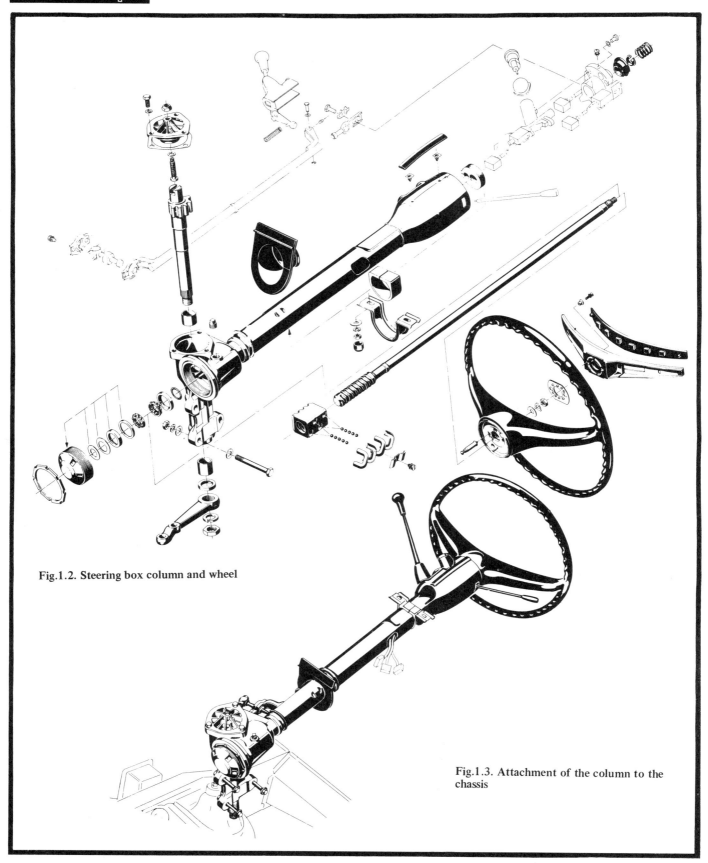

Fig.1.2. Steering box column and wheel

Fig.1.3. Attachment of the column to the chassis

Fig.1.4. Electrical connections to steering column from fuse box

Fig.I.5. Pitman arm and shaft

Fig.1.6. Attachment points of steering housing to front frame

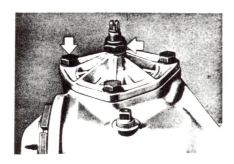

Fig.1.7. Backlash adjusting screw and locknut

Fig.1.8. Withdrawing Pitman shaft

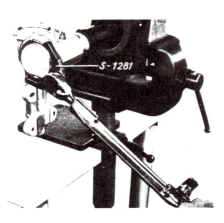

Fig.1.9. Bearing adjuster locknut removing with tool S.1281

Fig.1.10. Removing bearing adjuster

Fig.1.11. Removing bearing race from the bearing adjuster

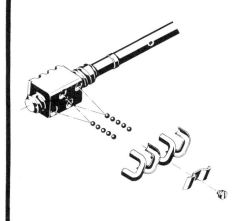

Fig.1.12. Ball set and guides

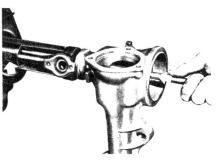

Fig.1.13. Pushing the felt from the steering column jacket

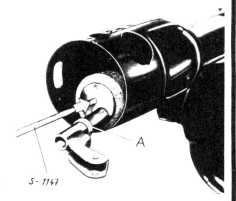

Fig.1.14. Control shaft anti-rattle rubber ring (A)

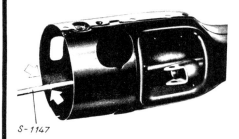

Fig.1.15. Positioning the anti-rattle ring in control shaft

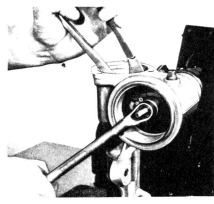

Fig.1.16. Inserting oil seal ring into steering gear housing

Fig.1.17. Position of ball nut and column (see text).

Fig.1.18. Half of a ball guide

Fig.1.19. Inserting steering column and ball nut assembly into the column jacket

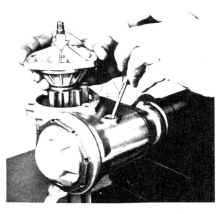

Fig.1.20. Using a screwdriver to position Pitman shaft

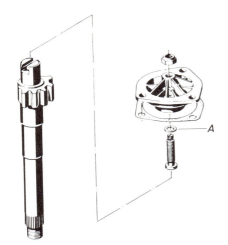

Fig.1.21. Exploded view of Pitman shaft

Fig.1.22. Adjusting the worm bearing

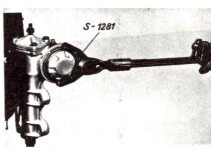

Fig.I.23. Worm bearing adjuster, (A) = dished washer, (B) = retaining ring

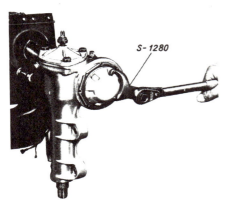

Fig.1.24. Using tool S-1280 to tighten worm bearing adjuster

Fig.1.25. Showing use of torsionmeter on steering wheel

Fig.1.26 Tightening locknut on adjuster

Fig.1.27. Adjusting the sector and ball nut backlash

Fig.1.28. Steering wheel items

Fig.1.29. Removing steering wheel from shaft with tools S- 1033, S-1258

Fig.1.30. Marking on steering shaft arrowed at horizontal.

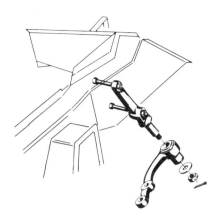

Fig.1.31. Idle lever and damper bushing assembly

Spacer sleeves for horn ring travel

Dimension to top of c/s	Colour
0.301 in	red
0.307 in	black
0.312 in	brown
0.319 in	blue
0.324 in	green
0.344 in	white

Table 1. Horn ring spacer sleeves

Fig.1.32. Removing ball joint of tie rod and relay rod from the idle lever

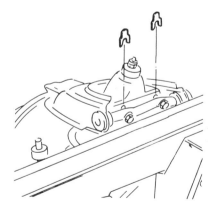

Fig.1.33. Shims used at upper control arm attachments

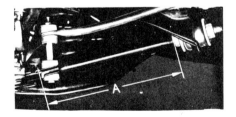

Fig.1.34. Tie strut adjustment dimension

point. Tighten the nut to 123 lb.ft. torque. Rub the sliding area of the shaft rod in the control shaft link with molybdenum disulfide paste and then fit the shaft control rod. Fit the cover plate, connect the parking brake cable and install the brake and clutch pedals. Fit the cables to the steering and ignition lock and signal switch connections at the fuse box. Fit and secure the front seats.

STEERING WHEEL - Removal and Installation

With reference to Fig.1.28, prise the horn push decorative cover away from the horn push bar then remove the screws securing the horn push and withdraw it from its position. Remove the nuts securing the steering wheel and use a drawer bar (or tools S-1033 and S-1258) to remove the steering wheel from its splined shaft.

Grease the direction signal switch return pins and their sliding return cams prior to refitting the steering wheel. When refitting the wheel ensure that the front wheels are straight ahead and that the marking on the shaft (Fig.1.30) is in an horizontal position. The cut-outs for the horn should be facing downwards and the direction signal and parking light switch in the centre.

Use a new lock plate when refitting the wheel and tighten the nut to a torque of 14 lb.ft. Insert the diaphragm with its convex side upwards into the wheel hubs.

When fitting horn bar use spacer sleeves (see Table 1) to give correct position. If horn sounds continuously select long sleeves. If horn travel is too long use short sleeves. Do not seat the spacer sleeves on to the diaphragm as jamming will result .

IDLER LEVER - Removal and Installation

Using a ball stud remover (tool S - 1255) and with reference to Fig.1.32 press the ball joint of the tie rod and the relay rod out of the idler lever. Ensure that no damage is done to the rubber bellows. Remove the split pins and castellated nuts and remove the idler lever and the damper bushing assembly.

When installing the idler lever tighten the castle nut to a torque of 29 lb.ft. and insert split pin to lock. If support was detached from frame side member tighten the bolts to a torque of 43 lb.ft. Insert the tie rod and the relay rod into the idler lever ball joint and tighten castle nuts to 29 lb.ft; insert split pin to lock.

CASTER,CAMBER,TOE-IN and ALIGNMENT - Inspection

Check that the car is on a level surface, that the steering is in the straight ahead position and that the front suspension and the steering linkage do not have excessive play. Ensure that the front wheel bearing is adjusted for correct clearance and the rims do not show excessive lateral or radial runout. Check the tyre pressures are correct for a full load, 21 p.s.i. front, 24 p.s.i rear.

If the check is to be performed using an optical indicator then read the indicator manufacturer's instructions carefully and drive the vehicle on to a measuring stand so that the front and rear are aligned. The settings required are as follows:-

Caster	-1° -	$+1^o$
Camber	$0^o05'$	$1^o05'$
Toe-in	0.08 in $0^o19'$	0.16 in corresponds to $0^o38'$ related to both wheels

Wheel turn angle - outer wheel $18^o31'$

Wheel turn angle - inner wheel $20^o00'$

CAMBER AND CASTER - Adjustment

The camber angle is adjusted by adding or removing fork shaped spacers or shims at the two upper control arm attachment bolts (Fig.1.33). The caster angle is adjusted at the tie struts on the front suspension cross member.

Prior to adjusting the caster angle and with reference to Fig.1.34, measure the dimension A: this is the fixed adjustment dimension and should be between 11.22 and 11.61 inches. All caster correction adjustments on the tie strut depend upon this measure as otherwise the front spring could be made to contact the front suspension cross member. An example of permissible adjustment measures is given as follows and shown at Fig.1.37 :-

Fixed adjustment dimension	11.22 to 11.61 in.
Measure adjustment dimension	11.5 in.
Permissible tie strut move for caster increase	11.5 minus 11.22 in.= 0.28 in.
Permissible tie strut move for caster decrease	11.61 minus 11.5 in.= 0.11 in.
The change of caster at a tie strut displacement of	0.08 in.=50' and at a tie strut
displacement of	0.2 in.= $1^o40'$

To increase the caster slacken the stabilizer bracket and the tie strut bolts and with reference to Fig.1.36 back off the inner nut (A). until the tie strut displacement dimension between the centre of the stabilizer support front bolt flat head and the inside edge of the inner tie strut attaching nut is a previously determined. Tighten the nut (B) to a torque of 65 lb.ft. so that the lower control arm is pulled towards the front by the tie strut.

To decrease the camber, slacken off the nut (B) and adjust the inner nut (A) as determined by the dimensions mentioned above. The control arm will be moved towards the rear by the tie strut. Tighten the nut (B) to a torque of 65 lb.ft. tighten the flat head bolt nuts to a torque of 47 lb.ft.

The caster can also be adjusted at the upper control arm by inserting shims NOT of equal thickness between the upper control arm shaft and the front suspension cross member at the front and rear. The maximum difference between front and rear is 0.03 in. Check the adjustment optically to ensure that it is at the correct setting.

To adjust the camber it may be necessary to rework two free-wheeling ratchets one for loosening and one for tightening. If rework is to be carried out refer to Fig.1.38. Jack the car up from below front suspension cross member and with loosening ratchet loosen the upper control arm on the front suspension cross member: further loosening requires a fork wrench as the bent ratchet cannot be removed at a later stage of adjustment. Lower the jack and then place shims of equal thickness between the upper control arm shaft and the suspension member at front and rear. Shims thicknesses obtainable are 0.016 in. 0.030 in,

105

Fig.1.35. Stabilizer bracket

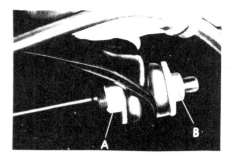

Fig.1.36. Tie strut caster adjustment

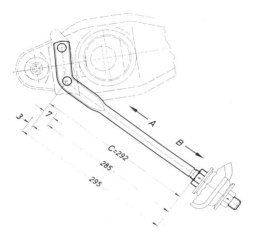

Fig.1.37. Tie strut dimensions shown in millimetres

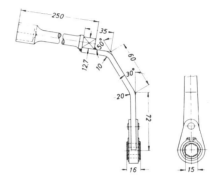

Fig.1.38. Dimensions for re-working free-wheel ratchets (dimensions are shown in millimetres)

Fig.1.39. Loosening the upper control arm on front suspension

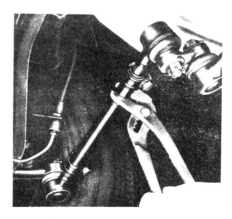

Fig.I.40. Loosening the clamp bolts on one side of the tie rods

0.059 in. and 0.118 in. A shim thickness of 0.030 in. corresponds to change of camber of 12'. Note that a total shim thickness of 0.127 in. must not be exceeded. Raise the jack again and tighten the upper control arm to suspension cross member bolts to a torque of 40 lb.ft.

TOE IN - Adjustment

Loosen the clamp bolts on the left and right tie rod and adjust the toe-in to the correct setting; adjustment should always be carried out on both tie rods. Tighten the clamp bolts to a torque of 11 lb.ft. and then check the adjustment optically. NOTE: the measured value for camber, caster and toe-in at the REAR wheels should be zero.

Technical Data

Camber	0o 05 - 1o 05'
Caster	-1o - + 1o
Toe-in	2-4 mm (.08 - .16 in.) corresponds to 0o 19' - 0o 38' related to both wheels
Turning angle of outer wheel assigned to turning angle of inner wheel = 20o	18o 31'

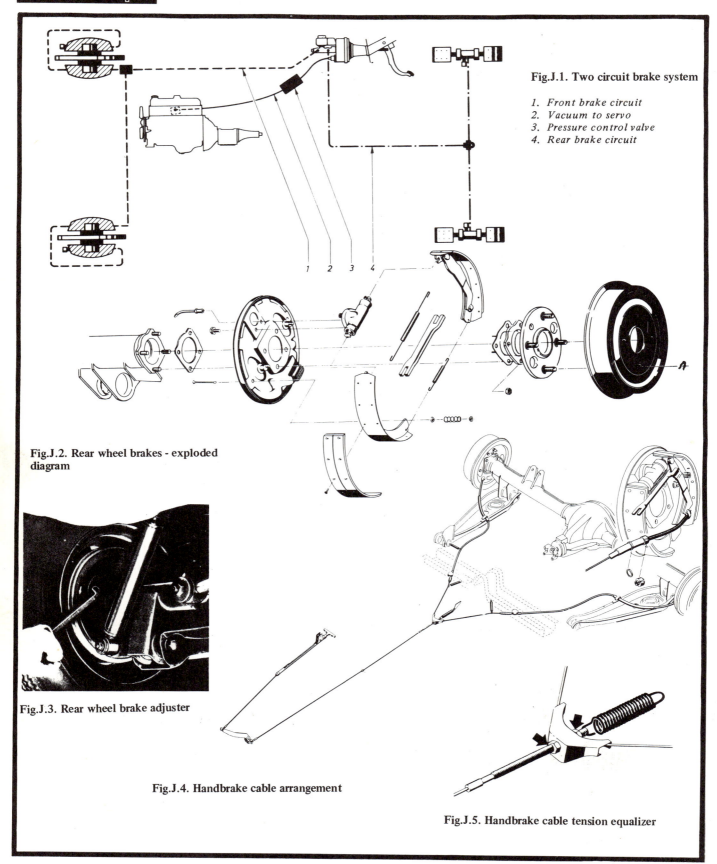

Fig.J.1. Two circuit brake system

1. *Front brake circuit*
2. *Vacuum to servo*
3. *Pressure control valve*
4. *Rear brake circuit*

Fig.J.2. Rear wheel brakes - exploded diagram

Fig.J.3. Rear wheel brake adjuster

Fig.J.4. Handbrake cable arrangement

Fig.J.5. Handbrake cable tension equalizer

Braking System

DESCRIPTION

The braking system is a hydraulically operated two - circuit system with servo booster. The brakes act on all four wheels with disc brakes at the front and drum brakes at the rear. The handbrake is independent of the hydraulic pressure and operates on the rear drum brakes through a system of cables and linkages.

On cars with automatic transmission the brake fluid has a higher boiling point due to the greater stress on the brakes. This fluid can be used in cars without automatic transmission and can be mixed with standard brake fluid. As the higher boiling point fluid is more hygroscopic it needs to be changed more often than the standard fluid.

Note that the front disc brakes need not be manually adjusted as the pistons in the callipers adjust automatically.

REAR WHEEL BRAKES - Adjustment

Chock the front wheels of the car, ensure that the gear selector/lever is in neutral and that the handbrake is released. Check that the reservoir is topped up to within half an inch of the top and then jack up the rear of the car until the wheels can be turned freely.

Use a brake adjustment spanner to turn the brake plate eccentric adjustment cam in a counter-clockwise direction until resistance is felt when trying to turn the wheel. Now turn the cam stage by stage in a clockwise direction until the wheel is just free to turn without rubbing.

Repeat the operation on the other rear wheel and then pump the foot brake pedal several times and then check that the wheels can still be turned without them rubbing. Adjust the handbrake after completion of the foot brake adjustment.

HANDBRAKE - Adjustment

Chock the front wheels of the car, ensure that the gear selector/lever is in neutral and that the handbrake is released. Jack up the rear of the car until the wheels can be turned freely. Check the handbrake cable for smooth operation by pulling down the front cable, near the equalizer, (Fig.J.6) until a braking action is noticeable at the rear wheels. Release the cable.

Pull out the ratchet until 5 notches are visible and then with reference to Fig.J.5 adjust the hexagon nuts at the equalizer until the brake shoe just contact the rear wheel drums. Release the jack and remove the chocks.

Road test the car to ensure that the car slows to a stop in a straight line when the brakes are applied and that the car is held by the handbrake alone on a steep gradient.

BLEEDING THE SYSTEM

If any of the brake hoses have been disconnected or renewed or if the brakes have a "spongy" feel, the brake system must be bled. Clean the area around each of the brake bleed nipples and around the reservoir to ensure that no dirt enter the system.

Ensure that the reservoir is topped up with the correct brake fluid then fit a transparent hose over the bleeder nipple furthest from the reservoir and submerge the other end of the hose into a dry and clean glass container partly filled with new brake fluid. Depress the brake pedal slowly and release slowly several times until no air bubbles are being forced from the hose into the brake fluid in the jar: depress the brake pedal fully, hold it in that position, tighten the nipple and remove the hose.

Top up the reservoir with clean fluid and then repeat the operation on the remaining wheels until each has been bled. Do not re-use the fluid in the glass container.

If it is possible to use brake bleeding equipment, prepare the bleeder according to the manufacturer's instructions and connect it, using adaptor S - 1261, to the tandem brake master cylinder. Subject the system to a pressure of 20 p.s.i. and then bleed the front and rear brake circuit. Leave the bleeder nipple open until the fluid flows in a steady solid stream, close the nipple and fill the reservoir with brake fluid B 040 032 (Standard), B040 880 (Auto Transmission).

Use a brake pedal compressor over a period of at least 10 minutes to test the system for leaks.

DISC BRAKE PADS - Removal and Installation

Renewal of the brake pads is necessary when the friction pad has worn down to a thickness of approximately 0.1 in. The car should be put into gear and jacked up at the front with the front wheels removed. The brake pads should be renewed on both wheels even if it is necessary only to renew one pad.

From outside to inside, drive the dowel pins out of the brake calliper and friction pads. Remove the cross-shaped retaining spring and withdraw the friction pads from the brake calliper.

If the pads have worn down to 0.1 in. or show signs of contamination by oil, or show cracks reaching down to the pressure plate, or have loosened over the complete circumference then they must be renewed.

Check the disc plate for signs of concentric scars. If the scars are not more than 0.02 in. then the new pads will adapt themselves to the disc, if they are deeper then the disc must be renewed.

Push the calliper pistons completely into the bore of the brake calliper. This operation can be carried out with tool MW 103 or with a piece of wood. Note the level of the brake fluid in the reservoir and if necessary drain off some of the fluid. Clean the discs and friction pad guides with alcohol and/or compressed air. Do not use cleaning agents using mineral oil as damage to the rubber seals with result. Renew all rubber seals which have hardened or cracked.

Install the new pads and check them for freedom of movement then fit new cross-shaped retaining springs and drive in the dowel pins. Dowel pins not having a tight fit should be renewed. Depress the brake pedal several times to adjust the pistons so as

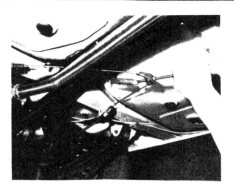

Fig.J.6. Equalizer location

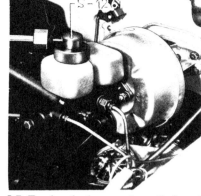

Fig.J.7. Tandem brake - master cylinder with pressure adapter fitted

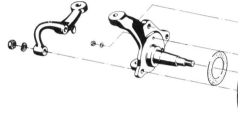

Fig.J.8. Hub, disc and pad assembly - front wheel

Fig.J.9. Driving out dowel pin on brake caliper

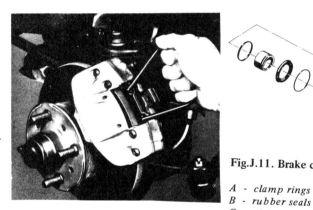

Fig.J.10. Removing friction pads

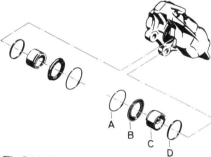

Fig.J.11. Brake caliper items

A - clamp rings
B - rubber seals
C - pistons
D - seal rings

Fig.J.12. Using compressed air to remove clamp rings and rubber seals

Fig.J.13. Removing piston using compressed air

Fig.J.14. Inserting pistons using hammer shaft

to allow the least clearance of the friction pads and then check the brake fluid level in the reservoir and top up as necessary.

Heavy braking should be avoided for at least the first 100 miles after new friction pads have been installed.

DISC BRAKE CALLIPER - Removal and Overhaul

To remove the brake calliper, remove the wheel ensuring that the vehicle rear wheels are chocked. Detach the brake line from the calliper and insert a plug into the line to prevent fluid from escaping. Unscrew the bolt securing the brake line support bracket and withdraw the bracket and the brake line.

Remove the friction disc pads from the calliper as previously detailed and then remove the bolts securing the calliper and remove the brake calliper assembly.

The brake calliper must not be dismantled: the pressing out of pistons, replacement of seal ring etc must be performed on an assembled calliper. Clean the assembly with brake fluid or alcohol.

With reference to Figs.J.11 and J.12, remove the clamp rings (A) and the rubber seals (B) and press the piston (C) out of the calliper half with compressed air. Apply compressed air to the brake line attachment to force the remaining piston from its guide. Mark the pistons and corresponding halves for re-assembly and then wash all parts in white spirit or alcohol. Check the pistons and cylinders for wear, if the cylinder is damaged or corroded, or shows signs of excessive friction, a complete new calliper assembly must be used.

When installing, handle both calliper halves with care so that no burrs are caused on the joint faces and coat all gaskets insides of rubber seals and sliding areas with brake cylinder paste. Always use new rubber seals and clamp rings. Prior to piston installation, position the rubber seals in the piston grooves and push the correct piston into the calliper mounting half. Push the remaining piston into the rim half of the calliper and then push both pistons into their cylinders using a hammer handle (Fig.J.14).

Check the correct piston position. The recessed part of the piston must be positioned at an angle of 20⁰ to the lower edge of the brake calliper shaft (viewed in installation position).

Attach the calliper assembly to the steering knuckle and insert the securing bolts and tighten them to 72 lb.ft. torque. Attach the brake line and the supporting bracket and then fit the disc pads. Bleed the brake calliper and road test the brakes.

REAR WHEEL BRAKE CYLINDER AND SHOES-
Removal, Inspection and Installation

Remove the wheel hub cap, slacken the wheel studs, chock the front wheels and engage the handbrake. Jack up the rear of the car and support it prior to unscrewing the wheel studs and removing the wheel. Mark the position of the drum for re-assembly by using a paint mark and then release the handbrake. Prise off the securing clips and remove the drum. Detach the handbrake cable at the brake lever remove the slotted guide bushings and remove the cable. Use pliers to remove the springs securing the brakes, then remove the connecting lever of the brake shoes and the hold down spring seat and remove the brake shoes.

Remove the screws securing the wheel brake cylinder and unscrew and plug the brake line connection at the rear of the cylinder before withdrawing the cylinder.

To overhaul the cylinder completely dismantle it and clean all the parts in brake fluid or alcohol only. Polish the cylinder bore with linen wrapped around a piece of wood of 1/2 inch diameter. Check the bore for rust spots, scores or other damage which require the renewal of the brake cylinder. Check the bore and the pistons for wear.

Largest permissible bore diameter 0.63 in.
Smallest permissible piston diameter 0.62 in.

Use a new set of rubber parts and on assembly thinly coat the rubber seals and the sliding areas with brake cylinder paste. Assemble the brake cylinder as a reverse of the dismantling procedure and install it as a reverse of the removal procedure.

Brake linings must be renewed if they are worn to less than half of their original thickness, or if an insufficient braking action is achieved after the brakes have been correctly adjusted.

Remove the rivets securing the worn linings to the brake shoes and remove the shoes. Two types of new brake linings are supplied, one of 0.2 in.thickness and one of 0.22 in.thickness. The thinner linings are for use when no brake lining grinder is available and the thicker linings when a grinder is available. After riveting the thinner linings can be installed immediately into the brake assembly but the thicker linings must be ground to size - radius 0.008 in.to 0.02 in.smaller than measured radius of the brake drum.

Assemble the brake shoes on to the back plate in the reverse order of the removal procedure, ensuring that all parts are clean and dry. Fit the handbrake cable and the brake drum and fit the wheel and tyre assembly. Bleed the rear brake circuit and adjust the brakes prior to removing the support and releasing the jack.

BRAKE SERVO FILTER - Replacement

Remove the split pin at the top of the brake pedal lever and remove the pin and washers securing the fork end of the servo piston rod. Unscrew the pipe connections and seal them to prevent the ingress of dirt; remove the bolts securing the servo and withdraw the servo together with its support and tandem brake master cylinder. Remove the master cylinder and reservoir. Remove the nuts securing the support bracket and detach it from the servo body; also remove the protective cap and its support (Fig.J.20). Slide off the noise deadener and then remove the filter.

No repairs can be carried out on the servo with the exception of renewing the filter.

Fit a new filter and slide on the felt noise deadener, note that the radial slots must be offset to each other by 180⁰. Fit the cap support bracket and seat the cap into it (ensure that it is properly seated). Locate and secure the support bracket and tighten the nuts to a torque of 11 lb.ft. Fit the protective cap and fork end together with the adjustment nut and locking nut

With reference to Fig.J.19, fit new sealing plugs (A) to the tandem brake master cylinder and fit the fluid container. Locate and secure the master cylinder to the servo using a new seal ring (B): tighten the bolts to 11. lb.ft.

H

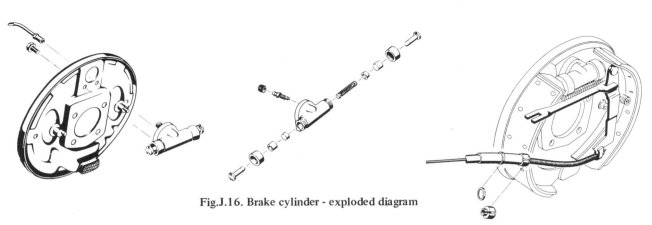

Fig.J.16. Brake cylinder - exploded diagram

Fig.J.15. Rear wheel brake plate and cylinder

Fig.J.17. Handbrake cable connection and operation

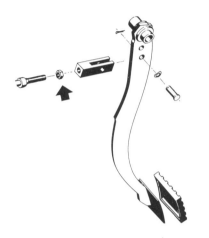

Fig.J.19. Servo - exploded diagram

A - foam rubber filter
B - noise deadener
C - support bracket
D - protective cap

Fig.J.18. Brake pedal and servo piston rod

Fig.J.20. Removal of servo filter

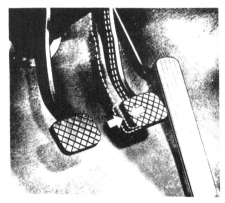

Fig.J.21. Brake pedal movement for servo adjustment

Fig.J.22. Location of vacuum control valve arrowed

Locate the servo into position turning the fork end until the bores in the fork end and in the brake pedal lever coincide. Note that the brake pedal must rest against the rubber stop: do not exert force when turning the fork end. Secure the servo and unseal and connect all lines.

Check that the servo is adjusted correctly by pushing down on the pedal until the vacuum part in the servo is closed: the measurement should be between 0.3 and 0.4 inches. Depress the brake pedal several times to clear the servo of any vacuum and take the measurement again. If the measure is not correct, then slacken the locknut on the piston rod and turn the piston rod with pliers to obtain the correct measure.

Bleed the brake system and check the system for leaks. Road test the car to ensure correct operation of brakes.

VACUUM CONTROL VALVE

The control valve is located adjacent to the inlet manifold and has a short hose from the manifold to the valve and a longer hose from the valve to the vacuum servo. Cars with automatic clutch or automatic transmission have the long hose installed behind the carburetter. Arrows on the control valve housing must point towards the intake manifold and all connections must be leakproof.

Note must be taken of the above points when the control valve is removed for the purpose of renewal etc. .

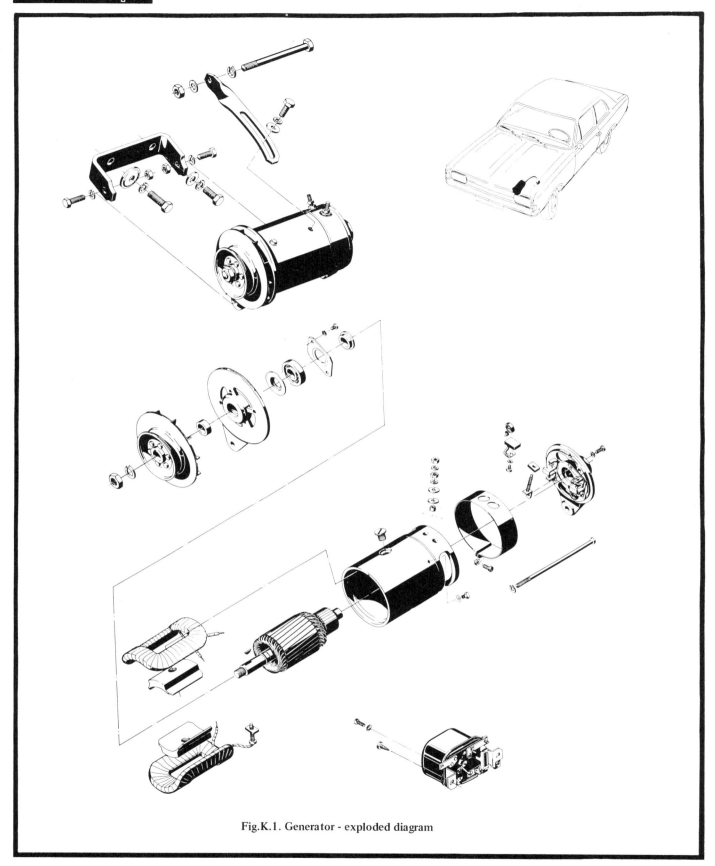

Fig.K.1. Generator - exploded diagram

Electrical Equipment

DESCRIPTION

The electrical system normally uses a conventional d.c. generator operating a 12 volt system with 8 circuits protected by 5 and 8 amp fuses. The fuse box is situated at the left side of the dash panel. The belt driven generator has a maximum output of 25 amps at a rated 14 volts and the voltage regulator is set at a cut-in voltage of 12.3 to 13.2. Refer to Technical Data for further information.

At special request an alternator can be fitted and if one is fitted in your car then it is essential that you read the following notes:

1. Never disconnect the regulator or battery when the engine is running.
2. Never allow the alternator field or its connection to be earthed.
3. Never use a 250 volt or 110 volt test lamp, only 12 volt.
4. Never use a Meggar to check the diodes.
5. Never operate the voltage regulator when it is connected to earth.
6. Never disconnect or remove the alternator prior to disconnecting the battery.
7. Never confuse the regulator leads.
8. Ensure that the negative (earth) terminal is connected to earth when replacing the battery.
9. Never charge the battery in-situ without first disconnecting both battery leads and remember that incorrect battery reconnection destroys the diodes and the regulator.

STARTER MOTOR - Removal and Installation

Disconnect the battery and then disconnect the starter connections. Loosen the two bolts at the bracket at the forward end of the starter and then remove the bolts securing the drive end of the starter: the bolt at the top outside of the starter may require to be driven out with a soft faced hammer or a wooden peg and hammer. Remove the bolt securing the front end bracket and withdraw the starter. An exploded view of the starter which may aid dismantling is shown at Fig.K.3.

To ensure a stress - free installation of the starter insert it into position and then tighten the bolts and nut at the drive end (Fig.K.6), then the bolt securing the commutator end bracket prior to tightening the two nuts, securing the starter to the bracket. Fit all connections ensuring that they are clean and free from grease or oil.

STARTER MOTOR - Checking In-Situ

Check that the battery is fully charged as this is a requirement of the test. Check that all battery and starter connections and the earth strap between the engine and the right front frame side member are clean and tight. Connect a voltmeter and ammeter in circuit on a VA tester as shown in Fig.K.7. Ensure that the parking brake is fully on, now engage gear and actuate the starter. Check that the voltage reading at starter terminal 50 is not less than 0.5 volts below the battery voltage (7 to 9 volt) Check that the amperage is approx. 300 amps, If the voltage drop is large, check the ignition lock contacts and plug connec-tions prior to removing the starter for further checks.

If the current consumption is much higher than 300 amps then it is likely that there is a short circuit in the starter. If the current consumption is substantially lower then check for a dirty commutator, worn brushes, dirty solenoid switch contacts or an open circuit.

GENERATOR/ALTERNATOR - Removal and Installation

Disconnect the battery and remove the connections from the generator/alternator (identify the cables to prevent incorrect reconnection). Remove the bolt (generator), nut and bolt (alternator) from the adjustment bracket and then loosen the remaining securing bolts and lift away the fan belt. Support the generator/alternator, remove the securing bolts and nuts and withdraw the unit.

Fit the generator/alternator as a reversal of the removal instructions and adjust the position until the fan belt can be depressed by half an inch at the centre of its longest run to obtain tension. Ensure that the electrical connections are clean and dry and then connect the generator/alternator. Connect the battery connections do NOT operate the alternator without first connecting the battery.

GENERATOR AND REGULATOR - Checking

No Load Check

Use a Volt-Amp tester and connect it according to the tester manufacturer's instructions; connect the earth connections of the tester to terminal B+ on the regulator. Start the engine and increase the revolutions until there is no further increase in the voltage, take the reading within 30 seconds of this condition. The reading should be between 13.6 and 14.5 volts.

Cut-in Voltage Check

Let the engine idle and connect a load resistor to terminal B+ set to the generator output (approximately 450 watts). Increase the engine revolutions until the voltmeter shows a sudden voltage drop and at this point read the cut-in voltage which should be between 12.3 and 14.2 volts.

Load Check

With the tester connected as in "Cut-in Voltage Check" above, increase the engine revolutions until a load current of 37 amps is obtained and at that time take the voltage reading. The reading should be between 12.8 and 13.8 volts.

Reverse Current Check

Connect the tester between the battery and the regulator terminal B+ and then increase the revolutions to approximately half maximum and then slowly decrease the revolutions. The needle on the ammeter should now return to zero and continue to a minus reading of between 2 and 9 amps: this is the reverse

Fig.K.2. Alternator - exploded diagram

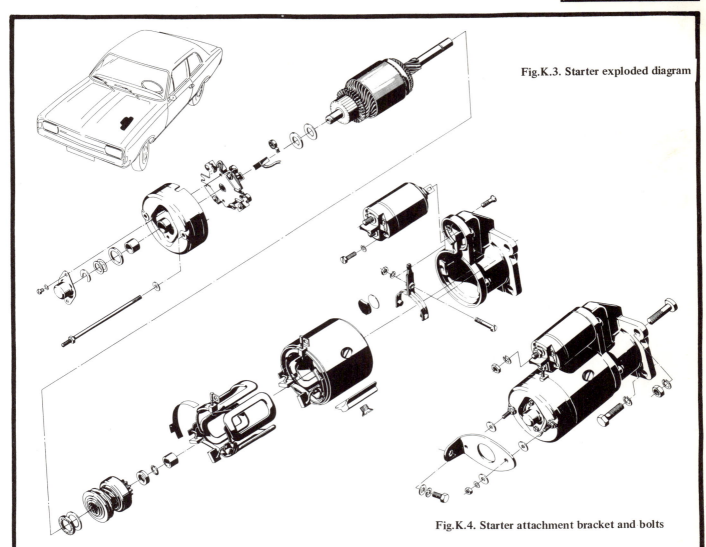

Fig.K.3. Starter exploded diagram

Fig.K.4. Starter attachment bracket and bolts

Fig.K.5. Driving out starter stud

Fig.K.6. Starter front attachment points arrowed

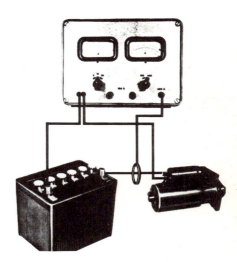

Fig.K.7. Tester connected to starter terminal 50

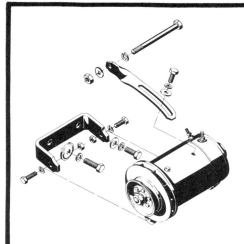

Fig.K.8. Generator attachment items

Fig.K.9. Tension adjustment strap and bolt

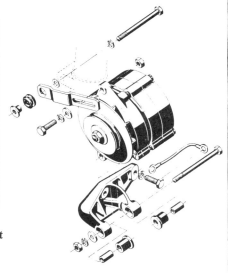

Fig.K.10. Alternator attachment items

Fig.K.11. Tension adjustment strap and nut & bolt

Fig.K.12. Coil and connections

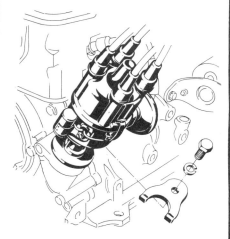

Fig.K.13. Distributor location

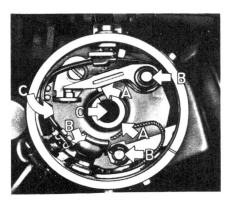

Fig.K.14. Grease points (see text)

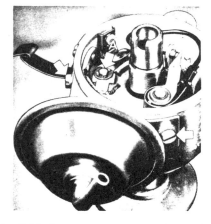

Fig.K.15. Grease control rod eye (A) with Bosch grease

Fig.K.16. Rotor arm identification

Fig.K.17. Crankshaft pulley and timing case markings

Fig.K.18. Alignment of distributor shaft and housing

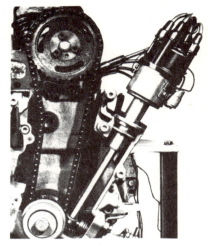

Fig.K.19. Location of distributor drive

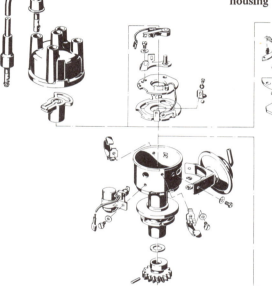

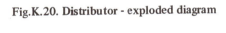

Fig.K.20. Distributor - exploded diagram

Fig.K.21. Distributor - oil pump drive

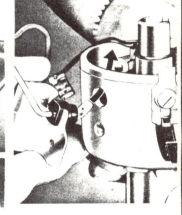

Fig.K.22. Ignition condenser

Fig.K.23. Use of stroboscope

Fig.K.24. A = advance the ignition, B = retard the ignition

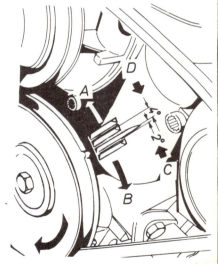

Fig.K.25. Timing marks (see text)

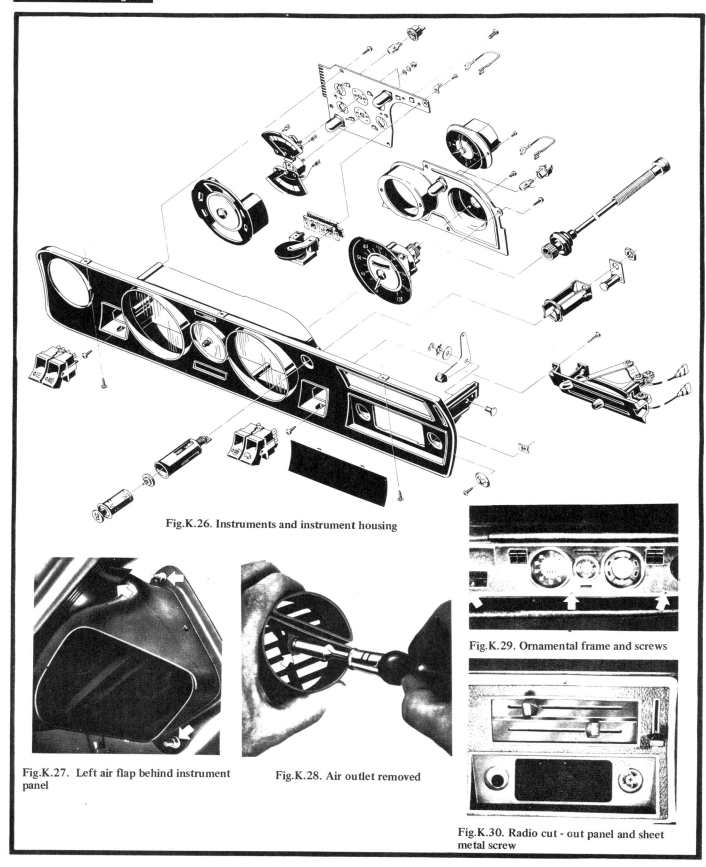

Fig.K.26. Instruments and instrument housing

Fig.K.27. Left air flap behind instrument panel

Fig.K.28. Air outlet removed

Fig.K.29. Ornamental frame and screws

Fig.K.30. Radio cut - out panel and sheet metal screw

current reading.

IGNITION COIL - Testing

After switching on the ignition, check with a test lamp that there is voltage at terminal 15 of the ignition coil: if a check is made with a voltmeter then the voltage at this connection should be the same as that of the battery. Connect an ignition tester according to the manufacturer's instructions and switch on the ignition and check the ignition voltage: the voltage should read between 10.000 and 14,000 volts. If no tester is available, withdraw the high tension lead from connection 4 at the distributor cap and hold it approximately 0.3 in.away from an earth point. When the starter is operated a spark should jump from the end of the lead to the earth point. If there is no spark, the ignition coil must be replaced.

IGNITION COIL - Removal and Installation

Remove the connections from the coil and identify them for reconnection. Remove the screws from the bracket securing the coil and remove the coil (Fig.K.12). Install the new coil and secure the bracket with the screws. Fit the connections using a new protective rubber cap on the high tension lead.

Test the coil circuit as previously described.

DISTRIBUTOR - Inspection

Remove the distributor cap and check it carefully for tracking prior to cleaning it. If a tester is available the test value of the individual wires should not exceed 1,000 ohms. Remove and clean the rotor arm and check that its resistance value is between 3,000 to 4,500 ohms. Check the contact breaker points and clean dirty or slightly burnt contacts with a contact file - do not use emery cloth. The contact points are manufactured from tungsten alloy and slight wear will not reduce their efficiency. Excessive wear means that the contacts must be replaced. Check that the contact breaker point measurement is between 0.16 and 0.2 in. using a clean and dry feeler gauge.

Grease the butting face of the breaker arm and lightly grease the cams and the breaker arm pivot pin. With reference to Fig.K.14 the identification letters refer to lubricants as follows:-

      A - Bosch grease Ft 1v 4
      B - Bosch grease Ft 1v 22
      C - Engine oil

Check that the connections to the ignition condenser are clean and tight. Check that the earth wire is not positioned so that it can be damaged by the vacuum advance control rod and then grease the control rod eye.

If a radio is installed then check that the rotor arm has the identification F and the interference suppression marking ⊼ on it.

DISTRIBUTOR - Removal and Installation

Remove the fuel pump (see Section "Fuel System") and then set No. 1 cylinder to the firing point. With reference to

Fig.K.17 align the markings on the crankshaft pulley and the timing case. Remove the distributor cap and align the cut-out in the distributor shaft with the notch in the distributor housing (Fig.K.18). Remove the distributor clamp and then withdraw the distributor from the cylinder block, immediately cover the bore in the cylinder block to prevent ingress of dust etc.

To install the distributor remove the cover from the bore and insert the distributor drive into the same position as noted during removal. It may be necessary to move the rotor slightly to start the gear but the rotor should align when the distributor is in place. Replace and tighten the distributor clamp and then replace the fuel pump. Check the position of the alignment marks previously detailed. Set the ignition timing.

DISTRIBUTOR - Dismantling and Assembly

Remove the distributor cap and rotor arm and then disconnect the vacuum advance unit wire and remove the snap ring securing the diaphragm link to the contact breaker base plate. Remove the adjuster cap and unscrew the screws securing the vacuum unit prior to withdrawing the vacuum unit.

Disconnect the condenser lead and the fixed contact and lift the fixed contact plate and the contact arm from the distributor. Remove the breaker plate screws and remove the plate from the distributor.
NOTE: Do not disassemble the breaker plate any further.

Remove the roll pin retaining driven gear from the main shaft and slide the gear from the shaft. Slide the cam and the mainshaft from the housing and then remove the weight cover and stop plate screws. Remove the weight springs and the weights and slide the cam assembly from the mainshaft. Release the drive gear from the shaft by removing the pin with a drift of suitable diameter and then sliding the drive from the shaft. Withdraw the shaft through the housing.

When assembling the distributor it is advised that the contact breaker points and the condenser are replaced with new items. The assembly of the distributor is the reverse of the dismantling process. During assembly lightly oil the distributor shaft, and smear grease on to the cam lobes and also into the groove in the upper part of the cam.

IGNITION TIMING - Setting

With reference to Figs. K.23 and K.24 and using a stroboscope connected according to the manufacturers instructions proceed as follows:- Remove the ignition wires from No. 2,3 and 4 spark plugs and tape the ends to prevent sparking against engine etc. Switch on the ignition and crank the engine with the starter and let the stroboscope flash on to the markings on the timing case and crankshaft pulley. Set the timing as required by turning the distributor housing in a clockwise direction to retard the ignition and counter-clockwise to advance the ignition.

Refer to Fig.K.25 and note that A=Advance; B=retardation; C=2° ATDC timing for 1.5 litre engines; D=4° BTDC timing for 1.7 and 1.9 litre engines.

If the ignition timing is too late then the engine will not develop its full output, the engine will become too hot and the fuel consumption will be excessive. If the ignition timing is too early then the engine will exhibit signs of pinking and will become

Fig.K.31. Screw hidden by switches

Fig.K.32. Heater control connections and attachment screws

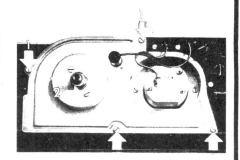

Fig.K.33. Speedo base plate

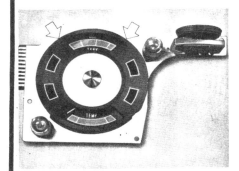

Fig.K.34. Indicator light housing

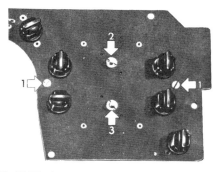

Fig.K.35. Attaching screws numbered 1,2,3. (see text)

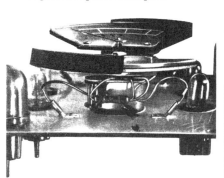

Fig.K.36. Fuel gauge - unit

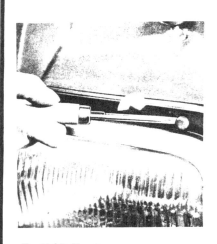

Fig.K.37. Headlamp screw caps

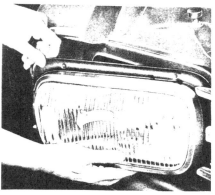

Fig.K. 38. Remove headlamp as shown

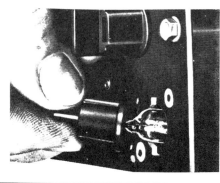

Fig.K.39. Headlamp adjustment screws

Fig.K.40. Instrument panel socket and bulb

excessively hot. In extreme cases of early ignition damage may be caused to bearings.

At the completion of engine timing adjust the engine idling by adjustment at the carburettor.

SPARK PLUGS - Removal, Inspection and Installation

Pull the spark plugs cables from the plug ends identify them and unscrew the spark plugs using a spark plug wrench. Check the spark plugs for cracks or chips on the insulators and then check the electrodes for excessive pitting and wear: If any one of these indications are noted then renew all the plugs. Note that all the spark plugs must be of the same make, type number and heat range. Always renew plugs at each 10,000 miles (16,000 kilometre) interval.

If the plugs are only dirty then clean by sand blasting, file the centre electrode flat and bend the earth electrode until the spark plug gap is 0.028 to 0.031 in. It is advisable to use a round feeler gauge when measuring the gap. When replacing the spark plugs ensure that there is a new copper washer inserted prior to inserting and tightening. Do not screw down too tightly and ensure that a good contact is made when the connector is pushed on.

The recommended plugs are as follows:-

1.5 and 1.7 litre engines	Bosch W 175T1
	AC 43FO
1.9 litre engine	Bosch W 225T1
	AC 43FO

INSTRUMENT HOUSING - Removal and Installation

Remove the padding at the lower left (left-hand drive) lower right (right-hand drive) at the instrument panel by removing the securing clamps. Unscrew the air flap behind the instrument panel and withdraw the connecting hose between the air flap housing and the air outlet.

Compress the air outlet lugs with a socket wrench and remove the air outlet from the panel. Remove the three screws as shown in Fig.K.29 and then withdraw the light switch and windshield wiper switch from the panel. Remove the radio cut-out panel and remove the sheet metal screw. Remove the radio, if installed and then on vehicles with automatic transmission remove the selector lever position indicator. Detach the speedo cable and remove the sheet metal screw covered by the switch. Unscrew the heater controls from the housing behind the instrument panel and remove the housing. Unscrew the choke bowden control cable and unhook it. Remove the instrument housing.

The installation of the instrument housing is the reverse of the removal procedure.

FUEL GAUGE - Removal and Installation

Remove the instrument housing as previously detailed and then remove the speedo base plate. Remove the printed circuit panel from the housing and then unscrew the indicator light housing.

Referring to Fig.K.35, (1) = indicator light housing screws,

(2) = fuel gauge screws, (3) = temperature indicator screws.

Remove the screws securing the fuel gauge to the panel and withdraw the gauge: disconnect the cables.

Installation of the fuel gauge is the reverse of the removal procedure.

HEADLAMP - Removal, Installation and Adjustment

Use a screwdriver to pry off the caps covering the headlamp securing screws and slide the headlamp from its housing as shown in Fig.K.38. Headlamp installation is the reverse of the removal procedure. The lamp must be adjusted to give an area of light that is consistant with the safety of the driver and other road users.

The adjusting screws are accessible without removing the rim. Stand the car on a lever surface and ensure that the tyre pressures are correct. Empty the luggage compartment of items not normally transported and place a load of 150 lb (10st 10lb) on the middle of the rear seat. Set up a screeen 35 feet from the front of the car and then measure the distance from the ground to the lower edge of the headlamp glass; subtract 4 inches from that measurement and draw a line on the screen that is that measurement from ground level. Switch on the headlamps at high beam setting and adjust them until the centre of the light beam is bisected by the line on the screen. Switch to dipped beam and ensure that no part of the light beam is above the line.

Align the headlamps so that the beams are slightly offset towards the kerb.

If it is possible to have the aim of the headlamps checked by an optical setter then the manufacturer's instructions should be followed.

INSTRUMENT LIGHT BULB - Replacement

Reach up behind the instrument panel, turn the bulb socket approx. 90° and then withdraw the bulb holder socket and bulb as an assembly. Pull the bulb from the socket and replace it with one of the same type and rating. Insert the socket into the aperture and turn it 90° to secure it in position.

For the bulb serving the speedometer and electric clock refer to Fig.K.41, and pull the bulb and socket out of the socket sleeve.

TAIL LAMP BULB - Replacement

Remove the three securing screws from the lens and remove the lens from the assembly. Withdraw the "dead" bulb and replace it with one of the same type and rating. Prior to refitting the lens ensure that the gasket is in good condition and use rubber cement to stick the gasket to the body rear panel. If the old gasket will not make a satisfactory waterproof seal then it must be replaced.

LICENCE PLATE BULB - Replacement

Push the lamp assembly out of the rear bumper from below. With reference to Fig.K.43 carefully tip the lamp socket out of

Fig.K.41. Speedo and clock light bulb

Fig.K.42. Tail lamp

Fig.K.43. Licence plate lamp socket (one of two)

Fig. K.44. Reverse lamp switch - 3 speed transmission

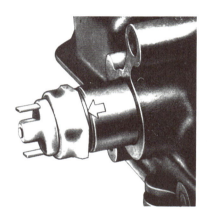

Fig.K.45. Reverse lamp switch - 4 speed column shaft

Fig.K.46. Reverse lamp switch - 4 speed floor shift

Fig.K.47. Windscreen wiper motor

Fig.K.48. Securing screws on wiper transmission cowl

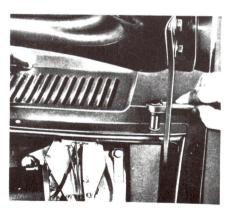

Fig.K.49. Wiper transmission cowl

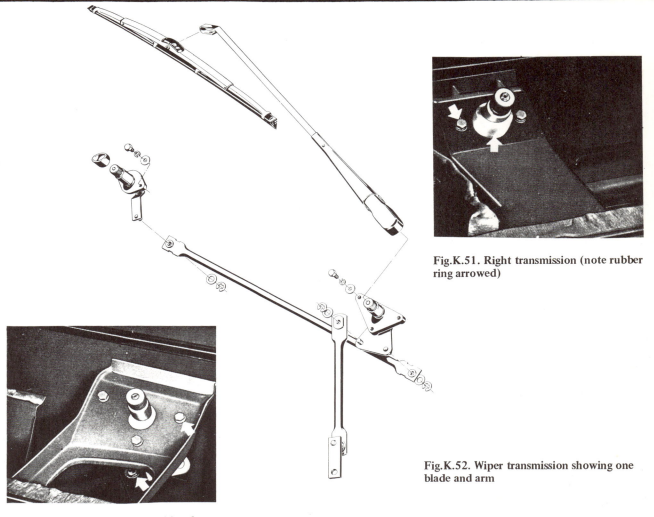

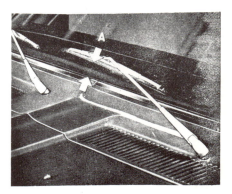

Fig.K.51. Right transmission (note rubber ring arrowed)

Fig.K.52. Wiper transmission showing one blade and arm

Fig.K.50. Left transmission and bracket

Fig.K.53. Rubber dampening locations arrowed

Fig.K.54. Blade clearance (A) to be approx. 2 inches

its housing until both lugs are free, then remove the socket. Replace the bulb with one of the same type and rating.

REVERSE LAMP SWITCH - Replacement

Refer to Figs. K.44 to K.46 for the type of switch fitted to your car. Fig.K.45 shows the 4-speed transmission (steering column lever) and the arrow refers to seal ring which should be renewed if it is damaged during replacement of the switch or if it shows signs of wear or perishing.

Fig.K.46 shows the 4-speed transmission (console shift) and the measure of gap (A) should be between 0.08 and 0.1 inch when 1st gear has been engaged.

WINDSCREEN WIPER MOTOR - Removal and Installation

Remove the windscreen wiper arms and unscrew the cowl as shown in Figs. K.48 and K.49. Remove the connecting rod from the transmission and unscrew the crank from the motor. Unscrew and remove the screws securing the motor to the dash panel and withdraw the plug from the motor prior to withdrawing the motor.

On installation pay attention to the correct arrangement of the rubber dampening parts and apply a plastic sealer to the cowl prior to fitting it into position. When installing the wiper arms refer to Fig.K.54 measurement (A) should be between 1.5 and 2.5 inches.

Technical Data

Nomenclature	Technical Specifications
Battery	12 Volts, 44 Amp. Hours
Generator, Type	EG 14 V 25 A 25
Identification number	0 101 206 109
Rated output on volts	14
Rated output r.p.m.	1850
Maximum current in amperes	25
Minimum diameter of commutator in mm (in.)	31 (1.22)
Brush spring pressure in ounces (p)	15.87-21.16 (450-600)
Minimum brush length in mm (in.)	12 (.47)
Voltage Regulator, Type	VA 14 V 25 A
Identification number	0 190 350 028
Regulator setting in volts - no load - within 30 seconds at 1/2 exciting current	13.6-14.5
Regulator setting in volts at a load of 37 amps. and 5900-6100 generator r.p.m. immediately after reaching load current	12.8-13.8
Cut in voltage	12.3-13.2
Reverse current in amps, with half-charged battery (12-12.2 volts)	2-9
Starter, Type	EF (R) 12 V 0. 8 PS
Identification number	0 001 208 023
No-load test:	
Volts	12
Amperes	45
RPM	6400-7900
Load test:	
Volts (minimum)	9
Amperes	200
RPM	1180-1350
Lock test:	
Volts (minimum)	7
Amperes	280-320
Maximum voltage required to close solenoid contacts	8
Armature brake torque in in. oz. (kpcm)	35-56 (2.5-4)
Overrunning torque in in. oz. (kpcm)	18-25 (1.3-1.8)
Minimum diameter of commutator in mm (in.)	32.8 (1.29)
Brush spring pressure in oz (p)	40.6-45 (1150-1300)
Minimum length of brushes in mm. (in.)	15 (.59)

Nomenclature		Technical Specifications
<u>Ignition Coil,</u> Type		K 12 V
Identification number		0 221 102 034
Resistance of primary coil in ohms		3.2-3.9
Spark gap at 12 volts and 3600 rpm in mm. (in.)		15 (.59)
Ignition voltage		10 000-14 000
<u>Spark Plug,</u> Type	1.5 and 1.7 ltr. engine	W 175 T 1 or AC 42 FS
	1.9 ltr. engine	W 225 T 1 or AC 42 FS
Spark plug gap in mm. (in.)		0.7-0.8 (.028-.031)
<u>Windshield Wiper Motor:</u> Bosch, Type		DH P 12
Identification number		0 390 346 050
Rated voltage		13
Current consumption in amps.		
No load Stage 1		3.8
Stage 11		5.5
Locked Stage 1		22
Stage 11		25
Minimum diameter of commutator in mm. (in.)		22 (.87)
Brush spring pressure in oz. (p)		5.29-8.82 (150-250)
Minimum brush length in mm. (in.)		7.5 (.30)
<u>Windshield Wiper Motor:</u> SWF, Type		SWM 400.839, SWM 400.840, SWM 400.841
Rated voltage		12
Test voltage		13
Current consumption in amps.		
No load Stage 1		1.7
Stage 11		2.8
Locked Stage 1		19
Stage 11		23
Minimum diameter of commutator in mm. (in.)		22.5 (.89)
Brush spring pressure in oz. (p):		
New brush		6.35-8.46 (180-240)
Used brush, minimum		3.53 (100)
Minimum brush length in mm. (in.)		6 (.24)

I

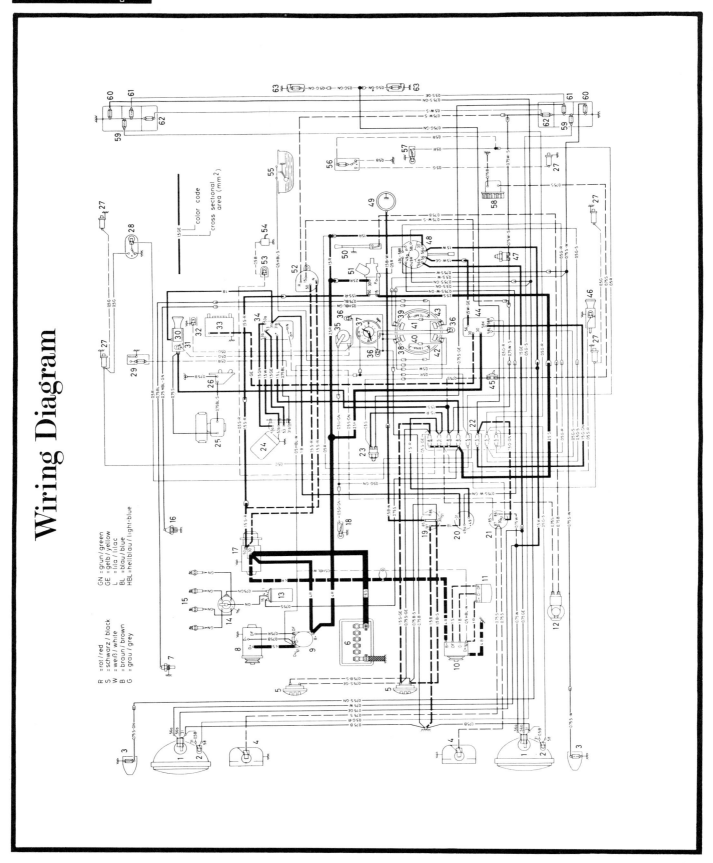

Wiring Diagram

color code
cross sectional
area (mm²)

R = rot / red
S = schwarz / black
W = weiß / white
B = braun / brown
G = grau / grey

GN = grün / green
GE = gelb / yellow
L = lila / lilac
BL = blau / blue
HBL = hellblau / light-blue

Light Bulb Set

Bulb for:	Designation	Part No.
Headlamp	A 12 V – 45/40 W	N–47950
Parking lamp	HL 12 V – 4 W	N–51200
Stop lamp)	K 12 V – 18 W	N–51230
Direction signal lamp)		
Back-up lamp	K 12 V – 15 W	N–58220
Tail lamp)	K 12 V – 5 W	N–15630
License plate lamp)		
Interior lamp	12 V – 6 W	12 24 627
Direction signal indicator lamp)		
Charging indicator lamp)	12 V – 3 W	N–59140
Oil pressure indicator lamp)		
Headlamp high beam indicator lamp)		
Cigar lighter lamp)	J 12 V – 2 W	N–31600
Ashtray lamp)		
Instrument lamp	12 V – 3 W	N–59140
Glove compartment lamp	12 V – 3 W	N–21840
Engine compartment lamp)	G 12 V – 10 W	N–47250
Luggage compartment lamp)		
Fog lamp	12 V – 35 W	N–30650

Code For The Large Numbers

1 Headlamp	22 Fuse box	43 Oil pressure indicator lamp
2 Parking light	23 Stop lamp switch	44 Light switch
3 Direction signal lamp, front	24 Windshield wiper motor	45 Demister motor switch
4 Fog lamp	25 Heater motor	46 Carburetor bowden control wire indicator lamp – Olymat
5 Horn or trumpets	26 Heater switch	47 Back-up lamp switch
6 Battery	27 Interior lamp switch	48 Signal switch
7 Temperature feeler	28 Interior lamp	49 Horn contact
8 Generator	29 Glove compartment lamp	50 Gearshift lever – Olymat
9 Regulator	30 Cigar lighter	51 Ignition lock
10 A.C. Generator	31 Cigar lighter lamp	52 Selector lever switch
11 A.C. Regulator	32 Ashtray lamp	53 Parking brake indicator lamp
12 Control valve – Olymat	33 Radio	54 Parking brake indicator lamp switch
13 Ignition coil	34 Windshield wiper and fog lamp switch	55 Fuel gauge tank unit
14 Distributor	35 Instrument lamp switch	56 Load compartment lamp
15 Spark plug	36 Instrument lamps	57 Luggage compartment lamp
16 Oil pressure switch	37 Electric clock	58 Demister motor
17 Starter	38 High beam indicator lamp	59 Tail lamp
18 Engine compartment lamp	39 Direction signal indicator lamp	60 Direction signal lamp, rear
19 Horn relay	40 Fuel gauge dash unit	61 Stop lamp
20 Passing signal relay	41 Temperature indicator	62 Back-up lamp
21 Fog lamp relay	42 Charging indicator lamp	63 License plate lamp

Trouble Shooting

Engine

SYMPTOMS

	a	b	c	d	e	f	g	h	i	j	k	l	m	n	o	p	q	r	s	t	u	v
ENGINE WILL NOT CRANK	*	*	*	*																		
ENGINE CRANKS SLOWLY	*	*	*																			
ENGINE CRANKS BUT DOES NOT START					*	*	*	*						*								
ENGINE STARTS BUT RUNS FOR SHORT PERIODS ONLY					*	*			*	*												
ENGINE MISFIRES AT LOW SPEED					*	*			*		*											
ENGINE MISFIRES AT HIGH SPEED					*	*				*	*											*
ENGINE MISFIRES AT ALL SPEEDS					*	*	*			*	*	*	*								*	*
ENGINE MISFIRES ON ACCELERATION AND FAILS TO REV.					*	*			*		*											*
ROUGH IDLE					*	*		*	*	*	*		*		*	*					*	*
RUNS ROUGH AT HIGH SPEED					*	*	*	*	*	*	*	*	*	*	*						*	*
LACK OF POWER			*		*	*	*	*	*	*				*	*	*						*
POOR ACCELERATION					*	*	*	*				*		*	*	*						*
LACK OF TOP SPEED					*	*	*	*		*		*		*	*	*						*
EXCESSIVE FUEL CONSUMPTION			*		*	*								*	*							
EXCESSIVE OIL CONSUMPTION																*	*	*	*			
PINKING					*	*																
COMPRESSION LEAK								*			*	*	*			*					*	*
	a	b	c	d	e	f	g	h	i	j	k	l	m	n	o	p	q	r	s	t	u	v

PROBABLE CAUSE

a. Fault in the starting system - Refer to the ELECTRICAL EQUIPMENT section for diagnosis.
b. Engine oil too thick.
c. Stiff engine.

d. Mechanical seizure.
e. Fault in the ignition system - Refer to the IGNITION SYSTEM section for diagnosis.
f. Fault in the fuel system - Refer to the FUEL SYSTEM section for diagnosis.
g. Incorrect valve timing.
h. Compression leak.
i. Air leak at inlet manifold.
j. Restriction in exhaust system.
k. Poor valve seating.
l. Sticking valves.
m. Leaking cylinder head gasket.
n. Worn camshaft lobes.
o. Incorrect tappet clearances.
p. Worn or damaged cylinder bores, pistons and/or piston rings.
q. Worn valve guides.
r. Damaged valve stem seals.
s. Leaking oil seal or gasket.
t. Incorrectly installed spark plug.
u. Cracked cylinder.
v. Broken or weak valve springs.

REMEDIES

b. Drain oil and replace with correct oil.
c. Add small quantity of oil to the fuel and run engine gently.
d. Strip engine and renew parts as necessary.

g. Retime engine.
h. Trace and seal.
i. Trace and seal.
j. Remove restriction.
k. Regrind seats.
l. Free and trace cause.
m. Renew gasket.
n. Fit new camshaft.
o. Adjust tappets.
p. Exchange engine.
q. Replace valve guides.
r. Replace seals.
s. Replace gasket.
t. Replace plug with correct one.
u. Renew cylinder block.
v. Replace springs.

Trouble Shooting

Lubrication System

SYMPTOMS

	a	b	c	d	e	f	g	h	i	j	k	l	m	n
EXCESSIVE OIL CONSUMPTION	*	*	*	*								*	*	
LOW OIL PRESSURE					*	*	*	*	*	*	*			*

PROBABLE CAUSE	REMEDIES
a. Worn or damaged cylinder bores, pistons and/or piston rings.	a. Regrind cylinder bores and fit new oversize pistons and rings.
b. Worn valve guides.	b. Replace valves and guides.
c. Damaged valve stem seals.	c. Replace seals.
d. Leaking oil seal or gasket.	d. Seal leak or replace gasket.
e. Faulty oil pressure gauge, switch or wiring.	e. Trace and rectify.
f. Relief valve defective.	f. Check and replace if necessary.
g. Oil pick-up pipe strainer blocked.	g. Remove blockage.
h. Oil filter over-flow valve defective.	h. Check and replace if necessary.
i. Worn oil pump.	i. Replace pump or parts.
j. Damaged or worn main and/or big-end bearings.	j. Renew bearings.
k. Incorrect grade of engine oil.	k. Replace oil with correct grade.
l. Oil level low.	l. Top up oil.
m. Oil level too high.	m. Drain off surplus oil.
n. Oil leak or the pressurised side of the lubrication system.	n. Trace and remedy.

Cooling System

SYMPTOMS

	a	b	c	d	e	f	g	h	i	j	k	l	m	n	o
OVERHEATING	*	*	*	*	*		*	*	*	*	*	*	*		
ENGINE FAILS TO REACH NORMAL OPERATING TEMPERATURE							*							*	

PROBABLE CAUSE	REMEDIES
a. Insufficient coolant.	a. Top up radiator.
b. Drive belt slipping or broken.	b. Tighten belt or renew.
c. Radiator fins clogged.	c. Unclog fins.
d. Cooling fan defective.	d. Trace fault, rectify or renew.
e. Water pump defective.	e. Replace water pump.
f. Thermostat jammed shut.	f. Replace thermostat.
g. Thermostat jammed open.	g. Replace thermostat.
h. Ignition timing too far retarded.	h. Retime ignition.
i. Excessive vehicle load or dragging brakes.	i. Unload car, check brakes.
j. Internal passage in the engine and/or radiator blocked.	j. Trace and clear.
k. Hoses blocked.	k. Trace and clear blockage.
l. Carburettor mal-adjustment	l. Adjust correctly.
m. Excessive carbon deposit in the cylinders.	m. Decarbonise engine, top overhaul.
n. Insufficient engine oil or use of inferior grade of oil.	n. Top up with correct grade. Drain if necessary.
o. Excessive radiator area.	o. Partially blank off in winter only.

Trouble Shooting

Fuel System

SYMPTOMS

	a	b	c	d	e	f	g	h	i	j	k	l	m	n	o	p	q	r	s	t	u	v
ENGINE CRANKS BUT DOES NOT START	*	*	*	*	*	*	*	*														
ENGINE STARTS BUT RUNS FOR SHORT PERIODS ONLY	*		*	*	*			*	*	*	*	*	*					*	*			
ENGINE MISFIRES AT LOW SPEED			*	*				*	*													
ENGINE MISFIRES AT HIGH SPEED	*		*	*				*	*					*								
ENGINE MISFIRES AT ALL SPEEDS	*	*	*	*	*	*		*	*			*	*	*								
ENGINE MISFIRES ON ACCELERATION AND FAILS TO REV.			*		*			*	*			*	*	*	*	*	*	*		*		
ROUGH IDLE				*				*	*	*	*	*	*				*	*		*	*	
ENGINE RUNS ROUGH AT HIGH SPEED				*				*	*			*	*	*				*		*		
LACK OF POWER				*					*			*	*	*	*			*		*	*	
POOR ACCELERATION				*					*			*	*	*	*	*		*		*	*	
LACK OF TOP SPEED				*					*			*	*	*	*		*	*		*	*	
EXCESSIVE FUEL CONSUMPTION			*	*					*						*	*		*		*	*	
PINKING															*				*	*		
BACKFIRE				*					*		*		*	*								

a	b	c	d	e	f	g	h	i	j	k	l	m	n	o	p	q	r	s	t	u	v

PROBABLE CAUSE

a. Fuel tank empty.
b. Fuel line blocked.
c. Fuel pump defective.
d. Blockage in carburettor.
e. Air lock in fuel line.
f. Fuel filter blocked.
g. Carburettor needle valve jammed.
h. Water in carburettor.
i. Erratic fuel flow due to blockage.
j. Idling speed too low.
k. Incorrect setting of choke control.
l. Incorrect carburettor fuel/float level.
m. Carburettor icing.
n. Air leak at inlet manifold.
o. Incorrect grade of fuel.
p. Carburettor accelerator pump defective.
q. Throttle linkage mal-adjusted.
r. Incorrect adjustment of idling mixture.
s. Air filter clogged.
t. Incorrect ignition timing.
u. Carburettor piston sticking.
v. Wrong carburettor jets fitted.

REMEDIES

a. Fill tank.
b. Blow out obstruction with compressed air.
c. Replace pump.
d. Remove blockage.
e. Trace and bleed out.
f. Clean filter.
g. Free needle.
h. Drain out water, dry out.
i. Remove blockage.
j. Adjust throttle stop screw.
k. Reset control.
l. Adjust level.
m. Wait for ice to melt. If persistent, trace cause.
n. Trace leak and seal.
o. Dilute fuel with highest octane rating obtainable.
p. Trace fault and rectify.
q. Adjust correctly.
r. Adjust mixture control.
s. Clean filter.
t. Retime ignition.
u. Oil carburettor.
v. Replace with correct jets.

Trouble Shooting

Clutch

SYMPTOMS

	a	b	c	d	e	f	g	h	i	j	k	l	m	n	o	p	q	r
CLUTCH SLIPPING (WILL NOT ENGAGE PROPERLY)	*	*	*	*	*	*												
CLUTCH DRAG (WILL NOT DISENGAGE PROPERLY)			*		*		*	*	*	*	*	*					*	*
CLUTCH JUDDER	*	*	*					*		*	*	*	*	*				
CLUTCH GRAB (ON ENGAGEMENT)	*	*	*	*			*	*		*	*		*	*		*		
CLUTCH NOISE - SQUEAL WHEN DEPRESSING THE PEDAL																*		
CLUTCH NOISE - RATTLE WHEN IDLING			*							*			*					
CLUTCH NOISE - CHATTER ON ENGAGEMENT										*			*					
	a	b	c	d	e	f	g	h	i	j	k	l	m	n	o	p	q	r

PROBABLE CAUSE

a. Insufficient free-play in release linkage.
b. Clutch disc facing worn or hardened.
c. Grease or oil on clutch disc facing.
d. Weak or broken pressure plate coil springs or diaphragm spring.
e. Air in hydraulic system.
f. Insufficient free-travel at clutch pedal.
g. Excessive free-play in release linkage.
h. Misalignment of clutch housing.
i. Clutch disc hub binding on splines of gearbox input shaft.
j. Clutch disc facing loose or broken.
k. Pressure plate mating surface warped.
l. Clutch cover distorted.
m. Looseness in transmission or suspension.
n. Clutch disc distorted.
o. Loose drive plate hub.
p. Release bearing defective.
q. Release arm bent.
r. Low hydraulic fluid level.

REMEDIES

a. Adjust linkage.
b. Replace clutch disc.
c. Clean and remedy cause.
d. Renew springs.
e. Bleed system.
f. Adjust travel.
g. Adjust or renew worn parts.
h. Realign housing.
i. Remove cause of binding.
j. Replace clutch disc.
k. Fit new parts.
l. Replace cover.
m. Take up play.
n. Renew disc.
o. Replace hub.
p. Renew bearing.
q. Straighten or renew.
r. Top up hydraulic fluid.

Trouble Shooting

Steering

SYMPTOMS

	a	b	c	d	e	f	g	h	i	j	k	l	m	n	o	p	q	r	s
STEERING STIFFNESS	*	*	*	*	*	*													
STEERING SLACK				*			*	*	*		*	*	*						
STEERING WANDER	*	*	*	*	*		*	*	*	*	*	*	*	*	*				
WHEEL SHIMMY				*	*		*	*	*			*	*	*	*	*			
CAR PULLS TO ONE SIDE	*		*					*		*					*	*	*	*	*
POOR RECOVERY OF STEERING WHEEL TO CENTRE	*	*	*	*	*													*	
EXCESSIVE OR ABNORMAL TYRE WEAR	*		*				*	*	*					*	*	*	*	*	*
	a	b	c	d	e	f	g	h	i	j	k	l	m	n	o	p	q	r	s

PROBABLE CAUSE

a. Tyre pressures incorrect or uneven.
b. Lack of lubricant in steering gear.
c. Lack of lubrication at steering linkage ball joints.
d. Incorrect wheel alignment.
e. Incorrectly adjusted steering gear.
f. Steering column bearings too tight or column bent or misaligned.
g. Steering linkage joints worn or loose.
h. Front wheel bearings worn or incorrectly adjusted.
i. Slackness in front suspension.
j. Road wheel nuts loose.
k. Steering wheel loose.
l. Steering gear mounting bolts loose.
m. Steering gear worn.
n. Shock absorbers defective or mountings loose.
o. Road wheels imbalanced or tyres unevenly worn.
p. Suspension springs weak or broken.
q. Brakes pulling on one side.
r. Chassis frame or suspension misaligned.
s. Improper driving.

REMEDIES

a. Inflate and balance tyres.
b. Inject lubricant.
c. Lubricate.
d. Check steering geometry.
e. Adjust correctly.
f. Adjust renew defective parts.
g. Tighten or replace joints.
h. Adjust or renew bearings.
i. Tighten to correct torque.
j. Tighten nuts to correct torque.
k. Tighten to correct torque.
l. Tighten to correct torque.
m. Replace worn parts.
n. Replace with new.
o. Balance wheels.
p. Renew springs.
q. Balance brakes.
r. Realign.
s. Arrange tuition on driving.

Trouble Shooting

Braking System

SYMPTOMS

	a	b	c	d	e	f	g	h	i	j	k	l	m	n	o	p	q	r	s	t	u	v	w
BRAKE FAILURE				*		*	*	*		*									*				*
BRAKES INEFFECTIVE	*	*	*	*	*	*	*	*	*	*							*		*				
BRAKES GRAB OR PULL TO ONE SIDE	*	*	*	*				*			*	*	*	*			*						*
BRAKES BIND						*								*	*	*		*		*			*
PEDAL SPONGY					*	*	*	*											*				*
PEDAL TRAVEL EXCESSIVE	*		*						*				*	*	*			*	*				*
EXCESSIVE PEDAL PRESSURE REQUIRED	*	*	*		*				*	*									*		*	*	
HYDRAULIC SYSTEM WILL NOT MAINTAIN PRESSURE								*	*										*		*		
BRAKE SQUEAL DEVELOPS	*	*	*	*												*		*					
BRAKE SHUDDER DEVELOPS	*	*	*	*								*	*	*			*	*					*
HANDBRAKE INEFFECTIVE OR REQUIRES EXCESSIVE MOVEMENT	*	*	*	*													*						
	a	b	c	d	e	f	g	h	i	j	k	l	m	n	o	p	q	r	s	t	u	v	w

PROBABLE CAUSE

a. Brake shoe linings or friction pades excessively worn.
b. Incorrect brake shoe linings or friction pads.
c. Brake shoe linings or friction pads contaminated.
d. Brake drums or discs scored.
e. Incorrect brake fluid.
f. Insufficient brake fluid.
g. Air in the hydraulic system.
h. Fluid leak in the hydraulic system.
i. Fluid line blocked.
j. Mal-function in the brake pedal linkage.
k. Unequal tyre pressures.
l. Brake disc or drum distorted or cracked.
m. Brake back plate or calliper mounting bolts loose or looseness in the suspension.
n. Wheel bearings incorrectly adjusted.
o. Weak, broken or improperly installed shoe return springs.
p. Uneven brake lining contact.
q. Incorrect brake lining adjustment.
r. Pistons in wheel cylinder or calliper seized.
s. Weak or broken pedal return spring.
t. Master cylinder defective.
u. Fluid reservoir overfilled or reservoir air vent restricted.
v. Servo vacuum hose disconnected or restricted, or servo unit defective.
w. Wheel cylinder or calliper defective.

REMEDIES

a. Replace linings or pads.
b. Replace with correct linings or pads.
c. Clean thoroughly.
d. Renew drums or discs.
e. Bleed out old fluid and replace with correct type.
f. Top up reservoir.
g. Bleed brake system.
h. Trace and seal.
i. Trace and clear blockage.
j. Correct as necessary.
k. Adjust and balance tyre pressures.
l. Renew disc or drum.
m. Tighten as necessary to correct torque.
n. Adjust wheel bearings.
o. Renew or install correctly.
p. Trace cause and remedy.
q. Adjust correctly.
r. Free and clean.
s. Renew spring.
t. Replace master cylinder and seals.
u. Lower fluid level. Clear air vent.
v. Check and replace hose. Renew servo unit if defective.
w. Replace as necessary.

Trouble Shooting

Ignition System

SYMPTOMS

	a	b	c	d	e	f	g	h	i	j	k	l	m	n	o	p	q	r
ENGINE CRANKS BUT DOES NOT START	*	*	*		*	*		*	*	*	*	*	*					
ENGINE STARTS BUT RUNS FOR SHORT PERIODS ONLY	*	*	*		*	*			*	*	*	*	*					
ENGINE MISFIRES AT LOW SPEED	*				*	*	*											
ENGINE MISFIRES AT HIGH SPEED			*	*	*	*	*		*	*	*		*					
ENGINE MISFIRES AT ALL SPEEDS			*	*	*	*	*		*	*	*	*	*					
ENGINE MISFIRES ON ACCELERATION AND FAILS TO REV.			*	*	*	*	*		*	*	*	*		*				
ROUGH IDLE	*	*	*		*	*	*	*	*	*	*	*	*	*			*	
ENGINE RUNS ROUGH AT HIGH SPEED			*	*	*	*	*		*	*	*	*		*	*		*	
LACK OF POWER			*	*	*	*	*	*	*	*	*	*		*	*		*	
POOR ACCELERATION			*	*	*	*	*	*	*	*	*	*		*	*		*	
LACK OF TOP SPEED			*	*	*	*	*	*	*	*	*	*	*	*	*		*	
EXCESSIVE FUEL CONSUMPTION			*	*	*	*	*	*	*	*	*	*			*	*	*	
PINKING	*	*		*	*		*				*	*			*	*		*

	a	b	c	d	e	f	g	h	i	j	k	l	m	n	o	p	q	r

PROBABLE CAUSE

a. Battery discharged or defective.
b. Contact breaker points need cleaning or renewing.
c. Incorrect contact breaker points.
d. Contact breaker spring weak.
e. Spark plugs need cleaning or renewing.
f. Incorrect spark plug gaps.
g. Wrong type of spark plug fitted.
h. Static ignition timing incorrect.
i. Coil or capacitor defective.
j. Open circuit or loose connection in the L.T. circuit.
k. Open circuit, short to earth or loose connection on the coil H.T. lead.
l. Open circuit, short to earth or loose connection on the spark. plug leads.
m. Plug leads incorrectly connected.
n. H.T. leak on coil distributor cap or rotor, due to oil, dirt, moisture or damage.
o. Centrifugal advance not functioning correctly.
p. Vacuum advance not functioning correctly.
q. Worn distributor cam or distributor shaft bush.
r. Using wrong grade of fuel.

REMEDIES

a. Recharge or replace battery.
b. Clean or renew.
c. Fit correct points.
d. Renew contact breaker set.
e. Clean or renew plugs.
f. Adjust gaps.
g. Fit correct plugs.
h. Retime ignition.
i. Replace as necessary.
j. Trace and rectify.
k. Trace and rectify.
l. Trace and rectify.

m. Connect correctly.
n. Clean with dry lint free rag.

o. Examine and oil sparingly.
p. Check and rectify.
q. Replace defective parts.
r. Change to correct grade of fuel.

Trouble Shooting

Electrical Equipment

SYMPTOMS

	a	b	c	d	e	f	g	h	i	j	k	l	m	n	o	p	q	r
STARTER FAILS TO OPERATE	*	*	*	*			*	*										
STARTER OPERATES BUT DOES NOT CRANK ENGINE		*	*	*			*	*	*									
STARTER CRANKS ENGINE SLOWLY	*	*	*															
STARTER NOISY IN OPERATION				*			*	*										
IGNITION WARNING LIGHT REMAINS ILLUMINATED WITH ENGINE AT SPEED			*							*	*	*						
IGNITION WARNING LIGHT FAILS TO ILLUMINATE WHEN IGN. IS SWITCHED ON		*	*						*			*	*					
IGNITION WARNING LIGHT STAYS ON WHEN IGN. IS SWITCHED OFF									*		*	*						
LIGHTS DIM OR WILL NOT ILLUMINATE		*	*								*		*		*	*	*	
BULBS BLOW FREQUENTLY AND BATTERY REQUIRES FREQUENT TOPPING-UP											*							
DIRECTION INDICATORS NOT FUNCTIONING PROPERLY		*	*										*		*		*	*
	a	b	c	d	e	f	g	h	i	j	k	l	m	n	o	p	q	r

PROBABLE CAUSE

a. Stiff engine.

b. Battery discharged or defective.
c. Broken or loose connection in circuit.
d. Starter pinion jammed in mesh with flywheel ring gear.
e. Starter motor defective.
f. Starter pinion does not engage with flywheel ring gear due to dirt on screwed pinion barrel.
g. Starter drive pinion defective or flywheel ring gear worn.
h. Starter solenoid switch defective.
i. Ignition/starter switch defective.
j. Broken or loose drive belt.
k. Regulator defective.
l. Generator/alternator defective.
m. Bulb burned out.
n. Mounting bolts loose.
o. Fuse blown
p. Light switch defective.
q. Short circuit.
r. Flasher unit defective.

REMEDIES

a. Add a small quantity of oil to the fuel and run the engine carefully.
b. Recharge or replace battery.
c. Trace and rectify.
d. Release pinion.
e. Rectify fault or replace starter motor.
f. Clean and spray with penetrating oil.

g. Replace defective parts.
h. Trace fault, renew if necessary.
i. Renew switch.
j. Replace belt.
k. Adjust or replace.
l. Adjust or replace.
m. Renew bulb,
n. Tighten bolts to correct torque.
o. Replace fuse after ascertaining cause of blowing.
p. Renew switch.
q. Trace and rectify.
r. Replace unit.

Lubricate and Clean

MO / MI / KM — 3 6 12 15 / 5 10 20 25

CAR UP

Component	Operation	Ref
ENGINE	Drain oil	1
Filter	Change element	2
	Clean element	3
GEARBOX	Check oil/top up	4
	Change oil	5
Overdrive Filter	Clean element	6
AUTOMATIC TRANSM.	Drain fluid	7
Filter	Clean element	8
DIFFERENTIAL	Check oil/top up	9
	Change oil	10
Limited Slip Differential	Check oil/top up	11
	Change oil	12
Sliding Joints(Drive Shaft)	Check oil/top up	13
	Change oil	14
SHOCK ABSORBERS	Check oil/top up	15
PROP./DRIVE SHAFT(S)	Lubricate	16
GREASE GUN POINTS	Lubricate	17
PEDAL SHAFT(S)	Lubricate	18
HANDBRAKE	Lubricate	19
GEAR LINKAGE	Lubricate	20

CAR LOWERED — WHEELS FREE

Component	Operation	Ref
WHEEL BEARINGS-Front	Repack	21
WHEEL BEARINGS-Rear	Repack	22
BRAKE FLUID	Renew/bleed syst.	23

CAR DOWN — BONNET OPEN

Component	Operation	Ref
ENGINE	Refill with oil	24
	Check oil level	25
Breather Cap	Clean	26
Air Cleaner	Service element(s)	27
	Replace element(s)	28
PCV-System	Clean filter	29
	Clean valve/hose(s)	30
	Replace valve	31
Carburettor(s)	Clean jets/bowl	32
	Top up pist. damper	33
	Lubricate linkages	34
Fuel Bowl/Filter(s)	Clean/replace	35
Fuel Injection Pump	Check oil level	36
Filter(s)	Clean/replace	37
AUTOMATIC TRANSM.	Refill with fluid	38
	Check fluid level	39
DISTRIBUTOR	Clean cap & ign.coil	40
Spindle/Cam	Lubricate	41
COOLING SYSTEM	Check/top up	42
	Flush system	43
Corrosion Inhibitor	Check solution	44
Anti-Freeze	Check	45
Water Pump	Lubricate	46
SCREENWASHER	Check/top up	47
BATTERY	Check/top up	48
	Check spec. gravity	49
Connections	Clean, grease	50
GENERATOR	Lubricate	51
STEERING	Check/top up	52
Power Steering	Check/top up fluid	53
	Grease ram	54
	Clean filter	55
CLUTCH/BRAKE	Check/top up fluid	56
BRAKE SERVO	Clean filter	57
	Renew filter	58
HYDR. SUSPENSION	Check/top up fluid	59
	Renew fluid	60
	Clean filter	61

CAR DOWN — EXTERNAL

Component	Operation	Ref
LOCKS, HINGES, ETC.	Lubricate	62
Door Drain Holes	Clean	63
WIPER SPINDLES	Lubricate	64

EVERY

MOnths / MIles (1000) / KMs (1000) — whichever comes first

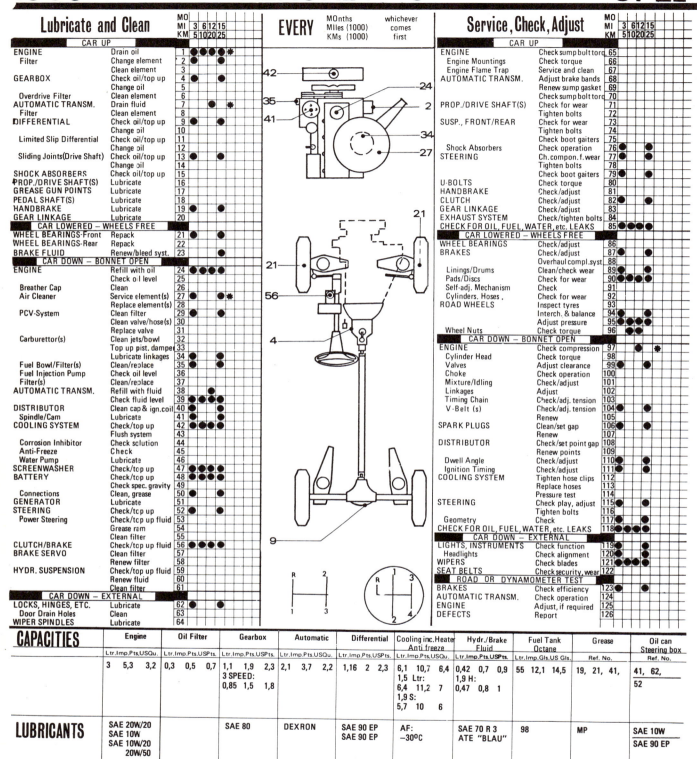

Service, Check, Adjust

MO / MI / KM — 3 6 12 15 / 5 10 20 25

CAR UP

Component	Operation	Ref
ENGINE	Check sump bolt torq.	65
Engine Mountings	Check torque	66
Engine Flame Trap	Service and clean	67
AUTOMATIC TRANSM.	Adjust brake bands	68
	Renew sump gasket	69
	Check sump bolt torq.	70
PROP./DRIVE SHAFT(S)	Check for wear	71
	Tighten bolts	72
SUSP., FRONT/REAR	Check for wear	73
	Tighten bolts	74
	Check boot gaiters	75
Shock Absorbers	Check operation	76
STEERING	Ch.compon.f.wear	77
	Tighten bolts	78
	Check boot gaiters	79
U-BOLTS	Check torque	80
HANDBRAKE	Check/adjust	81
CLUTCH	Check/adjust	82
GEAR LINKAGE	Check/adjust	83
EXHAUST SYSTEM	Check/tighten bolts	84
CHECK FOR OIL, FUEL, WATER, etc. LEAKS		85

CAR LOWERED — WHEELS FREE

Component	Operation	Ref
WHEEL BEARINGS	Check/adjust	86
BRAKES	Check/adjust	87
	Overhaul compl.syst.	88
Linings/Drums	Clean/check wear	89
Pads/Discs	Check for wear	90
Self-adj. Mechanism	Check	91
Cylinders. Hoses.	Check for wear	92
ROAD WHEELS	Inspect tyres	93
	Interch. & balance	94
	Adjust pressure	95
Wheel Nuts	Check torque	96

CAR DOWN — BONNET OPEN

Component	Operation	Ref
ENGINE	Check compression	97
Cylinder Head	Check torque	98
Valves	Adjust clearance	99
Choke	Check operation	100
Mixture/Idling	Check/adjust	101
Linkages	Adjust	102
Timing Chain	Check/adj. tension	103
V-Belt (s)	Check/adj. tension	104
	Renew	105
SPARK PLUGS	Clean/set gap	106
	Renew	107
DISTRIBUTOR	Check/set point gap	108
	Renew points	109
Dwell Angle	Check/adjust	110
Ignition Timing	Check/adjust	111
COOLING SYSTEM	Tighten hose clips	112
	Replace hoses	113
	Pressure test	114
STEERING	Check play, adjust	115
	Tighten bolts	116
Geometry	Check	117
CHECK FOR OIL, FUEL, WATER, etc. LEAKS		118

CAR DOWN — EXTERNAL

Component	Operation	Ref
LIGHTS, INSTRUMENTS	Check function	119
Headlights	Check alignment	120
WIPERS	Check blades	121
SEAT BELTS	Check security, wear	122

ROAD OR DYNAMOMETER TEST

Component	Operation	Ref
BRAKES	Check efficiency	123
AUTOMATIC TRANSM.	Check operation	124
ENGINE	Adjust, if required	125
DEFECTS	Report	126

CAPACITIES

	Engine	Oil Filter	Gearbox	Automatic	Differential	Cooling inc.Heater Anti freeze	Hydr./Brake Fluid	Fuel Tank Octane	Grease	Oil can Steering box
units	Ltr.Imp.Pts.USQu.	Ltr.Imp.Pts.USPts.	Ltr.Imp.Pts.USPts.	Ltr.Imp.Pts.USQu.	Ltr.Imp.Pts.USPts.	Ltr.Imp.Pts.USQu.	Ltr.Imp.Pts.USPts.	Ltr.Imp.Gls.US Gls.	Ref. No.	Ref. No.
values	3 5,3 3,2	0,3 0,5 0,7	1,1 1,9 2,3 3 SPEED: 0,85 1,5 1,8	2,1 3,7 2,2	1,16 2 2,3	6,1 10,7 6,4 1,5 Ltr: 6,4 11,2 7 1,9 S: 5,7 10 6	0,42 0,7 0,9 1,9 H: 0,47 0,8 1	55 12,1 14,5	19, 21, 41,	41, 62, 52

LUBRICANTS

	Engine	Gearbox	Automatic	Differential	Cooling inc.Heater	Hydr./Brake Fluid	Fuel Tank Octane	Grease	Oil can Steering box
	SAE 20W/20 SAE 10W SAE 10W/20 20W/50	SAE 80	DEXRON	SAE 90 EP SAE 90 EP	AF: −30°C	SAE 70 R 3 ATE "BLAU"	98	MP	SAE 10W SAE 90 EP

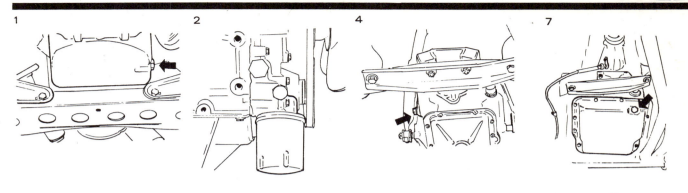

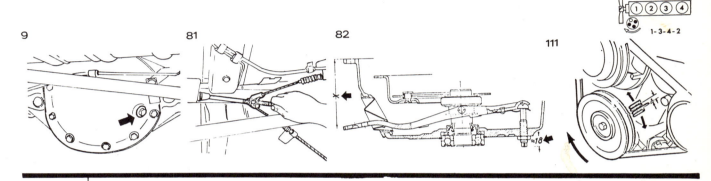

intereurope
1971 Copyright Intereurope - Without Liability

AUTOSERVICE DATA CHART

TECHNICAL NOTES

1 – In the case of intensive driving with frequent stops and starts - ENGINE OIL and FILTER should be changed more often.

7 – Under NORMAL DRIVING CONDITIONS, the transmission fluid should be changed at 45,000 KM/27,000 MI, then every 40,000 KM/24,000 MI.

27 – Also check SUMMER/WINTER adjustment of the pre-heated AIR - INTAKE.

97 – All ENGINE ATTACHMENTS - check for correct torque.

ENGINE DATA

COMPRESSION kg/cm²/psi	VALVE CLEARANCE INLET mm/in.hot(h)/cold(c) OUTLET	IDLING SPEED rpm.	SPARK PLUG GAP mm/inches	DISTR. POINT GAP mm/inches	DWELL ANGLE degrees	STATIC – IGN.-TIMING – STROB. degr.-BTDC degr.-BTDC/rpm.
	(h) 0,30 / ,012	700 - 750 1,9 H: 900 - 1000 AUT.: 600 - 650	0,7 / ,028	0,4 - 0,5/,016 - ,02	47 - 53	0

TYRES Pressure kg/cm²/psi

	STANDARD SIZE	FRONT PRESSURE normal/full	REAR PRESSURE normal/full	OPTIONAL SIZE	FRONT PRESSURE normal/full	REAR PRESSURE normal/full	BRAKES	MINIMUM THICKNESS SHOE mm/in. PAD
SALOON & COUPE	6,40 - 13 4 PR	1,4/20 1,5/22	1,5/22 1,7/24	6,40 S 13 4 PR 6,40 SR 13	1,4/20 1,5/22 1,6/23 1,8/26	1,5/22 1,7/24 2/29 2,2/32		
SPRINT	165 S 14	1,5/22 1,6/23	1,6/23 1,9/27	165 S 14	1,5/22 1,6/23	1,6/23 1,8/26		
CARAVAN	640 S 13 6 PR	1,5/22 1,6/23	1,7/24 2,8/40	640 SR 13	1,8/26 1,8/26	1,8/26 2,8/40		

STEERING GEOMETRY

TEST LOAD kg/lbs.	TOE-IN(i)/OUT(o) front-mm/in.	CAMBER degrees/min.	CASTOR degrees/min.	KING PIN INCLN. degrees/min.	TOE-IN(i)/OUT(o) rear-mm/in.	CAMBER degrees/min.	TOE-ON TURNS degr.at degr. LOCK
NIL	2 4/,079 - ,158	25' ± 30'	1 ± 1	6⁰ 45'			

TORQUE VALUES mkg/lb.ft.

65	80	84	86	96	98	V-BELT TENSION mm/inches	RAD. CAP. PRESS. kg/cm²/psi	CLUTCH PLAY mm/inches
						10 - 15/,4 - ,6		

TBA

6,40 - 13 4 PR 165 S 14 640 S 13 6 PR	12 V / 44 Ah	A 43 FO 1969 - 70/71: A 42 AC		FRAM PH 2800		FERODO V 958 V 4999		

Conversion Tables

|**LINEAR MEASUREMENT**					
INCHES		**M.M.**	**MILLIMETRES TO INCHES**		**INCHES TO MILLIMETRES**
FRACTIONS	**DECIMALS**		**MM.**	**INCHES**	**INCHES**	**MM.**

FRACTIONS	DECIMALS	M.M.	MM.	INCHES	INCHES	MM.
1/64	0.01563	0.3969	0.001	.00004	0.0001	.00254
1/32	0.03125	0.7937	0.002	.00008	0.0002	.00508
3/64	0.04688	1.1906	0.003	.00012	0.0003	.00762
1/16	0.0625	1.5875	0.004	.00016	0.0004	.01016
5/64	0.07813	1.9844	0.005	.00020	0.0005	.01270
3/32	0.09375	2.3813	0.006	.00024	0.0006	.01524
7/64	0.10938	2.7781	0.007	.00028	0.0007	.01778
1/8	0.125	3.1750	0.008	.00032	0.0008	.02032
9/64	0.14063	3.5719	0.009	.00035	0.0009	.02286
5/32	0.15625	3.9688	0.010	.00039	0.001	.0254
11/64	0.17188	4.3656	0.020	.00079	0.002	.0508
3/16	0.1875	4.7625	0.030	.00118	0.003	.0762
13/64	0.20313	5.1594	0.040	.00157	0.004	.1016
7/32	0.21875	5.5563	0.050	.00197	0.005	.1270
15/64	0.23438	5.9531	0.060	.00236	0.006	.1524
1/4	0.25	6.3500	0.070	.00276	0.007	.1778
17/64	0.26563	6.7469	0.080	.00315	0.008	.2032
9/32	0.28125	7.1438	0.090	.00354	0.009	.2286
19/64	0.29688	7.5406	0.10	.00394	0.010	.254
5/16	0.3125	7.9375	0.02	.00787	0.020	.508
21/64	0.32813	8.3344	0.30	.01181	0.030	.762
11/32	0.34375	8.7313	0.40	.01575	0.040	1.016
23/64	0.35938	9.1281	0.50	.01969	0.050	1.270
3/8	0.375	9.5250	0.60	.02362	0.060	1.524
25/64	0.39063	9.9219	0.70	.02756	0.070	1.778
13/32	0.40625	10.3188	0.80	.03150	0.080	2.032
27/64	0.42188	10.7156	0.90	.03543	0.090	2.286
7/16	0.4375	11.1125	1.0	.03937	0.10	2.54
29/64	0.45313	11.5094	2.0	.07874	0.20	5.08
15/32	0.46875	11.9063	3.0	.11811	0.30	7.62
31/64	0.48438	12.3031	4.0	.15748	0.40	10.16
1/2	0.5	12.700	5.0	.19685	0.50	12.70
33/64	0.51563	13.0963	6.0	.23622	0.60	15.24
17/32	0.53125	13.4938	7.0	.27559	0.70	17.78
35/64	0.54688	13.8906	8.0	.31496	0.80	20.32
9/16	0.5625	14.2875	9.0	.35433	0.90	22.86
37/64	0.57813	14.6844	10.0	.39370	1.0	25.4
19/32	0.59375	15.0813	11.0	.43307	2.0	50.8
39/64	0.60938	15.4781	12.0	.47244	3.0	76.2
5/8	0.625	15.875	13.0	.51181	4.0	101.6
41/64	0.64063	16.2719	14.0	.55118	5.0	127.0
21/32	0.65625	16.6688	15.0	.59055	6.0	152.4
43/64	0.67188	17.0656	16.0	.62992	7.0	177.8
11/16	0.6875	17.4625	17.0	.66929	8.0	203.2
45/64	0.70313	17.8594	18.0	.70866	9.0	228.6
23/32	0.71875	18.2563	19.0	.74803	10.0	254.0
47/64	0.73438	18.6531	20.0	.78740	11.0	279.4
3/4	0.75	19.050	21.0	.82677	12.0	304.8
49/64	0.76563	19.4469	22.0	.86614	13.0	330.2
25/32	0.78125	19.8438	23.0	.90551	14.0	355.6
51/64	0.79688	20.2406	24.0	.94488	15.0	381.0
13/16	0.8125	20.6375	25.0	.98425	16.0	406.4
53/64	0.82813	21.0344	26.0	1.0236	17.0	431.8
27/32	0.84375	21.4313	27.0	1.0630	18.0	457.2
55/64	0.85938	21.8281	28.0	1.1024	19.0	482.6
7/8	0.875	22.225	29.0	1.1417	20.0	508.0
57/64	0.8906	22.6219	30.0	1.1811	21.0	533.4
29/32	0.90625	23.0188	31.0	1.2205	22.0	558.8
59/64	0.92188	23.4156	32.0	1.2598	23.0	584.2
15/16	0.9375	23.8125	33.0	1.2992	24.0	609.6
61/64	0.95313	24.2094	34.0	1.3386	25.0	635.0
31/32	0.96875	24.6063	35.0	1.3780	30.0	762.0
63/64	0.98438	25.0031	40.0	1.5748	35.0	889.0
	1.0	25.40	45.0	1.7717	40.0	1016.0

UNITS	LIQUIDS				PRESSURES		SPEED OR DISTANCE		BRAKING DISTANCE	
	LITRES TO PINTS	PINTS TO LITRES	LITRS TO GALLS	GALLS TO LITRS	kg/cm² to lbs/in²	lbs/in² to kg/cm²	KILOS TO MILES	MILES TO KILOS	ON FIRM DRY GROUND, NO WIND	
									METRS	FT.
1	1.76	0.57	0.22	4.55	14.22	0.07	0.62	1.61		
2	3.52	1.14	0.44	9.09	28.45	0.14	1.24	3.22		
3	5.28	1.71	0.66	13.64	42.67	0.21	1.86	4.83		
4	7.04	2.27	0.88	18.18	56.89	0.28	2.49	6.44		
5	8.80	2.84	1.10	22.73	71.12	0.35	3.11	8.05		
6	10.56	3.41	1.32	27.28	85.34	0.42	3.73	9.66		
7	12.32	3.98	1.54	31.82	99.56	0.49	4.35	11.27		
8	14.08	4.55	1.76	36.37	113.79	0.56	4.97	12.88		
9	15.84	5.12	1.98	40.91	128.00	0.63	5.59	14.48		
10	17.60	5.68	2.20	45.46	142.23	0.70	6.21	16.09	4.58	15
15	26.40	8.52	3.30	68.19	213.35	1.05	9.32	24.14	7.62	25
20	35.20	11.37	4.40	90.92	284.47	1.41	12.43	32.19	12.19	40
25	44.00	14.21	5.50	113.65	355.59	1.76	15.53	40.24	16.77	55
30	52.79	17.05	6.60	136.40	426.70	2.11	18.64	48.28	22.88	75
40	70.39	22.74	8.80	181.80	568.90	2.81	24.85	64.37	36.59	120
50	87.99	28.50	11.00	227.30	711.20	3.52	31.07	80.47	56.40	175
60	105.58		13.20				37.28	96.56	73.18	240
70	123.18		15.40				43.50	112.65	96.04	315
80	140.78		17.60				49.71	128.75	128.05	420
90	158.38		19.80				55.92	144.84		
100	175.97		22.0				62.14	160.93		
110	193.57		24.20				68.35	177.02		
120	211.17		26.40				74.57	201.17		

NOTE:- Speeds are in miles per hour.

TORQUE - LOADING																	
UNITS ON TORQUE SPANNER	1	2	3	4	5	6	7	8	9	10	15	20	25	30	40	50	60
kg.m. to lb.ft.	7.23	14.47	21.70	28.93	36.17	43.40	50.63	57.86	65.10	72.33	108.45	144.66	180.75	216.99	289.20	361.5	433.8
lb.ft. to kg.m.	0.14	0.28	0.42	0.55	0.69	0.83	0.97	1.11	1.25	1.38	2.10	2.77	3.40	4.15	5.50	6.90	8.35

Printed in Great Britain by Page Bros (Norwich) Ltd